The Natural Heritage of
ILLINOIS

The Natural Heritage of
ILLINOIS

Essays on Its Lands, Waters, Flora, and Fauna

John E. Schwegman

Southern Illinois University Press
Carbondale

Southern Illinois University Press
www.siupress.com

19 18 17 16   4 3 2 1

Cover illustration: "Hill Prairies of Illinois" poster (detail) © 2016,
Illinois Department of Natural Resources; used with permission.
Artwork by Robert Eschenfeldt shows a typical Mississippi River bluff
in central Illinois with hill prairies dominating the southwest-facing
slopes; several native plants and animals appear in the foreground.

Library of Congress Cataloging-in-Publication Data
Names: Schwegman, John E.
Title: The natural heritage of Illinois : essays on its lands, waters, flora,
and fauna / John E. Schwegman.
Description: Carbondale : Southern Illinois University Press, [2016]
Identifiers: LCCN 2015051100 | ISBN 9780809334841 (pbk. : alk.
paper) | ISBN 9780809334858 (e-book)
Subjects: LCSH: Natural history—Illinois. | Natural areas—Illinois. |
Biotic communities—Illinois. | Wildlife conservation—Illinois.
Classification: LCC QH105.I3 S39 2016 | DDC 508.773—dc23 LC
record available at http://lccn.loc.gov/2015051100

Printed on recycled paper. ♻

This paper meets the requirements of ANSI/NISO Z39.48-1992
(Permanence of Paper) ∞

For Martha, John Andrew, and Christopher—my family

Their assistance and support through the years helped
make my life's work with nature possible.

CONTENTS

4. ECOLOGY, CONSERVATION, AND MANAGEMENT OF NATURAL FEATURES OF ILLINOIS 64

Contents

ILLUSTRATIONS

PREFACE

All but three of the essays in this volume originally appeared between August 1992 and December 1996 as part of a series of twice-monthly nature columns distributed by the Illinois Department of Natural Resources to newspapers within and bordering Illinois. As no newspaper ever published all of them, few, if any, readers will have seen every one. This is the first time they have been gathered together in book form. The goal of these columns was to develop public appreciation for the lands, waters, plants, and animals of Illinois. They seek to point out interesting facts that are little known to the general public and that will entice people to venture afield to observe nature and to help defend it when necessary. Some of the columns report news of interest to nature enthusiasts or mention people active in preservation efforts of the time. In this regard, these essays provide the reader with a historic perspective of happenings some twenty years ago.

The original writing was accomplished as part of my job as botany program manager for the Illinois Department of Natural Resources. I am grateful to the taxpayers of Illinois for their support during the writing of these essays and to the late Carl Becker, then chief of the Division of Natural Heritage, for his support of the column project. The series, as originally released, was edited by Carol Knowles, public information officer for the Illinois Department of Natural Resources. I wish to thank John (Jack) White for helpful comments on the manuscript and Herb Russell for urging me to undertake this project. My wife, Martha, and my sons, John and Christopher, accompanied me in the field for decades and helped with many discoveries, especially with their keen hearing and vision. Joe Devera provided suggestions on geology, especially on changes in terminology since the original writing. Jody Shimp and John Wilker updated me on the status of some programs at the Department of Natural Resources. Many people who provided information used in the essays are credited in them. Lastly, I want to thank my mentor, Dr. Robert Mohlenbrock, for his contagious enthusiasm for nature, which led me into the study of the wonders of Illinois' flora. That study prepared me for a career in nature preservation and the opportunity to help save many of Illinois' plants, animals, and natural communities.

As published here, all essays have been edited to fit the book format. Some have been slightly rewritten to give updated information, and all references to the Illinois Department of Conservation have been changed to Illinois Department of Natural Resources, even though some were written before the agency changed its name. Multiple essays on a single subject are merged into a single larger essay such as "The Way Nature Was in Early Illinois," with the original publication dates of the columns provided. New essays on spiders, dragonflies, and memorable moments with nature are published here for the first time. In keeping with the original newspaper format, these essays do not have source citations. Before writing, I would often call and discuss the topic at hand with an expert or would depend on public lectures I had attended or pertinent literature I had read. The people whose ideas and works influenced my writing on a given subject are mentioned in the text. Where new material is relevant or further reading is recommended, an author's note is added. Several suggested readings are in *Erigenia: Journal of the Illinois Native Plant Society*, which is available online. All photographs are by the author.

INTRODUCTION

The following ninety-three essays touch on Illinois' diverse natural inheritance and have been written to appeal to nontechnical readers throughout the state and beyond. Many features and phenomena are discussed that the reader can seek out for observation and study no matter where in Illinois (or elsewhere) he or she may reside. Often instructions and directions are given for how and where to observe specific aspects of nature. To a considerable extent this work functions as a naturalist's guide to understanding and experiencing Illinois' natural heritage.

When discussing plants and animals, common names are used rather than scientific names. For plants, common names come from the fourth edition of Robert Mohlenbrock's *Vascular Flora of Illinois: A Field Guide*, published by Southern Illinois University Press in 2014. For animals, they follow Philip Smith's 1979 edition of *The Fishes of Illinois* from the University of Illinois Press; Phillips, Brandon, and Moll's 1999 *Field Guide to Amphibians and Reptiles of Illinois* from the Illinois Natural History Survey; Donald Hoffmeister's 1989 edition of *Mammals of Illinois* by University of Illinois Press; and Cummings and Mayer's 1992 *Field Guide to Freshwater Mussels of the Midwest* by the Illinois Natural History Survey. Bird common names follow the seventh edition of the American Ornithologists' Union *Check-list of North American Birds*.

The essays in this book are organized into subject categories reflected in the titles of the book's seven chapters: "Lands and Waters of Illinois"; "Historical Accounts of Early Illinois"; "Natural Communities and Natural Diversity of Illinois"; "Ecology, Conservation, and Management of Natural Features of Illinois"; "Problem Exotic Species and Diseases Affecting Illinois"; "Animals of Illinois"; and "Plants of Illinois."

The Natural Heritage of
ILLINOIS

CHAPTER ONE

LANDS AND WATERS
OF ILLINOIS

The essays in this chapter deal with the nonliving aspects of Illinois' natural landscapes and how they came to be. The first two discuss how landforms such as hills and hollows developed, how river valleys came to exist, and how the rivers of the past have changed their location. Other essays deal with the geologic features of streams, the origins of Illinois' soils, and the breaks and folds in the bedrock of the state.

~~~~~~~~~~~~~~~~~~~~~~~

Illinois' Landforms

Hills, hollows, bottoms, flats, and mounds are all terms used to describe the land surface of Illinois. How these and other landforms came to be is the subject of this essay. Landforms are constantly being created, shaped, and eroded away or filled in, but like many geological processes the changes are slow and scarcely noticed. Most of Illinois' landscape features were created thousands of years ago and are gradually being modified today.

The most common and widespread landform in Illinois is the flat plain created by great ice sheets that covered most of Illinois' land surface twice in the past 170,000 years. The last glaciation ended just ten thousand years ago. These plains make up what many people think of as the typical flat landscape of the state. They were formed as vast sheets of ice up to a mile thick slid over the land grinding off high points, filling in low areas, and finally covering all with a layer of rock and soil from within the glacier's ice as it melted. This process is called glaciation.

We often see hills rising from these plains. Some are hard, old bedrock hills that were not completely worn down by the ice. Examples of these are hills around McLeansboro and Freeport and Lawrence County's Red Hills. More often, the hills on glacial plains are what geologists call kames or moraines. These were formed during glaciation. As glaciers melted, streams and small rivers formed on top of them. These streams picked up clay, silt, sand, and gravel from the melting ice as they flowed over and eroded into the ice. The flowing water separated the sand from the gravel and washed away the finer clay and silt. The streams carried the sand and gravel along as waterborne sediment until they found a hole in the ice or reached the edge of the glacier and dropped down to ground level. There they spread out under the ice or over the land, depositing a hill of sand and gravel. Where a stream continued under the ice, linear deposits of sand and gravel were formed. These hills of water-transported materials are called kames, while the linear deposits are called eskers. They are found throughout glaciated Illinois. Many of these features are mined today for their sand and gravel. Illinois communities on kames include Lebanon and Vandalia.

The other common hills on glacial plains are moraines. Moraines are formed when an advancing ice sheet stalls because its advance is balanced by its melting. Rock, soil, and other debris in the ice accumulate in a linear deposit along the edge of the ice sheet as the ice continues to advance and melt at the same place. Moraines are composed of a mixture of materials rather than water-sorted sand and gravel and are seldom mined. Bloomington, Champaign, and many of the suburbs of Chicago are on moraines.

Hollows are caused by stream erosion into a more or less flat surface. Hollows may be formed in sandstone as at Jackson Hollow in Pope County or in other rock types or softer glacial deposits. Hollows are generally smaller with intermittent streams, while larger eroded areas with permanent streams are usually termed valleys. Both are created by water eroding and carrying away material over a long period. Such erosion has progressed much farther on the old glacial plain south from Shelbyville and west from Peoria than on the younger plain north and east of these cities.

The materials of stream erosion are transported to the floodways of larger streams where they are deposited to form the flat flood zone of the stream—its floodplain. These lowlands are commonly called

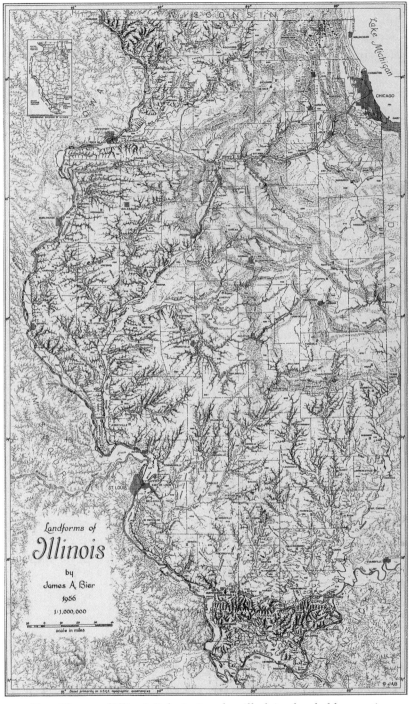

"Landforms of Illinois," depicting the till plains leveled by continental glaciers, as well as the stream valleys eroded into the plains and the moraines and kames deposited on them. The rugged topography of the unglaciated southern tip and northwestern corner of Illinois is apparent. © *James A. Bier.*

bottoms and often have ridges and swales representing past banks and channels of the stream that were left behind when the stream changed its location on the floodplain.

Lake plains are among the landforms covering the largest areas of the state. These are flat areas composed of the fine clay and silt that settled out of muddy lakes that are now extinct. Chicago is developed on a lake plain, as is Metropolis at the southern tip of the state. Chicago's plain formed beneath Glacial Lake Chicago, which was a higher level of Lake Michigan before its level lowered when drainage of the Great Lakes shifted from the Illinois River to northern rivers and eventually the St. Lawrence River.

Some of the flattest lands in Illinois in Livingston, Iroquois, and Grundy Counties are lake plains. The lakes in these areas were formed when glacial meltwater got trapped by moraines that acted as dams. The southern Illinois lake plains were created by large muddy lakes that formed each summer when glacial meltwater flooded the Mississippi, Wabash, and Ohio Rivers and backed into the drainages of the Big Muddy and Saline Rivers and other tributaries. The large flat areas around Harrisburg and northeast of Brookport are good examples of this landform.

Illinois' unglaciated areas have developed hills and valleys through water erosion of a variety of materials. Hard dolomite underlain by softer shales gave rise to the "mounds" of Jo Daviess County. Sinkholes—depressions caused by the collapse of underlying caves—are common in unglaciated limestone areas such as Monroe and Hardin Counties. Minor landform features include depressions (often ponds or lakes) in glacial till where large blocks of ice melted, wind-created dunes in sand areas, ridges and rock outcrops thrust up by fracturing (faulting) of bedrock, and a bedrock dome resulting from volcanic upheaval near Hicks in Hardin County.

Rivers of the Past

Being the center of the central lowland of North America leaves Illinois short on mountains, but since water runs downhill, much of the continent's water finds its way here in the form of large rivers. This big river heritage is part of what makes Illinois interesting to naturalists in spite of its generally flat landscape. The Mississippi, Ohio, Wabash, Illinois, and Rock are just some of these rivers. They are fascinating places to observe nature and to recreate.

We have been the central lowland of the continent for at least the last five hundred million years, so this river heritage is of long standing. However, when the ice age began some two million years ago the fact that ice also slides downhill had a major impact on Illinois and its rivers. Continental glaciers moved farther south in Illinois than anywhere else in the earth's northern hemisphere. As they did this they blocked and buried some rivers and gave rise to new ones. These "rivers of the past" and the new ones that replaced some of them play an important role in the landscape we see in Illinois today.

After the Nebraskan or first known glacier to reach Illinois retreated from northwestern Illinois, rivers eroded deep bedrock valleys. These included the ancient Mississippi and Teays Rivers in Illinois and the ancient Iowa on its western boundary. These valleys still exist, although some are buried and are not visible today. At that time, the Mississippi flowed south from the Wisconsin border as it does today, but from present-day Clinton, Iowa, it flowed southeastward to Hennepin, Illinois, and then southward down the valley now occupied by the Illinois River to Grafton, then down the present Mississippi valley to south of Cape Girardeau, Missouri, where it turned west rather than east to the Thebes Gorge, as it does today.

The present Missouri River flowed across Iowa as the Iowa River and joined the present Illinois border at the site of the city of Muscatine, Iowa. It then turned south and eroded the valley occupied by the Mississippi River today, joining the ancient Mississippi near present-day Grafton, Illinois. A major eastern river called the Teays drained much of today's upper Ohio River watershed. It crossed Ohio and central Indiana and Illinois to join the ancient Mississippi just south of Peoria. This junction area is now a broad valley occupied by Mason County, Illinois. The presently extinct Paw Paw and Ticona Rivers drained much of the area now drained by the Rock River and Illinois River east of Hennepin. Kentucky's Green River and other rivers from the east crossed southern Illinois in a valley now enlarged and called the "Cache valley."

About 480,000 years ago, the Kansan glacial advance descended on this landscape from both the Northeast and Northwest. It left the Mississippi relatively untouched in its course past the site of Peoria, but blocked and partially filled in the valleys of the Iowa River across Iowa and the Teays valley across Illinois, Indiana, and Ohio. The Iowa River was diverted south, as the Missouri River, along its present course down the western edge of Iowa and then turned east across central Missouri. The Teays was diverted to the west, south of the ice, and became the present Ohio River. It joined other smaller rivers and crossed southern Illinois in the present Cache valley. New rivers developed eastward from the Mississippi to drain much of northeastern Illinois.

Keeping this history in mind helps one interpret current landscapes in the state. The broad valley occupied by the Mississippi today, along Illinois' west-central border from Muscatine to Grafton, was not carved by it, but by the Iowa before it was blocked by the glacier and gave rise to the present Missouri River. The valley of the present Illinois River from Hennepin to Grafton was not carved by it, but rather by the Mississippi. This explains how the relatively little Illinois River has such a broad valley in this area.

The Kansan and two subsequent glaciers completely buried the Teays valley in Illinois. All that remains visible of it at the surface is the vast lowland that existed where it joined the ancient Mississippi. This area is now occupied by Mason County's sand areas and adjacent bottomland lakes of the Illinois River. The flat plain of east-central Illinois gives no hint of the Teays River bluffs that lie buried beneath it. Although out of sight, this buried valley remains significant to eastern Illinoisans as an important aquifer. The valley was filled with sand and gravel, which now holds large quantities of ground water, valuable as municipal and agricultural water supplies.

Our most recent glaciation, the Wisconsinan, diverted the Mississippi from its ancient valley past Peoria to its present course past Rock Island just 21,000 years ago. The site of this diversion is easily viewed just north of the Quad Cities at Port Byron. Here the Mississippi cuts through the uplands and has no floodplain or "bottom" on either side. It has not had time to erode these in just 21,000 years. West of Rock Island the Mississippi flowed into the valley carved by the ancient Iowa River and followed it south to Grafton, where it again entered the valley it had occupied for most of the ice age.

At the end of the most recent glaciation of the ice age, the Ohio River abandoned the Cache valley and shifted its course ten to twenty miles south to join the lower Tennessee and Cumberland Rivers and flow west past Metropolis as it does today. The Cache valley exists now as a lowland one to two miles wide across all of southern Illinois, abandoned by the Ohio and other rivers that carved it. Also at this time, the Mississippi River broke through the low upland at Thebes, Illinois, creating the Thebes Gorge of the Mississippi. Understanding these "rivers of the past" helps us comprehend how Illinois' landscape came to be.

September 1992

AUTHOR'S NOTE.—*The terms Nebraskan and Kansan glacial periods are no longer used because of the difficulty of identifying such early deposits. The pre-Illinoian glacial advance that began about 480,000 years ago is the glaciation that first blocked and partly buried the Teays and Iowa Rivers.*

Loess Soils

Most of the clay and silt that gave rise to Illinois' soils blew in on the wind. If this seems unlikely to you, read on and learn the fascinating story of loess.

Many people are aware that most of the state of Illinois was covered by great sheets of ice called continental glaciers during the ice age that paused just ten thousand years ago. Few realize, however, that while plowing and leveling the landscape, the glaciers gave rise to a dust that later covered most of the state to depths of up to 150 feet. This material, called loess, buried the rock, sand, and gravel left behind by the glacial ice and created the fine soil that makes Illinois one of the richest agricultural regions on earth.

Loess is a German word that the dictionary defines as "a fine-grained, extremely fertile loam deposited by the wind." This seems a simple enough description, but it does not begin to explain where it came from and how it buried most of the state. When I first heard that most Illinois soil was wind-deposited, I envisioned huge clouds of dust blown in from the western states as I had seen pictured from the Dust Bowl years of the 1930s. Only later did I learn that the source was much closer at hand.

Loess is a product of glaciers. Illinois' loess was derived from the continental glaciers that bore down on our state from the north during the ice age. Ice up to a mile high exerted tremendous pressure on the underlying rock and as it slid over the rock, it pulverized some of it into the consistency of dust. This "rock flour" was carried away from the glacier by numerous small "braided" channels of meltwater that flowed down the main stream valleys draining the glacier, where it was deposited as mud bars.

In the valleys of the Mississippi and Illinois Rivers these bars were as much as five miles wide and were nearly as wide in the Wabash. Because of the annual flooding each summer when the glaciers were melting, little if any vegetation grew in these valleys to hold or stabilize this material. As river levels dropped when winter freeze-up occurred, strong winds, mostly from the west, blew material from these bars across the state as loess. It is believed that the sharp temperature differences between air masses over the cold ice sheet and the warmer bare land to the south gave rise to a very windy climate during the ice age. Dust storms beyond anything we know today must have been common then. The loess depth is greatest near its source areas. Illinois' deepest loess is along the east sides of the Mississippi and Illinois Rivers. Some strong east winds also occurred, since a band of deep loess occurs along the west side of the Wabash in eastern and southern Illinois as well.

Soil scientists classify soil particles by size. Sand is the largest; silt is intermediate; and clay the smallest. This Illinois loess is composed mostly of silt-sized particles, ideal for the development of loose well-drained soils. Close to the source the particle size is larger, with some sandy loess immediately adjacent to river bluffs. The winds could not carry the large particles long distances, and the farther one travels from the river source, the smaller the particle size becomes. Soils in south central Illinois, such as in Effingham County, are composed of smaller particles. Their soils are denser, with more clay and less productivity than loess soils closer to major rivers.

Loess covers most of Illinois. The exceptions are bottomlands along rivers and streams, northeastern Illinois where a glacier stood when the last loess was being deposited, and areas where ancient lakes existed at the time of loess deposition. The latter areas include much of the Saline and Big Muddy River basins in southern Illinois. Here,

Wind blowing loess from mud bars deposited by a river draining the
St. Elias mountain glacier at Kluane National Park, Yukon, Canada.

soils of tight clay are derived from small particles that settled from
muddy waters to the bottom of ancient lakes.

The rock ground into "flour" by Illinois' glaciers was mostly limestone and dolomite. This loess is naturally limed or "sweet" and ideal
for plant growth. The result of loess deposition over most of Illinois
is the creation of ideal soils for agriculture but also the masking of
natural substrate diversity, and a lessening of biological diversity over
much of the state. The relatively great biological diversity we see in
northeastern Illinois is in part due to its lack of loess. Gravelly ridges,
old sandy beach lines, and bouldery till are all at the surface there
because of the lack of loess. This diversity of substrates supports a
greater diversity of plants and animals.

The story of loess becomes clearer and more relevant when one
observes modern glaciers. While smaller than continental glaciers,
mountain glaciers in the Canadian Rockies and Alaska also give rise
to streams with milky water rich in rock "flour" that produce braided
stream beds choked with silt. At the edge of the giant St. Elias mountain glacier in Canada's Yukon Territory, you can see winds sweeping
down from the glacier, raising clouds of loess, just as occurred in
Illinois thousands of years ago.

January 1993

~~~~~~

Streams in Balance

June is rivers-appreciation month, and one aspect of rivers and streams that is not generally appreciated is the degree to which humans have a physical impact on streams. While human-caused pollution, exotic organism introductions, and shade removal have greatly affected stream life, physical alterations of streams and their watersheds have serious implications for streams as well.

The "balance of nature" is an ecological concept that refers to natural ecosystems in which predators, prey, and plants are in balance with each other and their physical environment. It is also a term that can be used to describe natural streams. Few habitats in nature are so delicately balanced, and at the same time, so easily disturbed by man as streams. Over thousands of years of natural development, streams create channels the size needed to carry their normal and flood flows of water and sediment. They also establish a slope of their bed in harmony with their erosive forces and sedimentation rate. Upsetting this balance of the stream with its watershed can lead to vast changes in water quality, erosion rates, sediment loads, flood events, and floodplain alterations affecting wetlands, croplands, and forests.

As humans have cleared land for agriculture, and especially as we have paved over and "developed" the land, we have greatly accelerated the speed of rainwater runoff. Where much rainfall once soaked into the soil, it now runs rapidly off roofs and parking lots and plowed land that lacks permanent vegetation. The balance between stream-channel capacity and the runoff rate of the watershed is thus destroyed. Water enters the natural stream from the altered watershed faster than its channel can handle it, and this increases the frequency and severity of floods. Altering this balance has happened to some degree to almost every stream in Illinois. Some alterations are minor, but many are severe for both man and nature.

Another delicate balance that humans can interrupt is that between the stream's slope and its length. The downward erosive force of its flowing water and sediment such as sand and gravel that the water carries along to replace the eroding stream bottom are in balance. Streams that meander over a floodplain naturally increase their length and reduce the speed of their water flow and downward erosion. When a stream is channelized, straightened, and shortened for human purposes, this balance is broken. As the stream length is shortened the slope of its bed increases, accelerating the water flow rate and the erosive force of its water. This often results in downward erosion of the steam bed through a process called entrenchment.

An entrenching stream literally cuts itself into the ground until a new stable gradient is established, a process that may take centuries. Tributaries of an entrenching stream also can begin their own downcutting and gully erosion as the elevations of their mouths are lowered by the entrenchment of the primary stream. Channelizing a stream at the lower end of a watershed can set off a vast process of gully soil erosion throughout an entire watershed. This process has been set in motion at southern Illinois' Cache River watershed, where channelization has greatly shortened the river length. As the upper Cache River cuts itself deeper into the ground, it leaves unique wetlands, such as Heron Pond Swamp, high above it and thus vulnerable to drainage. The channelized Cache River has already drained and destroyed some wetlands, and conservationists are now struggling to save Heron Pond.

Reservoir construction also disrupts a stream's balance and does so in two ways: by trapping much of its sediment load; and by reducing the height and volume of flood flows. Reservoirs act as settling pools that remove silt, sand, and gravel from the water, and then pass clear water over the spillway. The natural stream below a dam is balanced for replacement of eroded stream bed with sediment that is now trapped in the reservoir. Such streams begin entrenchment and increased bank erosion for some distance below a dam until new sediment is created from its increased erosive actions. Such areas suffer removal of finer sediment such as sand and silt to the detriment of their sandbars and natural character.

When the federal government tried to correct a dam-generated stream problem on the Colorado River through the Grand Canyon, it made a massive release of water from Glen Canyon Dam to simulate predam flooding. While this action stirred up some new sediment and helped somewhat to restore sandbars, it will never replace the sediment from the entire watershed that settles out in the reservoir (Lake Powell).

11

Streams support an important part of Illinois' natural heritage, and we should be aware of their intricate balance with their environment as we work to conserve them.

June 1996

AUTHOR'S NOTE.—*Man-made rockbars have been established in Cache River to slow its entrenchment and, together with riverbank stabilization, have protected Heron Pond from drainage.*

~~~~~~~~~~~~~~~~~~~~~~~~~~~~~~~~~

Our Geologic Faults

Illinois' bedrock layers mostly lie flat with few of the folds and faults or cracks in the rock characteristic of mountainous regions. Nevertheless, faults and folds are widespread and play a role in the state's economy and natural diversity. The term *fault* was coined by British coal miners to describe a vein of coal they were mining that would suddenly be displaced up or down at a bedrock break leaving the miner "at fault." Fault is now accepted geological terminology for such breaks and movement of rock.

Unlike California's San Andreas fault that has lateral movement as two of the earth's surface plates slide past one another, Illinois is in the middle of a continental plate, and faults here are mostly cracks created when one block of rock rose or fell relative to another. Such displacement or movement in Illinois can be from a few feet to over 3,400 feet.

Most Illinois faults are the result of uplifts or movement of the earth's crust involving large areas, but some are the result of localized events such as meteor impacts and volcanic activity. Many faults in the state are buried beneath glacial drift and other deposits that hide them from view except where they are exposed in river valley walls or road cuts. One of Illinois' most interesting hidden faulted areas is the Des Plaines disturbance, which lies buried under glacial deposits beneath the city of Des Plaines. This circular area of faulted rock is five miles in diameter and resulted from a meteor strike less than 280 million years ago. It might well be a tourist attraction if it were visible at the surface. Other atypical faults occur in southern Illinois' Hardin County. Here, curving faults encircle the west and north slopes of an old volcanic bulge in the bedrock known as Hicks Dome.

The longest fault in northern Illinois is the Sandwich fault, which stretches from Mount Morris in Ogle County southeastward beneath Sandwich to southwest of Joliet. It is most visible where it crosses the Rock River adjacent to Castle Rock State Park. Here, a feature along the fault is known as Devil's Backbone.

The LaSalle anticlinorium is a sharp fold rather than fault in the bedrock where it crosses the Illinois River in Starved Rock State Park. A strongly inclined sandstone layer, locally known as Little Rock, marks the anticline where it sticks out to the river from the south river bluff just a mile east of the Interstate 39 bridge. East of the anticline in the park are towering cliffs of sandstone while west of it the bedrock is limestone giving the bluff a gentler slope. Ohio Buckeye trees are common on the west side of the anticline but are absent east of it. Farther south in Illinois, this arch in the rock led to the development of major oil fields.

The Lincoln fold system stretches east–west from Missouri past Pere Marquette State Park to near Edwardsville. The fold's sharply inclined rock strata are visible behind the park's nature center and east along Route 100 to Grafton. Some downward bend to the south of rock strata is evident all along Route 100 from Grafton to Alton. This dip in the rock helped conserve the relatively low-elevation coal and shale rocks of the bluffs of the Mississippi valley below Alton. These low bluffs form the site for St. Louis, Edwardsville, and other cities. These relatively soft rocks also allowed the river to erode an exceptionally wide floodplain in this area, known as the American Bottom, which is rich in wetland wildlife.

Farther down the Mississippi is the Ste. Genevieve fault zone, which divides the Ozark Uplift from the Shawnee Hills. It enters Illinois from Missouri at the city of Grand Tower and extends southeast to Mountain Glen in Union County, Illinois. This fault is best viewed at Grand Tower, where it is exposed at Devil's Backbone Park and at Devil's Bake Oven. The latter is a prominent rock that juts into the Mississippi River.

Southeastern Illinois is the most heavily faulted region of the state and one of its most active earthquake zones today. Earthquakes indicate movement along a fault, so faulting is still actively occurring here. This large fault zone enters the southern tip of Illinois from the direction of New Madrid, Missouri, to the southwest and angles northeastward across Pope and Hardin Counties then branches off into the Wabash fault zone that extends up the Wabash valley to Lawrenceville. The most heavily faulted area is in Hardin County, where many of the bedrock cracks have been filled with minerals such as fluorite, galena, zinc, sphalerite, barite, and minor amounts of silver. Fluorite is Illinois' state mineral, and until deposits were depleted, it was actively mined.

The road cut on the north side of Route 146 just west of the canyon highway bridge in Dixon Springs State Park is a good place to see a fault in cross section. The mountain-like terrain of Cave Hill, visible to the southeast from Harrisburg, is a highly visible example of a faulted landscape. This range of hills lies along the southeast side of the Shawneetown fault and tilts away from it. Displacement or movement along this fault reaches 3,400 feet in this area.

Faults have played an important role in shaping Illinois. Winter is a good time to search them out and see what they look like.

February 1996

CHAPTER 2

HISTORICAL ACCOUNTS
OF EARLY ILLINOIS

The essays in this chapter recount natural conditions in early
Illinois, discuss some of the state's first natural scientists, and
describe ancient species surviving in the state.

～～～～～～～～～～～～～～～～

The Way Nature Was in Early Illinois

Biting horseflies so abundant they could kill a horse, flights of
Passenger Pigeons so dense that they darkened the sun, and flocks
of wild parrots flitting along the banks of Illinois' major rivers are
just a few of the ways it used to be in the Prairie State. John White
and Lisa Bell at Ecological Services in Urbana have uncovered a
wealth of information on early Illinois natural history in the course
of their study of how to design large nature preserves in Illinois.
Their findings help us understand just how close to the real thing our
present nature preserves are and how close we can expect to come
with planned restorations. They found these accounts of early Illinois
in county histories and various other early descriptive writings. Their
findings go beyond the well-known descriptions of game abundance
to describe various fish, nongame wildlife, and even insects.

Most surprising are the accounts of the green-headed flies (actually
it is the eyes of the fly that are green) that made life on the prairie
nearly unbearable for livestock during daylight hours from early June
until frost. About half an inch long, with a brown body, green eyes,
and clear wings, the flies would rise from the prairie grass in swarms
ahead of grazing stock or horses on a trail and descend on the animals
in great numbers. The pain the flies caused as they bit and obtained

their blood meal could stampede animals; and some animals died from loss of blood. John James Audubon attributes the death of the horse he was riding across southern Illinois in the summer of 1811 to these flies. In spite of having his horse's head and body clothed in light linen for protection, the flies got through gaps in the cloth and bit the horse in such numbers that it stampeded for the Big Muddy River. After emerging from the river the horse went but a short distance before dying.

Don Webb, fly expert at the Illinois Natural History Survey, says these were probably one or more of the seven to eight species of green-headed horseflies native to the state. They have greatly declined due to the drainage and destruction of the wetlands and wet prairies where their larvae live. We notice them today when one seeks a blood meal from us at the swimming pool or beach.

While green-headed flies were the most frequently described insect pest of the early prairies, John James Audubon also mentions the clouds of buffalo gnats that hovered like swarms of bees over the southern Illinois prairie. If you think that black flies are only creatures of northern lakes you will be surprised to learn that the buffalo gnat, a large blood-feeding black fly, was common on all of Illinois' early prairies. They would land on livestock in densities of over one hundred per square inch.

Mosquitoes were terrible as well. The Duke of Württemberg, on a tour of early America, describes a stop at Wilkinsonville on the Ohio River in Pulaski County on the night of April 27, 1823: "Since the region along Cash River and in the vicinity of the mouth of the Ohio River was still inundated, there were billions of mosquitoes and flies there, making our stay an inexpressible torture." In describing life on a homestead north of Monticello in Piatt County, Emma Piatt recounts how in the summer of 1824 all but one of the five horses they had were killed by fly and mosquito bites. They turned to their oxen to plow the fields.

Remarkably, some of the most notable and abundant wildlife described by these early observers were species that are now extinct. The Passenger Pigeon and Carolina Parakeet are examples of this. The parakeet was generally reported along riverbanks, which were its preferred habitat. It occurred along the Illinois River as far north as Mazon Creek in Grundy County and was conspicuous along the Wabash, Ohio, and Mississippi Rivers. It appears to have been a year-round resident. Noisy flocks of fifty to sixty of these tame birds were common along most large rivers, where they fed on the fruits of sycamore trees and other seeds. A little larger than Mourning Doves, these yellow, green, and red birds were described as of uncommon beauty. They were reported to commit depredations on wheat at harvest time, and large flocks were observed feeding in a cornfield in White County in January 1833. Their taste for crops and their tameness contributed to the parakeet's extinction.

Passenger Pigeons mostly nested north of Illinois. The great flocks and roosts were seen in Illinois mostly during migration although some did winter here. Zebulon Pike reported a nesting colony on islands in the Mississippi River in Pike County in 1806. Migrating flocks were so large that they were said to pass over Will County in clouds rather than flocks. In Madison County they were said to darken the skies. A forty-acre roost near the site of Cairo was in willows, while a six-hundred-acre roost near Crow Creek in Marshall County was in oaks. Both were characterized by trees with limbs broken off by the sheer weight of perching birds. The pigeons fed on acorns and beech nuts from the vast forests of the day, but spring migrants in Kane County were said to clean out a newly seeded spring wheat or oat crop as well. Their decline was caused by market hunting, which was made easy by their colonial roosting and nesting. By 1894 they were such a rarity that when one was spotted in Chicago's Lincoln Park the *Chicago Tribune* reported the sighting under "Last of His Race." One of the last reports of a wild Passenger Pigeon from Illinois was by Professor J. H. Moore in Chicago on July 11, 1911.

By 1850 Prairie Chicken populations had increased in response to early farming. The increased food from waste grain in crop fields coupled with large remnant prairies nearby for roosting and nesting led to a population explosion. Huge flights between roosting prairies and feeding fields occurred each morning and evening, which became the favored time for shooting them. A market hunter near Thornton in southern Cook County reported killing two thousand "chickens" by October in 1850. He sold them in Chicago for one dollar per dozen.

The Illinois River was one of the richest in fish life in the early days. In 1819 Edmund Dana attributed this richness to "the superior transparency of the water caused by the gentleness of its current" as compared to the Mississippi and other rivers. This clarity of water seems impossible to one who sees the river today, turbid with silt from soil erosion kept in suspension by barge traffic. Dana said Illinois River catfish weighed up to 170 pounds, and the "Spoonfish" (now called Paddlefish) reached four feet in length. Describing the river at Peoria Lake in 1838, Edmund Flagg reported Alligator Gars "about seven feet in length, a yard in circumference, and encased in armour of hornlike scales impenetrable to a rifle-ball." He estimated their weight at several hundred pounds. The Alligator Gar, a southern fish, is now very rare in Illinois waters if it lives in the state at all.

Other fish stories include the 1803 account by Lewis and Clark who pulled their boat ashore at the mouth of the Ohio to scout the area before entering the Mississippi. They returned to their boat to discover that their men had caught a giant catfish. While they were accustomed to thirty to sixty pounders, this one amazed them. They had to cut it into pieces to weigh it and finally determined it weighed 128 pounds. It was probably a Flathead Catfish, as it was thirteen inches between the eyes with a head weighing forty-four pounds. Elsewhere a forty-two-pound Muskellunge was pulled from Pistakee Bay in McHenry County, and many forty-to-sixty-pound Lake Trout were caught in Lake Michigan. Large catches include seining and salting ten barrels of fine pickerel in one day from the Fox River at St. Charles and a single seine haul from the Rock River at Rockford that produced enough fish to last the population of the town for several days. The latter haul included eighty-pound catfish and four-foot sturgeon.

William Keating describes the birds he saw on a trip through a prairie northwest of Freeport on June 15, 1823. The Sandhill Crane was common, the Long-billed Curlew occasional, and they even saw a Swallow-tailed Kite. Among these species, only the crane still nests in Illinois. One bird that captured the imagination of early Illinois explorers was the Trumpeter Swan. Lewis and Clark recorded these huge majestic white birds passing their Madison County camp in abundance on February 7, 1804. Others reported 107 swans in a single flight near Rock Island, where resting "swans whitened the sand bars" of the Mississippi. They were reported to have nested at Lima Lake north of Quincy.

Several accounts of wildlife in and near Chicago in the early years are notable. Bald Eagles nested along the bluffs at Lake Forest, and quail were so abundant that as many as seven thousand were packed in a single shipment by a merchant and sent via the Erie Canal to the

New York market. In 1834 a sizable strip of timber grew along the east side of the South Branch of the Chicago River from Madison Street south. In the fall of 1834 a large Black Bear was discovered in these woods, and the townspeople turned out in great numbers for the hunt. The bear was treed and killed near the corner of Market and Jackson Streets. This bear-hunt site of 1834 is part of Chicago's Loop today.

February 1993

AUTHOR'S NOTE.—*A breeding population of Trumpeter Swans has been established in Wisconsin, which now winters regularly in southern Illinois.*

Pioneer Botanists in Illinois

Illinois began the nineteenth century as the American frontier and ended it a civilized state. At its beginning, little was known of the plants inhabiting Illinois, but thanks to several botanists among our early settlers, this soon changed. These "botanists" came from diverse backgrounds, which reflect the variety of pioneers moving to Illinois. Some were from eastern states, while others came directly from Europe. Most were trained professionals who practiced medicine or other professions. Their botany was often self-taught and practiced as an avocation. They settled in all parts of the state, where they set about studying and documenting the variety of interesting plants about them. Since many of the plants they saw were new to science, they corresponded with the great botanists of the day who were mostly in Boston and New York. The eastern experts would identify known plants and give names to the new or unknown plants. Often they named the new species in honor of their collector back in Illinois.

Samuel Mead was a Connecticut Yankee who moved to Hancock County, Illinois, in 1834 after graduating from a New York medical school. His log cabin was the first house erected in the newly platted town of Augusta, where he became the first resident plant collector of Illinois. His medical practice covered a large area of scarcely settled land, which he reached by horse and buggy. Having a background

19

Mead's Milkweed, a prairie plant discovered by and named for
Illinois' first resident botanist, Dr. Samuel B. Mead, of Augusta.

in botany from his medical training, he made collections of the native plants he saw as he made his rounds. Of his discoveries, Mead's
Milkweed and Mead's Sedge are prairie plants that were named in his
honor. The milkweed is now on the endangered species list.

George Vasey was born at Scarborough, England, but obtained
his medical education in Massachusetts. He moved to Ringwood,
Illinois, in 1848 and practiced medicine in McHenry County until
1866. His love for plants led him to leave medicine and join John
Wesley Powell's 1868 Colorado River expedition through the Grand
Canyon. He eventually moved to Washington, DC, where he was
curator of the national plant collection there. Some of the many

plants named for him are Vasey's Rush and Vasey's Pondweed. Both are endangered in Illinois today.

Frederick Brendel immigrated to Peoria in 1852 after graduating from medical school in his native Erlangen, Germany. As he practiced medicine in Peoria he explored the rich plant life of the middle Illinois River valley and wrote a flora booklet for the Peoria region. He also kept meticulous climate records, which provide some of the earliest climatological data from the state.

Jacob Schneck was born in 1843 at New Harmony, Indiana, and practiced medicine at Mount Carmel, Illinois, from 1871 to 1906. He collected plants mainly near his home county. The Schneck Oak is just one of the plants named in his honor.

John Wolf was a self-taught naturalist and linguist from Bavaria who immigrated to America and settled in Canton, Illinois. He was born in 1820 and died at Canton in 1897. Among his many discoveries were Wolf's Bluegrass and Wolf's Spike-rush. The former is endangered in Illinois today.

George Hazen French was born at Tully, New York, in 1843. He moved to Illinois before 1868 and joined the faculty of Southern Illinois University at Carbondale in 1874. His interests included insects and plants. He discovered one of Illinois' most notable wildflowers, French's Shooting-star in what is now Giant City State Park.

Elihu Hall was a self-taught plant explorer and professional collector who was born in rural Virginia in 1822. After years of plant collecting on the frontier in Oregon, Colorado, Texas, and other western states, he turned to farming at Athens, Illinois. He said "he could make more money raising 'taters' than drying plants." Hall continued collecting plants in central Illinois, but most of the many plants named for him are from the west. Hall's Bulrush is an exception, however, having been found by him around the sand ponds in Mason County, Illinois.

Harry Patterson was born at Oquawka in Henderson County, Illinois, in 1853 and lived most of his life there as a printer and avid botanist. He corresponded with the great field botanists of his day because he printed plant collection labels for these professional collectors who explored the west during the last half of the nineteenth century. He discovered Patterson's Bindweed in the sands near Oquawka.

E. J. Hill was born in rural New York in 1833 and moved to Illinois after the Civil War to become a schoolteacher in Kankakee and Englewood. He discovered and named the Hill's Oak in south Cook County and discovered the very rare Kankakee Mallow on an Island in the Kankakee River. The mallow is one of only two plants thought to occur naturally only in Illinois. Hill's Pondweed is named in his honor.

These accounts remind us that Illinois has a rich heritage of native plants and an important historic heritage tied to their discovery and naming.

November 1993

FURTHER READING.—Afield with Plant Lovers and Collectors, *edited and published by Alice Kibbe of Carthage College, Carthage, Illinois, in 1953. "Elihu Hall, Illinois Botanist and Plant Explorer," by John Schwegman in* Erigenia *Number 25, Spring 2012.*

Prairie Fires in Illinois

The coming of Indian summer heralds the fire season on the Illinois prairie as it was practiced by Indians at the time of European settlement. After autumn's first frosts and freezes had killed the grasses and flowers down to ground level, the warm sunny days of fall dried and "cured" them. By late October and early November, some twenty-one million acres (61 percent of the state) were "clothed" in highly flammable fuel. Only a spark was needed to start the annual conflagration.

Biologist Bill McClain of the Department of Natural Resources, Division of Natural Heritage scoured county histories, old letters, and early explorer reports to document when and how Illinois prairies burned at the time of the Europeans' arrival. McClain found over seventy-five descriptions or discussions of prairie fires from 1673 to 1873. During this period, prairie fires invariably burned in the fall, almost as soon as their grasses were dry. McClain only found four references to fires in the spring, when most prairie managers burn prairie today. He found one reference to prairie fire started by lightning in Livingston County, but the other references were to fires set by Indians and later by early European settlers. On Illinois' flat landscape, a single fire could burn for scores of miles and cover thousands of acres. In November 1836 a fire started at ten o'clock in the morning on the Spoon River in Stark County northwest of Peoria. Driven by a strong south wind, it burned all the way to the present site of Rockford by sunset. Traveling about ten miles an hour, its eight-mile-wide front had covered ninety miles in a day. This single fire probably burned close to three hundred thousand acres. Such prairie fires are among the most spectacular and humbling sights in nature. People caught in their path on foot had little chance of outrunning them. Their only escape was to set a fire of their own and stand in its burned out area as the fire roared by.

According to early written accounts, the Indians set fires to hunt buffalo and other game. They set a partial ring of fire around the animals, leaving a gap where some of the hunters were stationed to shoot animals with arrows as they fled the flames. The Indians also used fire as a weapon against warring tribes and to protect themselves from vengeful fires. In the latter case they burned the prairie from around their lodges and villages so they did not have to worry about wildfire. The natives also burned favored hunting grounds not burned in ring fires so they would green up early in the spring and attract grazing game and to remove brush that hindered their movement through prairie and forest. Early settlers continued the practice of wildland burning to protect themselves from wildfire, to improve grazing, and to prepare the sod for plowing.

Once a tract of prairie was plowed, fire danger was greatly reduced. Breaking up the blanket of prairie fuel into ever-smaller tracts, settlers soon eliminated the wide- ranging fires that had blackened the Illinois landscape annually. It is generally agreed by ecologists that frequent fire was one reason that Illinois was mostly prairie at the time of European settlement. Our climate had adequate rainfall to support forest growth, which it did on steep topography and other sites protected from fire. But on flat lands, where wind-driven fires reigned, the trees could make little headway.

In addition to keeping trees and brush out of the prairies, fires help prairies by stimulating prairie plant flowering and seed production and creating an open sunny environment for seedling establishment. Today, most prairie managers burn prairie in the spring. Long days, higher temperatures, and the lower humidity of late winter and early spring make this the easiest time to accomplish prescribed burning. It also leaves the grassy cover as winter shelter for wildlife. McClain's research shows that the prairies that greeted our European settlers were the result of fall burns squeezed into the short period between the first killing frosts and the cool temperatures and high humidity of late November. Ecologists are now studying the comparative effects of fall and spring burning on prairies. Preliminary findings indicate that there may be significantly different ecological effects from burning at different times.

If you see smoke rising from a prairie remnant or restoration on a beautiful Indian summer day in Illinois, you may be witnessing a bit of our natural and cultural heritage as described by the earliest explorers of the state.

October 1992

AUTHOR'S NOTE.—*Although fall management burns are more common today, prescribed fire is still most common in the spring.*

Illinois' Living Fossils

Roaming the byways and waterways of Illinois and growing in its wildlands are creatures and plants little changed over tens or even hundreds of millions of years. These "primitive" species are a minor component of the present flora and fauna, but the fossil record indicates that they and their relatives once dominated our landscape. By chance, as their relatives died out one by one, these creatures found a niche in which they could compete with the more advanced forms. Today, these "living fossils" provide a glimpse of what life was like long ago in Illinois.

Illinois' six lamprey species are truly living fossils. Often considered fishes, they are far more primitive than the true fishes. They and their ancestors have apparently never had jaws or a backbone like "higher" animals. They feed without jaws by sucking nutrients from fishes that they parasitize or by filtering plankton from stream bottoms. In place of a backbone, lampreys have a stiffening rod of cartilage called a notochord. This rod is considered the forerunner of the backbone of modern vertebrate animals. The lamprey's paired gill slits appear in the development of a chick embryo, but are lost by the time the chick hatches. These slits are a primitive or "fossil" feature of the chick's ancestor that survives today only in lampreys.

Living fossils among fishes include sturgeons and the Paddlefish. Like the shark, they have primitive cartilage skeletons rather than bone. Also like sharks, they have primitive tail fins (called heterocercal by biologists) that consist of fin tissue along the lower side of the backbone with just a weak lower lobe of tail fin tissue. Modern fishes have a tail fin with equally developed upper and lower lobes.

Even among the fishes that have advanced to a bony skeleton from cartilage, the gars and Bowfin are reminders of earlier times. Both have tails intermediate in shape and structure between the most primitive fishes and modern fishes. Gars also have thick bony scales for protection that are not seen in modern fishes.

While the amphibians and reptiles as a group are all primitive and ancient forms, it is difficult to call any single species a living fossil relative to the others. The whole group looks much as it has for millions of years. The jumping ability of frogs and the protection of the turtle's shell are examples of special adaptations that have allowed these cold-blooded animals to survive in the age of birds and mammals.

Few or none of our birds qualify as living fossils, but one mammal surely does. This is the Virginia Opossum. This marsupial has a remarkably small brain and retains a primitive reproductive system, using a pouch to nurture young born just barely beyond the embryo stage. Marsupials are ancient creatures that died out as more advanced mammals developed in Africa, Eurasia, and North America, but survived on the island continents of Australia and South America. When a land bridge joined South America to North America some three million years ago, opossums found their way northward to Illinois. Primitive as they are, opossums seem to compete well in the modern world by their prolific reproduction rate, their habit of feigning death when attacked ("playing possum"), and their willingness to eat just about anything. I once watched a Virginia Opossum feeding on earthworms on a pavement after a rain. It would eat a worm, then a twig that slightly resembled a worm, then another worm. I was amazed that it did not spit out the twigs. This convinced me that they can and will eat just about anything.

Living fossils among Illinois' native plants include the horsetails and clubmosses. Relatives of these plants were among the dominant trees and herbs that grew in the state's coal-age forests over two hundred million year ago. The survivors of this group are generally smaller than their ancestors but retain the same general structure.

Bald Cypress trees are another of our living fossils. Closely related to the Dawn Redwood of China and the redwood and sequoia trees of California, our cypress and its relatives were widespread right up to the beginning of the ice age (Pleistocene epoch) about two million years ago. Bald Cypress has fared better than most of its relatives and is the most widespread member of its family surviving in North America today. Recognizing our living fossils helps us understand and appreciate the diversity and importance of our natural heritage.

December 1992

~~~~~~~~~~

Relict Species and Communities

The Plains Hognose Snake, Barren Strawberry plant, and Iowa Pleistocene Snail have one thing in common. In Illinois they all exist as relicts—plants and animals living on in an area as survivors of an earlier climatic period. Illinois has been subjected to four major climatic regimes over the past thirteen thousand years, three in addition to the one we now live in. Relict plants and animals from these former periods survive in unique minor habitats that mimic these climates of the past.

Just thirteen thousand years ago Illinois was still subjected to a cold ice-age climate with spruce forests covering much of the state and with some areas supporting tundra. About twelve thousand years ago the climate turned warmer and moister than our present conditions. This melted the continental glaciers and allowed a forest adapted to warm and moist conditions to become established in Illinois about nine thousand years ago. Some eight thousand years ago this warm, moist climate gave way to a warm climate much dryer than our present climate. This dry period lasted some three to four thousand years, and led to the spread of western prairie and plains plants and animals eastward into Illinois. Prairie exists in Illinois now, but these western plants and animals included species that are widely distributed today only in the short-grass plains of western Kansas and Nebraska. Climatologists call this dry period the Xerothermic Period.

This Xerothermic Period was followed by a shift to the cooler and moister climate we have today. Our present climate supports temperate deciduous forests, tallgrass prairies, and a variety of wetland communities. But scattered within this mosaic of plants and animals adapted to the present climate are relicts of three past climates—the ice age, warm-moist forests, and the very dry Xerothermic Period. Relatively small patches of unique habitat have allowed these reminders of Illinois' past to survive.

Ice age or cold-climate relicts have mostly survived on cool, shaded, north-facing rock ledges, often above the water of a stream in a canyon or gorge. The Barren Strawberry, various clubmosses and sphagnum mosses are examples of cold-climate relicts in the Shawnee Hills of southern Illinois. Others are found in canyons in east-central and northern Illinois. Some northern relicts are also found in seeps, where cool groundwater creates cold conditions over a small area. The Birds-eye Primrose in northwestern Illinois and Alder Buckthorn in northeastern Illinois are examples. Perhaps Illinois' most notable ice age relicts occur on north-facing rocky hillsides in the northwest called Algific Slopes. Ice forms in some of the jumbled boulder piles in winter and remains throughout the summer. Cool air draining from the ice refrigerates the slope, mimicking the climate of the ice age. The Iowa Pleistocene Snail, an animal that was widespread in the ice age, survives today only on these small cool slopes in Illinois and adjacent states. This habitat also supports Illinois' only Mountain Clematis and Beaked Hazelnut plants.

Relicts of the warm, moist forest period are frequently found on moist, protected slopes and ledges. Most are plants of the eastern forests that spread into the state only to die out except in these special sites when the climate turned dry during the Xerothermic. American Barberry and Pink Valerian plants are examples. The barberry survives only on ledges in southern Illinois and on moist shaded slopes in Tazewell County. The Valerian's native range includes the southern tip of the state and the Wabash River border counties, but isolated ravine populations in Greene and Pike Counties in western Illinois are relicts. Another relict of this period is an isolated population of American Beech trees in a protected rocky ravine in western Effingham County. Growing with it, and providing evidence that the trees

Mountain Clematis, a woody vine relict of a past colder climate. It is now known in the state only from an Algific Slope in the Driftless Area of northwestern Illinois.

were not just transported there by Indians, is a relict population of Harvey's Buttercup. These plants probably migrated together up the Kaskaskia River valley to this location. Areas close to the lower Kaskaskia are the nearest location where they grow together today.

Relicts of the Xerothermic Period have mostly survived in loose sand that provides a dry environment because of its low moisture-holding capacity. A few species also survive on exposed high and

Central Illinois sand dune at Sand Prairie Scrub Oak Nature Preserve in Mason County. Sand areas often support relict populations of western plants and animals. The Yellow Puccoon in the foreground is a western species.

dry prairies and bluffs. Western animals such as the Plains Hognose Snake, Bull Snake, Yellow Mud Turtle, and Strecker's Chorus Frog have survived here in sandy areas. Scientists believe the latter two species have evolved into new subspecies since being isolated here just five to six thousand years ago. Relict western plants include Grama Grass, Silvery Bladderpod, and Prairie Dandelion. Grama Grass grows in sand prairie, Silvery Bladderpod grows in Illinois only on a high sand dune in Mason County, and Prairie Dandelion survives on a few high and dry hill prairies in central and northern Illinois.

Relicts add much to Illinois' diversity of natural wonders. They are a living heritage from the past that reminds us just how much our climate and wildlife have changed over the past centuries.

January 1993

AUTHOR'S NOTE.—*Illinois' only known population of Barren Strawberry has disappeared, and it is now considered extirpated. It disappeared after a period of extreme drought.*

CHAPTER 3

NATURAL COMMUNITIES AND NATURAL DIVERSITY OF ILLINOIS

The essays in this chapter describe the diversity of Illinois' natural communities, such as forests and prairies, as well its variety of plant and animal life. Some descriptions of individual communities and sites are also included, especially those that are unique or especially interesting to the naturalist. Other essays describe the loss of community diversity through human exploitation and species extinction. Still others describe the contribution to diversity of man-made habitats such as highway rights of way and the continuing change in nature as it adjusts to changing conditions.

~~~~~~~~~~~~~~~~~~~~

The Natural Diversity of Illinois

Natural diversity refers to the variety of living things occupying a geographic area. Susan Post of the Illinois Natural History Survey estimates there are 53,754 native species in Illinois, not including three very poorly known groups of microscopic creatures. Published in the survey's *Our Living Heritage: The Biological Resources of Illinois* in 1991 in celebration of Earth Day 1990, the estimates came mostly from survey staff experts on various groups of plants and animals.

This was perhaps the first time that scientists had attempted to estimate the number of species in an area the size of Illinois and provide some interesting facts. The count shows only 2,574 kinds of plants but 29,662 animals. The plant count does not include 20,000 kinds of mushrooms and other fungi, which are no longer considered plants. However, it does include 385 mosses, 75 ferns, and 1,955 flowering plants. Algae and largely microscopic forms such as protozoa are also not considered plants or animals and number 1,518.

Within our "natural diversity" are a wide variety of unexpected forms of life. There are four hundred kinds of bread mold, fourteen sponges, twenty kinds of soil-dwelling earthworms, and one freshwater jellyfish. Now it immediately comes to mind to anyone familiar with Illinois waters that he or she has probably never seen a sponge or jellyfish in the state. That is because Illinois' species are small when compared to their Florida relatives.

Insects are the most numerous animals in Illinois, with about 17,000 native species. Most abundant among these are some 5,000 kinds of beetles, 4,100 types of flies and mosquitoes, 2,000 kinds of moths and butterflies, and 2,000 ants and wasps.

We have ninety-eight kinds of dragonflies, but only nine types of cockroaches, five walking sticks, and one praying mantis. Our five termite species manage to cause considerable structural damage in spite of their low diversity. A bit of a surprise to me are the 10,600 kinds of spiders and their relatives native to the state. These include 530 spiders, twenty ticks, nineteen daddy longlegs, and one scorpion. Most numerous of this group, however, are the estimated ten thousand species of mites. They feed on everything from plants to insects and large animals. Most of us are familiar with the Chigger, a mite that feeds on humans if it gets the chance. Of the more repulsive critters, there are thirty-two kinds of leeches, thirty-three fleas, and 298 lice. Most of these parasitize animals other than man.

In the mollusk group, Illinois has 170 kinds of snails and originally had 104 species of mussels. Sixteen of the latter have disappeared from the state, and four of these have become extinct. Their decline is in response to man's severe alteration of Illinois' waterways.

Among the "higher" animals, Illinois has 6 lampreys, 181 fishes, 39 frogs and salamanders, 59 reptiles, 297 birds, and 67 mammals. The above list includes some species that are now extinct and others that no longer occur in the state. Post notes that her list of 53,754 species does not include an estimate for bacteria, one-celled animals (protozoa), or roundworms (nematodes). Too little is known about them. Bacteria are not as identifiable to species as are other forms of life. While we are very aware of the bacteria that cause disease in humans, most bacteria live in soil and water where their numbers and characteristics remain a mystery. The same is true for many one-celled animals. Nematodes include some fairly large worms, such as the roundworm parasite of man, but for the most part are small microscopic animals of the soil. They are present in such vast numbers on and in the soil that it is said that if everything but nematodes were removed, you could still see the outline of the land in nematodes. Because of their great numbers and small size, no one can even guess how many kinds of nematodes there are.

Illinois has great natural diversity, and thanks to Susan Post and the Illinois Natural History Survey, Illinois is one of the few states with an actual estimate of its species.

November 1992

FURTHER READING.—Illinois Natural History Survey Bulletin *Volume 34, Article 4, April 1991.*

AUTHOR'S NOTE.—*As of July 2015 no comprehensive update to the number of species in Illinois has been compiled. New floras have added 644 additional species and hybrids of vascular plants to the state list, but most of these are introductions by humans, not native species.*

The Natural Divisions of Illinois

In spite of its generally flat terrain, Illinois has a variety of natural landscapes and biological diversity. From Lake Michigan beaches and rolling prairies to cool, forested ravines and cypress swamps, the Prairie State has a lot of natural diversity to offer.

Scientists concerned with conserving Illinois' natural diversity have divided the state into fourteen "natural divisions," each with its own distinctive landscapes, flora, and fauna. These divisions provide a framework for viewing nature in Illinois. Let's take a look at each division and a few natural areas where their primary features can be seen.

The Wisconsin Driftless Division comprises the hill country of Jo Daviess County and the northwest corner of Carroll County in northwestern Illinois. It escaped the ice age glaciers that flattened most of

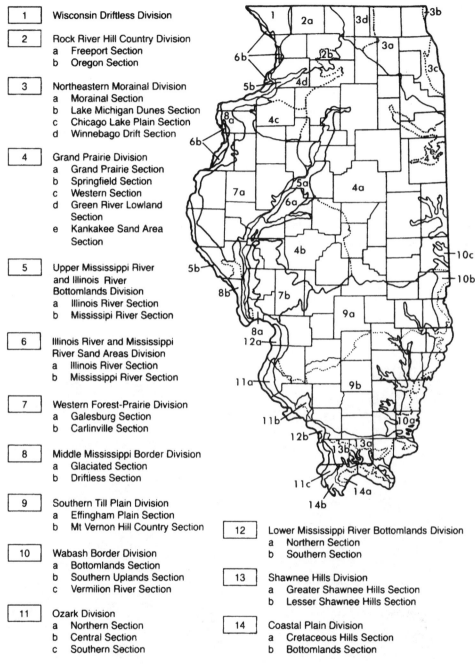

1	Wisconsin Driftless Division
2	Rock River Hill Country Division
	a Freeport Section
	b Oregon Section
3	Northeastern Morainal Division
	a Morainal Section
	b Lake Michigan Dunes Section
	c Chicago Lake Plain Section
	d Winnebago Drift Section
4	Grand Prairie Division
	a Grand Prairie Section
	b Springfield Section
	c Western Section
	d Green River Lowland Section
	e Kankakee Sand Area Section
5	Upper Mississippi River and Illinois River Bottomlands Division
	a Illinois River Section
	b Mississipi River Section
6	Illinois River and Mississippi River Sand Areas Division
	a Illinois River Section
	b Mississippi River Section
7	Western Forest-Prairie Division
	a Galesburg Section
	b Carlinville Section
8	Middle Mississippi Border Division
	a Glaciated Section
	b Driftless Section
9	Southern Till Plain Division
	a Effingham Plain Section
	b Mt Vernon Hill Country Section
10	Wabash Border Division
	a Bottomlands Section
	b Southern Uplands Section
	c Vermilion River Section
11	Ozark Division
	a Northern Section
	b Central Section
	c Southern Section
12	Lower Mississippi River Bottomlands Division
	a Northern Section
	b Southern Section
13	Shawnee Hills Division
	a Greater Shawnee Hills Section
	b Lesser Shawnee Hills Section
14	Coastal Plain Division
	a Cretaceous Hills Section
	b Bottomlands Section

"The Natural Divisions of Illinois," a classification of the natural lands and waters of the state. This recognition of geographic areas within Illinois having similar natural characteristics helps in planning for the development of a comprehensive state nature preserves system. *Courtesy of the Illinois Nature Preserves Commission.*

Illinois and the upper Midwest. Mississippi Palisades State Park near Savanna and Apple River Canyon State Park north of Stockton are good places to view the natural features of the Driftless Division. Look for the white trunks of paper birch trees along the bluffs at Mississippi Palisades and wildflowers in seepage areas of cliffs along Apple River. Pasque Flowers can be found in bluff-top prairie at Hanover Bluff Nature Preserve west of Hanover.

The Rock River Hill Country Division occupies the land from just east of the Rock River north and west to the Wisconsin Driftless Division. It is rolling land with a thin mantle of glacial soil. Rock outcrops and forests are common near the rivers and streams, while prairies formerly occupied much of the uplands. A visit to Castle Rock and White Pines Forest State Parks near Oregon, Illinois, gives a glimpse of the unique vegetation and landforms of the division. Notice northern relict plants, such as White Pine, on the cliffs.

The Northeastern Morainal Division includes Chicagoland (the Chicago metropolitan area) and northeastern Illinois out to Rockford.

Pasque Flowers in Illinois, at the very east edge of a distribution stretching back across Siberia into Europe. They grow in open upland prairie in northern Illinois. The specimen pictured here was in Hanover Bluff Nature Preserve in the Wisconsin Driftless Division.

It is mostly hilly to rolling, but not because of underlying bedrock. Its hills are made of glacial moraines—soil and rock ridges left by glaciers. Bedrock outcrops are rare. The division's diversity includes sand dunes along Lake Michigan, bogs, glacial lakes, marshes, forests, and prairie. Glacial landforms such as kames and "kettle holes" are common. Visit Illinois Beach State Park at Zion to explore dunes, beach, and prairie communities. Volo Bog in northwest Lake County is the best bog and good for marsh, while the best place to see glacial landforms is McHenry County's Glacial Park near Wonder Lake.

The Grand Prairie Division is the largest natural division in the state. Stretching from DeKalb south to Springfield and Shelbyville, it is level and largely treeless. Goose Lake Prairie State Park near Morris offers an impressive prairie vista and interpretation of the prairie vegetation. Funks Grove southwest of Bloomington is one of the division's best remaining prairie forest groves. Drive out through its virgin forest to the church and view the huge ancient oaks along the way.

The Upper Mississippi River and Illinois River Bottomlands Division stretches from the Grafton area northward along those rivers. This landscape of lakes, big rivers, and former prairies can best be seen at areas such as Anderson Lake Fish and Wildlife Area in Fulton County and Rip Rap Landing in northwestern Calhoun County.

The Sand Areas Natural Division harbors sand prairie, dunes, and scrub oak forest with cactus galore. Sand Prairie-Scrub Oak Nature Preserve east of Bath and Big River State Forest near Oquawka are good viewing spots.

The Western Forest-Prairie Division has rugged, sometimes rocky topography in the west-central part of the state. Siloam Springs State Park near Quincy and Beaver Dam State Park near Carlinville are good spots to see these forests, which contain Flowering Dogwood among other more southern and western plants. Siloam Springs also has stands of native prairie on rolling topography.

The Middle Mississippi Border Division includes the bluffs along the Mississippi and lower Illinois River valleys from East St. Louis northward. Steep sloping prairies called hill prairies and forests occur on these bluffs, which are also important as migration ways for soaring birds such as hawks. Pere Marquette State Park west of Grafton has good examples of all these unique features and vegetation types. Another accessible hill prairie is at the Department of Transportation rest area between Dallas City and Niota in Hancock County.

The Southern Till Plain Division is a flat plain dissected by stream valleys that once contained a mix of forest and prairie. It stretches from Shelbyville south to Marion and from Belleville east to Olney and Fairfield. Clay soils make this a region of rigorous conditions for plant growth. Flatwoods are a unique community of Post Oak and Pin Oak occurring on flat poorly drained uplands. Ramsey Lake State Park near Ramsey has examples of the forest and prairie vegetation. Prairie Ridge State Natural Area southwest of Newton in Jasper County has prairie vistas and a chance to see some of our remaining Prairie Chickens and other rare grassland birds.

The Wabash Border Division is a strip of land bordering the Wabash and Vermilion Rivers in eastern Illinois. Visit Beall Woods State Natural Area near Mount Carmel to see both upland and lowland virgin forests of this division and to walk along the Wabash River. Lincoln Trail State Park near Marshall and Middlefork Woods at Kickapoo State Park near Danville are good places to view the Wabash Border Division's upland forests. Look for the smooth gray-barked American Beech trees in these forests that are more typical of eastern states.

The Ozark Division is composed of the Illinois portion of the Ozark Uplift, which is along the southwestern border of the state. Visit Fults Hill Prairie Nature Preserve near Fults in Monroe County to see prairies that harbor Ozark plants such as Missouri Brown-eyed Susan and animals such as the Striped Bark Scorpion. The Pine Hills area of northwestern Union County is the best place to see native Shortleaf Pine trees, and look for flowering pink azaleas here if you visit in early May.

The Lower Mississippi River Bottomlands Division extends from the mouth of the Missouri River south to Cairo. It includes the Illinois part of the Mississippi River and the river's adjacent floodplain. The LaRue Swamp that lies adjacent to the Pine Hills in northwest Union County is an outstanding example of this division's forests and wetlands. At LaRue, look for the whorled pink flowers of the Swamp Loosestrife shrub in summer. Also listen for calls of the southern Green Treefrog from the swamp.

The Shawnee Hills Division consists of mostly unglaciated hills stretching across southernmost Illinois. Deep ravines, canyons, and rocky glades are among its outstanding features. Bell Smith Springs west of Eddyville offers a view of many of the division's habitats in a small area. Be sure to inspect the bluff-top vegetation and descend the steps to walk along Bay Creek. Limestone glades supporting prairie plants are present in the southern part of the division. Climb the hill at Cave Creek Glade Nature Preserve on the east side of Route 45 some three-and-a-half miles south of Vienna.

The Coastal Plain Division occupies the southern tip of the state. It contains both low hills and swampy land. The lowland forests and swamps are rich in southern species such as Bald Cypress and Tupelo Gum trees and a host of southern oaks. Visit the Heron Pond Nature Preserve south of Vienna to view this diversity from well-maintained trails and a boardwalk that leads out into the swamp. Visit the Barkhausen Cache River Wetlands Center on Route 37 some three-and-a-quarter miles south of Cypress, Illinois, for interpretation of the division and directions to other natural areas.

From northern bog to southern swamp and from desert-like sand dunes to prairies and cool beech forests, Illinois' natural divisions have much to offer those willing to explore.

July 1994

FURTHER READING.—Comprehensive Plan for the Illinois Nature Preserves System, Part 2, The Natural Divisions of Illinois *by John E. Schwegman et al., published by and available from the Illinois Nature Preserves Commission.*

Points of Inspiration in Illinois

Illinois has many sites of exceptional natural beauty, grandeur, and relevance to its wild natural heritage. They are capable of inspiring us with a sense of awe and wonder at nature's splendor. Some provide us with a sense of isolation that lets us experience what it must have been like to be a Native American in the area a thousand years ago. Others crowd our senses with sounds and sights of wildlife or just provide exceptional, beautiful views. A few require an understanding of natural forces at work to gain that sense of awe.

Fort Defiance Park at Cairo Point falls into this latter category. Standing in the park at the junction of the Mississippi and Ohio Rivers, the immediate scenery is not that exceptional. But with understanding you realize that at your feet the waters from much of the continent are mingling for the first time. Waters that plunged over Wyoming's Yellowstone Falls meet that which tumbled down Little River through the virgin forests of the Great Smoky Mountains of the east. Contemplating this stirs emotion and adds to the aura of Fort Defiance Park.

The shore of Lake Michigan at Illinois Beach State Nature Preserve moves me to wonder as well, especially when an east wind is blowing. Here in relative solitude and isolation near millions of people you can walk the shore with the surf pounding and the "sea" stretching to the horizon. It changes your sense of relevance.

A historic perspective helps in appreciation of some of our natural wonders. Anyone can appreciate the view from the top of Starved Rock; the sandstone bluffs cloaked with native White Pine and White Cedar and the Illinois River with its massive lock and dam. But an understanding of the Native Americans who perished there adds to the experience. Similarly, standing at the Lewis and Clark memorial south of Wood River and looking directly across the Mississippi to the mouth of the Missouri River is impressive. But realizing that in 1804 the brave explorers of an unknown wilderness camped near this very spot waiting for the spring thaw to cross and ascend the Missouri just adds to the ambiance.

The floating boardwalk into the swamp at Heron Pond south of Vienna is another site capable of inspiration to awe. Take it into the midst of a grove of cypress trees in spring, which includes some giants perhaps a thousand years old. Now with the wavering call of the Bird-voiced Treefrog in the distance, sit quietly and let the sense of nature primeval soak in. Try closing your eyes and identifying the natural sounds around you. Other sites where giant trees bring home the sense of the primeval are Beall Woods south of Mount Carmel and Funks Grove southwest of Bloomington. At both sites trails lead you among the living giants that sprouted before Europeans arrived.

A completely different but moving experience is the vastness of the prairie. Goose Lake Prairie Nature Preserve near Morris is the best place to experience this once common but now rare Illinois landscape. Here you can look out over prairie stretching well over a mile into the distance and get some sense of the awe it inspires—both as a stark and empty landscape stirring fear and with understanding of it as a rich community full of life. Visit in the spring when migrating waterfowl abound or in late summer when the prairie blooms its best. Try lying on your back in the tall grasses of summer for a mouse's eye view of the prairie. It adds interesting perspective.

High vistas have a place among Illinois' most inspiring natural sites. My favorites are the Pine Hills of northwestern Union County, McAdams Peak in Pere Marquette State Park, and Mississippi Palisades State Park at Savanna. Although the Pine Hills have an "Inspiration Point," it looks down on a road, and I prefer the view from one of the overlooks farther south in this Forest Service ecological area. A visit in April is especially rewarding with multitudes of frogs calling from the swamps below the bluffs. McAdams Peak is up the hill behind the lodge at Pere Marquette. Surrounded by waving prairie grasses, the view to the west is of the Illinois River valley and the broad, shallow Stump Lake. Spring and fall offer good views of migrating hawks from this spectacular vantage point. Mississippi Palisades offers many bluff-top views of the Mississippi River far below. It is part of the rugged Wisconsin Driftless Division, and vistas from these heights are hard to find elsewhere in northern Illinois.

Among the most moving wildlife displays in Illinois are the eerie booming of Prairie Chickens at Prairie Ridge State Natural Area near Newton and the clamor of wintering geese at Horseshoe Lake near Cairo. The Prairie Chickens are active from March into early April, while any time in the winter is good for Horseshoe Lake. At Horseshoe I like the view from the spillway best, with geese and an occasional Bald Eagle over the lake against a backdrop of cypress trees.

Illinois has many special places capable of inspiring and stirring our inner emotions. Plan to visit and experience some of them in the coming year.

March 1996

AUTHOR'S NOTE.—*The great flocks of geese at Horseshoe Lake have dwindled to a fraction of their former size as Canada Geese have begun wintering farther north. To some extent they have been replaced with large flocks of Snow, Blue, and White-fronted Geese.*

~~~~~~~~~~~~~~~~~~~~~~~~~

Memorable Moments with Nature

A lifetime spent observing and working with nature has led me to surprising and unexpected glimpses of seldom-seen natural phenomena. From unexpected sounds and sights to new and rare species of plants and animals, I continue to marvel at the wonders of nature.

In the spring of 2014, while visiting Heron Pond along the Cache River of southern Illinois, our group at the end of the boardwalk kept hearing an otherworldly croaking call from far off in the swamp. Finally we caught a glimpse of a cormorant-like bird making the call. A check of our bird-call recordings revealed that it was an Anhinga, sometimes called snakebird. We may be hearing more of the strange call of this immigrant from the south in the future. It has recently started nesting in southern Illinois.

While I was studying mussels along the North Fork of the Saline River I was startled by a strange frog call coming from weeds along the shore. A careful look at the point it was coming from revealed a Southern Leopard Frog being swallowed rear end first by a Northern Water Snake. As the snake kept extending its mouth over its prey, the frog made this unique "croak" that another frog sometimes answered nearby. Herpetologist Ronald Altig advises me that this is the death call of the frog. He said the amazing thing is that many different species of frogs make it as they are being eaten in this manner and that the calls sound about the same for all species. I have heard it just four times in all my time afield.

A group of friends and I were hiking on a trail in the Shawnee National Forest when we heard a dog driving an animal toward us. Soon a doe deer appeared heading right at us. We were spread out more than normal along the trail, and when the deer saw us it stopped. It looked back toward the barking dog and then at the long stretch of people before it and suddenly collapsed no more than thirty feet from us. Its legs spread out in all directions, its chin was laid on the ground and its ears flopped low as well. Its eyes were wide open and staring at us. It was hiding in plain sight! I took photos of it, and it got up after the dog had passed and slipped away.

Another deer story I have has to do with the birth of fawns. As I walked across an open field toward a patch of tall grass I saw a doe run out the other side of the patch. As I got closer I saw two wobbly fawns standing in an area of trampled grass. I walked up to the trampled area and one of the fawns looked at me and came over bleating and rubbed against my leg! I got my camera out and got pictures of this unexpected behavior. The two fawns had just been born and apparently one thought I was its mom. Amniotic fluid on the rear half of the fawn that rubbed my leg indicated that its birth had just happened and the doe had not had time to lick its coat clean.

Over the years I have come upon animals trapped and killed by dangers in their natural habitat. The first that comes to mind is a half-grown Eastern Cottontail, dead in a prairie with a morning glory vine wrapped around its neck. Another time I saw a Raccoon carcass hanging with its head stuck in a hole in the end of a stubby

White-tail fawn, just minutes old, and not having had all of the amniotic fluid licked from its coat by its mother. When I approached the fawn it ran to me and rubbed against my leg, apparently thinking I was its mother.

tree branch just five feet above the ground. The Raccoon had apparently pursued something into the hole, got its head in the hole, and then lost its grip on the limb. More recently, I saw a Common Yellowthroat warbler that was fluttering with its foot caught in its perch. Grape vines grab for support with tendrils that wrap around and around a limb to hold the vine up. If the limb it grabs dies and rots away, this leaves a round structure that looks like a compressed spring with small spaces between the coils. The bird had its middle toe caught in one of these spaces and could not get it out. I was able to free it only when the toe pulled off. I am sure it would have died had I not happened along.

After conducting a prescribed prairie burn on a Mississippi River bluff hill prairie, I was walking over the burn to check that all the fire was out. At a point near the top of the prairie, where the grass fuel was especially dense, I found a dead mole on the burned ground. It was not singed or burned in any way but had apparently come out of the safety of its burrow in search of oxygen. It appeared that the fire had consumed all of the local oxygen and the mole had suffocated.

The Gray Petaltail dragonfly is an ancient insect with fossils of it that show it was alive 150 million years ago. It is a living species that was a contemporary of dinosaurs. It is both a rare and a tame species that lives in and around seepage areas rather than ponds and streams like other dragonflies. When I entered its habitat to photograph one I was amazed when a Gray Petaltail landed on my shoulder. I have no doubt that its ancestors landed on dinosaurs just as this one had landed on me!

Mead's Milkweed is an endangered plant that I worked to conserve during my career as a nature conservationist. Late one afternoon I was sitting next to a flowering Mead's after having pollinated it by hand in an effort to enhance seed production (see essay titled "Milkweed Pollination" in chapter 7 ["Plants of Illinois"]). This milkweed has green flowers that hang upside down and depends on odor rather than color to attract pollinators. The wind was still, and I was on a hillside with cool evening air a foot or two deep draining downslope past me. As I watched the sun setting I noticed a bumblebee about fifty feet downslope flying slowly toward me. It was following the milkweed's stream of scent in the air toward the milkweed. As I watched, it proceeded slowly and lost the scent stream several times. When this happened, the bee searched back and forth until hitting the scent again and then proceeded toward the plant. It came right to my side and collected nectar from the milkweed.

A final memorable moment came when I realized that I had discovered a new species of plant in Illinois. I had found a new wood sorrel (genus *Oxalis*) that had hidden right under our noses because it was somewhat similar to an eastern species. I first collected the new plant along Little Lusk Creek in Pope County and keyed it out to the Large Yellow Wood Sorrel of the east. I noticed that the botany manuals did not mention the tubers on its roots and said that the leaves had brown margins on them that the Illinois plant lacked, but I thought this must be an oversight by the manuals. When I finally saw Large Yellow Wood Sorrel in the Blue Ridge Mountains of North Carolina, I realized Illinois' plant was not the same and that it was a new undescribed species. I named it the Illinois Wood Sorrel.

If you spend a lot of time in the field, you are sure to have many interesting encounters with nature; some that are new, unexpected, and exciting.

February 2015

Unexpected Plants and Animals in Illinois

Scorpions, wood rats, and the Red Squirrel are just a few of the creatures most would never think of as Illinois wildlife. Better think again! These are just a sampling of the unexpected critters that make their home in our forests, prairies, wetlands, and bluffs—an important part of the natural diversity of life in the Prairie State.

Illinois' scorpion is the Striped Bark Scorpion. They live on the dry rocky bluffs of the Mississippi River in Monroe and Randolph Counties just south of the St. Louis area. These scorpions are not often seen since they only come out at night to search for food. By day they hide under rocks and in burrows in the soil. If you visit their habitat at night with a "black light," you should find them by their glow. They fluoresce under ultraviolet light. Their sting is no worse than a wasp's.

Striped Bark Scorpion, the only native scorpion in Illinois. It is found in the Illinois part of the Ozark Uplift (Mississippi River bluffs) in Monroe and Randolph Counties.

The Red Squirrel is that little scolding tree squirrel that is so common in the pine and spruce forests of the north. Anyone who has camped in northern Wisconsin or Michigan has probably seen them scurrying about looking for scraps of food. They are about half the size of a Gray Squirrel. Their range extends south through Indiana and enters Illinois along the Kankakee River drainage. The best place to see them is in the city park in Momence.

The pack rat native to Illinois, more properly called the Eastern Wood Rat, conjures up visions of the arid west, where wood rats are most common. The name pack rat comes from their habit of "packing" in material to build nests. These structures resemble piles of sticks about two feet across, but they include a variety of food items and shiny materials like bottle caps and plastic as well. They are now found in Illinois only in the Mississippi River bluffs of Jackson and Union Counties. Their abandoned houses and droppings under and along bluffs across the Shawnee Hills indicate they were formerly much more widespread in southern Illinois than they are now.

A mouse that hops along like a kangaroo may be a surprise to most Illinoisans. But believe it or not, Illinois has one, and it occurs throughout the state. The Meadow Jumping Mouse can reach tremendous speeds for its size using its powerful hind legs for long jumps and its extra-long tail for stability. Meadow Jumping Mice can be found in a variety of grassy and brushy habitats, especially wet areas. But do not look for them in winter as they hibernate.

The Snowy Egret is a small white heron of the south. About two-thirds the size of our common Great Egret, this beautiful bird has more filmy plumes than its larger cousin and yellow feet to boot. In Illinois, the Snowy Egret nests mainly in the lowlands along the Mississippi River opposite St. Louis in the area known as the American Bottoms.

Terns are waterbirds that we most often think of as cruising along above the seashore making quick dives into the surf for fish. It's a surprise to learn that four kinds of terns actually nest in Illinois. The Black, Forster's, Common, and Least Terns all nest in the state. The first three raise young only in the glacial lakes and wetlands of northeastern Illinois and along Lake Michigan. However, the Least Tern may nest along any of Illinois' large rivers where sandbars occur. All Illinois terns occur in such low numbers that they are listed as endangered species.

A surprise in the aquatic world is a small fish that lives only in springs and adjacent cave waters. Called the Spring Cavefish, it has small eyes covered by skin and spends some of its time in the total darkness of caves. It is found only in the Shawnee Hills and Ozarks of the southern tip of the state.

Unexpected species are not limited to the animal world. You might be surprised to learn that Illinois is home to forty-six kinds of wild orchids. Orchids reach their greatest diversity in tropical forests but are by no means limited to the tropics. There are native orchids in most of Illinois' natural habitats. There are also carnivorous (insect-digesting) plants in the state. Illinois does not have the Venus Flytrap, but sundews and pitcher plants are in the bogs and damp sandy areas of northeastern Illinois. Sundews catch insects on sticky hairs on their leaves and absorb their nutrients through the leaf. The leaves of pitcher plants hold water that drowns insects. The insects are then digested in the fluid and absorbed by the plant.

Illinois holds a great diversity of living surprises. This natural heritage can be a source of enjoyment and education for those who take the time to seek it.

May 1993

Hill Prairies

Hill prairies are dry upland grasslands that occur on hillsides and the tops of ridges. They represent a large percentage of the remaining Illinois prairie because they are too steep to plow or develop. They typically occur on west- and south-facing slopes where the afternoon sun is hottest and the prevailing westerly winds strike them with full force. Because of their high location and short, open vegetation, hill prairies offer some of the most spectacular natural vistas in Illinois. The cover of this book is of a hill prairie scene..

Hill prairies are found in all parts of Illinois where there is enough topographic relief to support them. They are best developed along the Illinois and Mississippi Rivers but occur on many tributaries to these rivers. They also occur on limestone outcrops across the Shawnee Hills, along eastern Illinois rivers such as the Embarrass

Northeast Meredosia Hill Prairie in Morgan County with Pale Coneflowers in the foreground. Hill prairie extends into the distance on smooth slopes of loess soil with the Illinois River floodplain beyond.

and Vermillion, and on gravel knobs and hills in northeastern Illinois. They occupy a microclimate that is hotter and drier than surrounding, usually forested, land. In addition to being exposed to the more direct rays of the afternoon sun and wind, which evaporates moisture more rapidly, much rainfall runs off the hill rather than soaking into the soil. The result is a prairie of shorter grasses and drought-adapted wildflowers more like the mixed-grass prairies of central Kansas or Nebraska than the tallgrass prairies of Illinois.

In addition to their unique hillside location, hill prairies are seldom found on acid (sour) soils, growing mainly on sweeter neutral-to-alkaline substrates. Loess, wind-deposited silt, is the typical soil they grow in along major rivers, but some occur on glacial till and others on exposed limestone and dolomite bedrock outcrops. Illinois' loess has so much calcium carbonate or sweetness in it that moisture moving through it often picks up the lime and concentrates it into stone-like calcareous concretions, not unlike the material composing stalactites in caves. These concretions are usually very conspicuous to visitors and can be identified by their sculpted-to-rough prickly appearance.

Native Americans lived along Illinois' rivers. During the middle woodland period, before the time of Christ, many of them chose bluff tops with beautiful hill-prairie vistas for burial of their dead. Small burial mounds are a feature of many of these prairies today. Like other prairies, hill prairies are dependent on periodic fire to maintain grass and herb dominance over trees and shrubs. Many in private ownership today are disappearing from lack of fire. Hill prairies typically give way to forest on adjacent north- and east-facing slopes protected from the hot sun, drying wind, and wind-driven fire.

Most hill prairie is dominated by Little Bluestem and Sideoats Grama, both mid-height, warm-season grasses that do their growing and flowering in the heat of summer. These grasses give the prairie its short appearance relative to the Big Bluestem of Illinois' tallgrass prairie. One of the most scenic times to visit these prairies is in mid-June. The display of Pale Coneflowers is usually awesome then. But early autumn, when the Little Bluestem turns orange and various sunflowers, asters, and blazing stars bloom is also an impressive season.

Hill prairies provide habitat for some of Illinois' most interesting wildlife. The Slender Glass Lizard, a legless lizard that resembles a snake until you notice that it can close its eyes, is a typical inhabitant throughout most of Illinois. The only scorpion in the state and many western creatures such as the Plains Hognose Snake and Coachwhip Snake make their homes on hill prairies in southwestern Illinois.

Good places to see these prairies are scattered throughout Illinois. In northwestern Illinois, try Hanover Bluff Nature Preserve near Mississippi Palisades State Park or some small prairies in the park itself. In central Illinois, Revis Nature Preserve east of Kilbourne in southern Mason County and Pere Marquette State Park are good bets. In southern Illinois, Fults Hill Prairie southeast of Fults in Monroe County and Cave Creek Glade Nature Preserve four miles south of Vienna on Route 45 are good.

October 1993

Nature's Icebox

Most everyone knows that Illinois has prairies, forests, and wetlands, but did you know it also has small areas where ice never melts in summer and where the climate mimics that of the ice age of long ago? Scientist Terry Frest of the University of Iowa coined the term *Algific Slope* for this unique habitat and the cold climate it maintains over a small area. Such areas are limited to the Wisconsin Driftless Area and are most common in northeast Iowa but are also found in Minnesota, Wisconsin, and Illinois. To date only nine such sites have been found in Illinois, and only two of these seem to hold ice all summer. All are in Jo Daviess and Carroll Counties in the northwest corner of Illinois.

Algific Slopes are jumbled piles of rock at the base of dolomite rock cliffs. The rocks average about three feet or less in diameter and are piled at the base of cliffs that face north to northwest. The rocks have broken off the bluff and are called talus. Because of the jumbled nature of the rock pile, there are many spaces for air and water to move through it. Many of the associated rock outcrops and bluffs have cracks and fissures in the bedrock near the face of the bluff. During winter these rocks, even those deep within the pile, are chilled to below freezing by cold air driven into the pile by the north wind and from cold air drainage from shallow fissures in the adjacent bluff. As snow melts and rain falls in the spring they drain into the rock pile and freeze, forming ice within it. Sometimes the ice may be fed by groundwater as well. During summer, the rock pile and its ice cools warm air that enters the top of the pile as heavier cold air drains from holes between the rocks from about midway down the slope to its base.

Our largest Algific Slope is about one hundred yards long and forty yards wide or high. These habitats are open areas devoid of trees for the most part due to their rocky nature and the permanent ice in the tree-root zone. They are covered with mosses, ferns, and herbs that grow in the thin layer of black organic-rich soil that has accumulated on top of the rocks. Occasional Paper Birch trees grow in apparent warm spots on the slopes, and various shrubs and trees thrive in the cool habitat along the lower edge of the slope.

I took a temperature reading at our largest slope on July 30, 1985, and found the temperature on the surface of the slope to be forty-two degrees Fahrenheit at two o'clock in the afternoon, when the temperature away from the slope was sixty-five degrees. At a depth of ten inches down between the rocks, the temperature was thirty-three degrees, indicating the presence of ice nearby. The cold air flows in a layer only six to eight inches deep on the surface of the slope. You can be standing in summer's warmth, but placing your hand on the surface of the slope is like sticking it into a refrigerator. The cold air slows plant flowering to a remarkable degree while not freezing or killing them. I found spring-flowering plants such as Columbine still blooming on July 30, and Canada Violets bloomed from spring to at least September 25.

As a botanist, I was struck by the unique plants I found growing on these slopes when I first discovered them in 1981. The two-inch-long blue blossoms of the Mountain Clematis vine first caught my eye. A closer look revealed Needle Rose and Beaked Hazelnut as well. None of the three had ever been found in Illinois before. Many of the other plants found here are rare species of the north that survive in Illinois only in this and other unique cold habitats.

Biologists think that these slopes are not just remnants of natural communities that are common farther north. They seem to represent small examples of how the climate was at some distance from the glacier during the ice age. The ice age climate was probably cool all summer but not as cold in winter as the boreal forests

Iowa Pleistocene Snail, widespread in Illinois during the Pleistocene geologic epoch that saw many glacial advances in the last 2.6
million years. As shown by its fossil shells, it was widespread during
glacial periods. It now exists only in a unique cold habitat created
by ice that persists throughout the summer months. The species
is presently limited to the Wisconsin Driftless Area.

of modern-day Canada. The evidence for this is the survival of the
Iowa Pleistocene Snail on these slopes today, whose shells are found
as widespread fossils in ice age deposits. These snails cannot live in
Canada's boreal forest today because temperatures of minus-for-
ty-degrees Fahrenheit, common there today, kill them. The Iowa
Pleistocene Snail now survives only on these tiny Algific Slopes,
where it awaits the next ice age and the chance to once again spread
out over the Midwest.

These small, unique habitats are truly refugia for the future as
well as reminders of the past and contributors to the present diversity
of Illinois' natural heritage.

September 1993

AUTHOR'S NOTE.—*The Needle Rose has disappeared from this habitat
and the state since 1993, apparently due to deer browsing.*

FURTHER READING.—*"Algific (Cold Producing) Slopes in Illinois and
Their Vascular Flora," by John Schwegman in* Erigenia *Number 7,
July 1986.*

~~~~~~

Sandbars

Sandbars along Illinois' large and medium-sized rivers are fascinating places to observe nature. They provide ideal habitat for feeding and resting birds, habitat for foraging mammals, and the opportunity to see a variety of aquatic creatures, other wildlife, and their tracks and signs. Typical habitats include expanses of moist-to-dry barren sand, a shoreline with wave-impacted beach, deep-to-shallow waters adjacent the bar and inlets, and pools partly-to-completely separated from the river. Some have high and dry, loose sand habitats. Being inundated by the river most of the year, they are often devoid of vegetation except on their highest points. Low annual herbs sometimes spring up on them in late summer and rush to make seed before frost.

Sandbars are exposed best during low-water periods such as late summer and fall. Their fringing shallow waters are ideal for foraging by herons and migrating shorebirds such as sandpipers. Their isolated and open points and beaches are important resting and loafing sites for migrating waterfowl and gulls. If you visit a sandbar, be sure to take along binoculars for viewing birds. You will not be able to approach them closely because of the lack of cover.

The smooth surface and shore of a sandbar are ideal for interpreting animal tracks and signs. The concentrated webbed tracks of loafing gulls, ducks, and geese stand in sharp contrast to the unwebbed large tracks and long stride of the hunting heron visible in the shallow water. These all contrast with the many small tracks of Killdeers and sandpipers that forage along the shore. Crow tracks are common around dead fish that have floated up on shore. Both Common Crows and Fish Crows are opportunists and often make a meal of dead fish. The tracks of predator mammals such as Raccoons and Mink can usually be seen following the shore searching for stranded fish and mussels to eat. You might even find mussels recently opened and eaten by Raccoons. I recently saw the tracks of a River Otter on a sandbar along the Illinois River near Banner. This is an animal sign that had long been missing from this part of Illinois until recent reintroductions. During warmer periods, tracks of turtles that have come ashore to sun themselves or even ventured inland to lay eggs are common. If willows are present you might see the massive foot tracks and tail track of Beaver and the scratches where one has dragged a cut tree across the sand to be eaten in the river.

You are bound to come upon several dead fish along the shore, as these wash up constantly. They usually represent a good cross section of the fish species present in the river. One does not have to be an expert to recognize gar, catfish, and game fish, but occasionally something unusual such as a Paddlefish or sturgeon is spotted. Sometimes it is best to check your nose at the shore when you venture on a sandbar as the odor can be strong near some of the carrion.

Look for the tracks of mussels and aquatic snails in pools and near the shoreline. These single, linear-to-meandering tracks in the sand should have the animal present at one end or the other. If you are lucky enough to find a mussel actively crawling, take time to notice how it does it. First the "foot" is narrowed and pushed forward into the sand. Then the mussel expands the end of the "foot" to anchor it and contracts the foot that pulls the shell up to the anchor. Old dead shells of mussels and snails are commonly incorporated into the sand of the sandbar. See how many kinds you can find.

As you leave a sandbar in August to early September, you may encounter a large and very noisy cicada emerging from the roots of riverbank willow trees. I call this the Willow Cicada because of its apparent food preference. It is our largest cicada.

Sandbars are among my favorite places. I am sure they will become yours too if you take the time to visit one.

October 1996

Highways as Habitat

Highway rights of way play an important role in the natural world of Illinois. They provide wildlife habitat, wildlife migration corridors, and, on the negative side, can be sources of wildland weed problems. The interstate highway system, with its broad medians and borders, covers about 40,000 of the 139,000 acres in state-maintained highways in Illinois. Its network of grassy and brushy habitat and associated borrow-pit lakes and ponds reaches into every corner of the state. While these lakes and ponds are often privately owned, this generally does not diminish their value to wildlife. As we travel along these interstates through the otherwise vast croplands of the flat regions of Illinois, it is easy to see how their grassy habitat and ponds act as a partial surrogate for the prairie and its "pothole" wetlands of ages past. The habitat value for birds includes nesting, feeding, and migratory rest stops. Permanent resident wildlife such as mammals, amphibians, reptiles, and fish all find homes here year-round.

We have all seen hawks perching along our highways, nature's testimony to the good habitat they provide for their preferred diet of mice and voles. The dense grassy cover along highways usually produces good populations of these rodents, which are important food for raptors and mammal predators alike. During winter, large Rough-legged Hawks that have migrated from nesting grounds on the northern tundra often hunt from low perches like fence posts along our highways. Permanent resident raptors such as the Red-tailed Hawk and the American Kestrel are common but prefer higher perches.

House cats are probably the most frequent mammals observed hunting mice here, but weasels, foxes, and Coyotes do so as well. Highways in general, not just the interstates, are very important to the survival of ground squirrels in Illinois. These herbivores survive in cropland areas that are otherwise unsuitable for them by feeding on grasses along the roads and denning in the road banks. Interstates provide us with one of the surest signs of spring as Red-winged Blackbirds return in March and set up nesting territories at regular intervals along them. They are probably the most numerous birds to nest here, but increasingly roadside ditches are also being used for nesting by Mallard Ducks, and borrow pits support regular nesting by Canada Geese. Although valuable habitat to some, many grassland songbirds are unable to nest along highways because traffic noise prevents them from hearing and responding to their songs.

The strings of ponds along interstates are good rest stops for migrating waterfowl and other wetland birds. Another migration-corridor effect of interstates stems from the fact that they provide a continuous corridor of similar habitat over hundreds of miles. Probably the most striking response to these corridors by mammals is the spread of the Western Harvest Mouse. This grassland mammal was restricted to the northwest corner of the state in 1959, when construction began on the interstate system. It has now spread throughout the northern half of Illinois, where its rapid range expansion seems to have been facilitated by the strips of grass along the interstate highways.

Highway habitat corridors also allow for the spread of hard-to-control exotic wildland weeds. These exotic invaders and degraders of wildlife habitat are a fairly recently recognized problem. One such weed of prairies and other sunny habitats is Cut-leaved Teasel. This tall thistle-like biennial from Europe seems to have used the highways as a major route for rapidly spreading over eastern North America. Control of such pest plants is a growing concern for highway agencies and conservation biologists.

All in all, highway rights of way are important wildlife habitat, especially in areas where other wildland is scarce. However, they need special attention by managers to prevent them from becoming sources of weeds that degrade other wildlife habitats. As we drive and enjoy seeing wildlife along the interstates and other highways of Illinois, let's keep an eye out for animals on the road. Given our roadway's value to wildlife, the least we can do is minimize road kill by careful driving.

December 1994

Extinctions

Most of us realize that Elk, Passenger Pigeons, Gray Wolves, and Black Bears no longer inhabit the Prairie State, but few realize that extinction has taken a much bigger toll from our wildlife. Extinctions can be total or local. Total extinctions are forever and represent the loss of species and the genealogy spanning millions of years that produced them. Local extinctions are more properly called extirpations and refer to the loss of a species from a region or state. Susan Post of the Illinois Natural History Survey consulted experts and published records in 1991 and concluded that we have lost at least 115 native species from Illinois. Considering how little we know about groups like the insects and fungi, the number is probably higher. Post's list of extirpated species contains fifty-nine plants, sixteen mussels, twelve fish, nine mammals, eight birds, seven insects, and one kind each of snake, salamander, crayfish, and shrimp.

Of this list, only nine are thought to be total extinctions. These are the Leafshell, Round Combshell, Tennessee Riffleshell, and Wabash Riffleshell mussels; the Passenger Pigeon, Carolina Parakeet, and Ivory-billed Woodpecker; the tiny Thismia plant; and the Chewing Louse that parasitized the Passenger Pigeon. The other 106 species are thought to still exist outside of Illinois. The destruction or alteration of habitat as exhibited by siltation, land clearing, prairie plowing, and wetland drainage seem to be the main causes of our native species loss. However, a few species of birds and mammals were hunted to extinction here for their food value or because they were considered pests. Those exterminated largely for their food value were the Passenger Pigeon, Trumpeter Swan, Sharp-tailed Grouse, Elk, and Bison. Perceived pests included Gray Wolf, Mountain Lion, Black Bear, and Carolina Parakeet. They were often killed, but also suffered from habitat alteration and loss.

Slightly over one-third of our extirpated species were aquatic, living largely in water. Their loss reflects the decline in water quality in Illinois since settlement. The aquatic organisms include the sixteen mussels, twelve fish, Hellbender Salamander, Broad-banded Water Snake, Rusty Crayfish, Ohio Shrimp, and twelve of the plants. The single biggest problem with our water quality is siltation or turbidity created by soil erosion resulting from plowing the land. Turbidity cuts off light to submerged plants, often killing them. It clogs the filter-feeding mussels and, if the silt is deep enough, can bury and kill mussels outright. Siltation also impairs feeding and reproduction of some fishes.

Among the fishes we have lost are the Alligator Gar, Muskellunge, Bigeye Chub, Northern Madtom, Ohio Lamprey, and Bluehead Shiner. The latter species was extirpated by a chemical spill into its only known habitat. The Blackfin Cisco has disappeared from Lake Michigan along with four darters from our streams. Many darters inhabit clean, fast riffles in small rivers and creeks, a habitat that is becoming rare in Illinois today.

Of our total plant losses, two were mosses, one a quillwort, one a scouring rush, two were ferns, and fifty-three were flowering plants. Habitat loss, particularly the plowing of prairies and the drainage of wetlands contributed heavily to our loss of plants. Many of them had very limited distribution in Illinois, and some occurred in the Chicago area, where they disappeared as the city grew and their habitat was paved over. Seven of the lost flowering plants were native orchids, which are noted for their rarity and fidelity to unique habitats. The Dragon's Mouth Orchid was the most beautiful of these, and its occurrence in Chicago sealed its fate.

In addition to the birds that were totally exterminated and hunted to extirpation, we have also lost the Roseate Spoonbill, Common Raven, and Eskimo Curlew. Other mammals lost in addition to those hunted to extirpation are Porcupine, Marten, Fisher, and Cotton Mouse. In addition to the Passenger Pigeon Louse, the known insects that no longer live in Illinois include the Brown Lacewing and five butterflies—the Dakota Skipper, Simple Prominent, Mustard White, Indiana Schinia, and Diana Fritillary.

The extirpation of many birds, flowers, and butterflies has cost Illinois some of its most beautiful and interesting wild species. Let us all support efforts to keep our remaining natural beauty and diversity.

August 1994

AUTHOR'S NOTE.—*Bachman's Warbler was formerly found in Illinois and is now considered extinct. The Ohio Shrimp and Northern Madtom, which were considered extirpated, have been rediscovered living in Illinois.*

~~~~~~~~~~~~~~~~~~~~~~~~~~~~~~

Springtime

Spring heralds two of nature's grand annual shows in Illinois—the blooming of spring wildflowers and the annual songbird migration. This is written in hopes of motivating the reader to get out and enjoy these wondrous events. You can be a part of Mother Nature's rites of spring by getting out to the woods sometime in the first half of May.

As the song says, "the best things in life are free." Any local park, preserve, or woods down the road will have this show of flowers and songs free for your enjoyment. Of course, ask before entering private lands. It is a good idea to have field guides for the birds and flowers to help identify what you are seeing and a pair of binoculars to bring those colorful little warblers up close. A recording of bird songs is another helpful identification aid. All of this flowering and singing is crowded into the short period of spring for some very basic biological reasons.

Let's consider the plants first. Most of the plants of the forest floor crowd their flowering into the short period after it gets warm enough for plant growth but before the leaves come out on the trees and cut off the direct sunlight. These plants need this sunlight to produce energy for seed production and food to carry them over until the next spring. This causes the overlapping of flowering time for many plants resulting in a "carpet" of colorful flowers in many different hues and forms. Almost any ungrazed woods should have several dozen kinds in flower at once. Try to identify as many kinds of flowers as you can. Notice how the Dutchman's Breeches flower resembles its name. See the spur on that larkspur, how buttery the buttercup looks, and locate Jack in that Jack-in-the-pulpit. Another thing to watch for is the habitat selection of different kinds of plants. Some will be only in wet areas, others will prefer slopes facing one

Bloodroot, a common early spring woodland wildflower found throughout Illinois. It is our most common member of the poppy family and gets its name from the blood-colored sap of its root.

direction or another, and still others will grow on dry ridgetops and rocks. Check out the base of north-facing slopes and ravine bottoms for the richest assemblage of flowers.

Of course, all of these beautiful flowers are not here just to please us. Their real and important function is to attract insects for pollination and seed production. Take a minute to see what is pollinating the flowers. You will probably see a few honeybees (not native in North America), but mostly you should see bees a little darker than honeybees. These are solitary ground-nesting bees, the primary native pollinators of our spring flora. One last thing to notice is the seeds of most of these plants. Generally they are small and have a white spongy appendage on one end. You can usually find a few by picking apart a fruit of an early flowering specimen. Don't bother looking on the ground. The white spongy piece is key to the dispersal and planting of the seeds of these plants. It is a delicacy for ants, which pick up the seeds about as fast as they hit the ground and carry them back to their underground dens. Here the ants eat the delicacy and discard the seed, which is now not only dispersed away from the parent plant but planted in the soil and ready for growth. Look around for ants. You will surely see some, and you may even see one carrying a seed. This is just another example, along with the pollinators, of the interdependence of life within the forest ecosystem.

The spring bird concentration is caused by the annual passage of songbirds returning from their wintering grounds to the south. Some will nest here, but many are just passing through on their way to habitats in the Great Lakes states and Canada. While American Robins, Common Grackles, and a few other migratory birds are back by March and April, the great concentration of song and color arrives with the warblers and other small songbirds in early May. They mostly migrate at night and seem to arrive in "waves," filling our treetops with a diversity of song and species that goes unmatched the rest of the year. During the two weeks when new oak leaves are about the size of a squirrel's ear, it is possible to see one hundred or more kinds of birds in a day. While a similar migration passes through Illinois in fall, at that time the birds are drab and mostly silent. In contrast, these spring migrants are in full breeding colors and are singing profusely.

Of course, this musical "show" is not for our enjoyment but rather because the birds have nesting and rearing families on their minds.

The songs and flashy colors of the males allow them to attract a mate and establish and defend a nesting territory. Also notice how many of the warblers, vireos, and other small birds are flitting about at the ends of the branches high in the tree canopy. They are feeding on insects that concentrate in these newly opening leaves and flowering catkins. It is not hard to see how they fit into the forest's web of life. They greatly reduce the number of insects that prey on the tree's fruits and leaves. If you only take one nature hike a year, try to make it into the woods in spring. You will be glad you did.

May 1993

Wildlife Watching from Trees

The fall season finds me setting up in trees a good bit, looking for deer and seeing a lot of other wildlife in the process. In thirty-five years of bow hunting from a tree stand, I have seen a lot of nature that I would never have seen otherwise and saw many common species from new perspectives. Just as deer do not normally look up in trees for humans, most other wildlife does not expect us up there either. This gives the tree-sitter a much better chance at viewing elusive animals than someone on the ground might have.

Deer stands are often only fifteen to twenty feet off the ground, but my favorite stand is thirty feet up, putting my head about halfway to the top of the canopy of a large, spreading White Oak. I got a whole new perspective on the Sharp-shinned Hawk when one flashed through the tree canopy about a yard in front of my nose! After the start it gave me, I have an appreciation of the terror it must hold for its prey—the warblers and other songbirds foraging among the treetops. I had another Sharp-shin land about ten feet from me on the very limb I was standing on. I watched as it shifted its weight from foot to foot and could even see its eye blink. I do not think any amount of bird-watching from the ground could give you the feel and understanding of this hawk that I got by actually seeing it on its own turf.

I gained a better understanding of songbird foraging after holding still as mixed flocks of chickadees, titmice, and kinglets fed their way through a tree canopy with me setting in their midst. Deer hunters have to be careful in such situations since these birds are quick to scold and raise a fuss if they notice you, and that could scare off any game in the area.

Among rarely seen wildlife I have viewed from tree stands are nocturnal species such as skunks, opossums, and Gray Fox making their way home just at the crack of dawn. I once watched a young Raccoon fall out of a tree as it inched to the end of a thin branch in an effort to reach persimmons. It ran off, apparently uninjured, after falling more than twenty feet. Foraging Coyotes are also occasionally seen from tree stands in the early morning hours, while I have never managed to get close to them while on the ground.

Squirrels are perhaps the most common mammal seen from the high vantage point of a deer stand. They do not expect to encounter danger in the trees either and often come within a few feet before noticing me. I once had one come right up to me and smell my boot. The only observation I have ever made of a Red-tailed Hawk trying to capture a Gray Squirrel occurred from a deer stand. The hawk grabbed the squirrel while it was out at the end of a limb gathering acorns. Both crashed to the ground, and after ten minutes trying to subdue the squirrel, the hawk let it go, and it ran away. Raptors kill much of their mammal prey by suffocation as their talons squeeze the chest. Squirrels must be a little too large for the talons of a Red-tail.

On an afternoon stand, I once watched two woodpeckers going to roost in a tree cavity. At what was apparently a choice cavity, I first observed a Northern Flicker enter. About ten minutes later a Pileated Woodpecker arrived at the same hole. After peering inside and craning its neck from side to side to make sure no predator was watching it go to roost, the Pileated popped into the hole. A moment later, both woodpeckers came out squawking and startled, each surprised by the presence of the other. One bit of Blue Jay behavior I have viewed only from trees involves the jays flitting silently from branch to branch about four feet above an animal moving on the ground. In one instance, the "monitored" species was a Mink, and in another it was a hen Ring-necked Pheasant. The pheasant was clearly bothered by this, but the Mink paid no attention to the jay. I never figured out what the jays were trying to accomplish.

I have also learned some about arboreal insects by setting long hours up in trees. I never noticed tree crickets before entering their habitat in the tree canopy. Since I had never seen one from the ground, I was surprised at how commonly I see them crawling on the bark of the trunk and larger limbs well into the cold weather of late autumn.

All in all, wildlife watching is an important side benefit of spending time in a tree stand. If I could just get motivated to spend time up there at seasons other than autumn, my list of memorable wildlife moments would probably expand greatly. I can only imagine what I would see from the old oak tree during the spring songbird migration. A change of perspective and season can make all the difference in the world.

November 1995

The Changing Face of Nature

Illinois' natural world is constantly changing as new species move in, some old ones die out, and some animals change their habits. Of course massive human-induced changes such as land clearing and draining and urban development are going on, but this essay is about more subtle changes brought about by plants and animals as they adapt to changing environmental conditions.

The most conspicuous changes going on are those involving natural vegetation, where whole communities are taking on a different character. Our oak woods are changing to Sugar Maple forests, and our hill prairies are converting from prairie grasses to shrubs and trees, both because of the lack of fire. Widespread landscape fires that maintained these communities in the past are not compatible in much of our modern landscape.

Many bulrush and sedge marshes in northeastern Illinois are changing to cattail marshes because of soil disturbance and increased nutrients and fertility in their water. Others are being invaded by the introduced exotic Purple Loosestrife plant and Reed Canary Grass, which replace the native sedges and flowers. Whole forests are changing their character as their native wildflowers are replaced by exotic plants such as Garlic Mustard and Dame's Rocket. Prairies are being overrun by the exotic White Sweet Clover plant.

Conservation biologists are working to control these changes in managed natural areas, while the overall landscape continues its face change. At the species level, exotic animals such as the Zebra Mussel are changing the nature of our rivers and Lake Michigan in a major way. Because of their massive numbers, Zebra Mussels lower the oxygen levels in the water, and their filter feeding consumes much of the microscopic food needed by fish fry and other creatures. They may kill out native mussels by attaching to them in such numbers that they smother them.

Newly introduced fish such as the Round Goby of Lake Michigan and the Bighead Carp and Silver Carp in the Mississippi River may eventually trigger big changes in these aquatic habitats. The two-inch-long Chinese Mystery Snail that has recently established itself in the Illinois River drainage and Lake Michigan is quite a change in nature just by its presence. Its impact on native snails may cause further changes.

Exotic animal introductions such as the House Sparrow and European Starling have been stabilized for many years, and no new invasions are under way. However, our native wildlife continues to change its range and abundance. That pink-tinged "sparrow" that shows up at your bird feeder now is the House Finch of southwestern American deserts that man introduced on the east coast of North America. Since establishing there, it has spread westward to now inhabit all of Illinois.

The Coyote is now common throughout Illinois, while it was not even present when I was growing up in southern Illinois. The open habitats created by agriculture in the state proved to be suitable habitat for this "prairie wolf" of the plains. With its increase in Illinois, there has been a decline in the numbers of Woodchucks and Red Foxes in the state. Coyotes successfully prey on these mammals. The Giant Canada Goose, a subspecies of the Canada Goose that was nearly exterminated early this century, has adapted so well to our lakes and ponds that it is now a common nester statewide. In urban areas it has become a pest. Wild Turkeys are now common almost statewide where they were absent within my memory, and our deer herd is locally so abundant now that it changes the vegetation on large areas by overbrowsing the trees and shrubs for food. This change of nature is greatest in urban areas where deer numbers are difficult to control.

Native migrant birds are also changing their ways. White Pelicans that normally just fly over Illinois in route to nesting grounds in the northern Great Plains now sometimes stop for the summer on the Mississippi River in northern Illinois. Snow Geese that once wintered only on the Gulf Coast of Texas and Louisiana now stop and spend the winter along major rivers and lakes of the southern half of Illinois. Since the turn of the twenty-first century, White-fronted Geese of the central plains have begun wintering in southern Illinois as well. The presence of these new geese in winter is a very conspicuous change in the face of nature.

The appearance of the Striped Mullet in the Mississippi and Ohio River waters of Illinois since 1990 represents another change in range for a native species. Normally a fish of coastal salty waters, for some reason this fish has decided to move into fresh waters up the Mississippi River. Since they reach three feet in length, they will obviously be a conspicuous addition to our fauna. In the mid-1980s, wild American Holly trees began appearing in southern Illinois forests. This native tree of the south had been cultivated in the area for probably a century without spreading to the wild. The appearance of wild populations now may be in response to the warming climate.

The changes in nature include behavior changes as well as migrations to new areas. One of the most noticeable of these is the foraging of gulls on parking lots in the last few years. Gulls have learned that discarded French fries and other food items can be found on these lots and now soar over them searching for food as they once searched rivers and lakes for fish.

Someone familiar with the natural scene in Illinois just forty years ago would be amazed to see the changes that have occurred in nature since that time. Most of this change is due to human activities such as the introduction of species and habitat alterations. One thing seems sure—the face of nature will continue to change.

December 1996

AUTHOR'S NOTE.—*Many animals and plants have expanded their ranges northward in Illinois since 1996. Birds include Scissor-tailed Flycatcher, Black-necked Stilt, Anhinga, and Mississippi Kite. Amphibians include the Green Treefrog, and plants, the Powderpuff.*

CHAPTER 4

ECOLOGY, CONSERVATION, AND MANAGEMENT OF NATURAL FEATURES OF ILLINOIS

This chapter contains essays on the concepts of ecology and the application of ecological principles and methods to nature conservation. There are also essays on conservation practices and descriptions of conservation problems.

~~~~~~~~~~~~~~~~~~~~~~~~~~~~~~~~~

Ecosystems

Anyone who listens to the news or reads the papers is familiar with the terms *ecology* and *ecosystem*. They are mentioned in just about every news story about the environment, but few Illinoisans have a real understanding of the terms. Ecology is the scientific study of interrelationships between living organisms and between organisms and all aspects, living and nonliving, of their environment. The statement "the ecology," sometimes used by the media, is pretty much meaningless unless further defined as, for instance, the ecology of a Robin or a forest. For example, the ecology of a Cardinal includes the plants that produce the seeds it eats and its nesting and roosting sites. It also includes the sunlight, air, rain, and soil needed to grow its food and shelter plants, the insects necessary to pollinate the flowers of the plants, and on and on.

Ecologists realize that all life is so interdependent that one can hardly study a single species without getting involved in the entire living system of which it is a part. This has led to recognition of the concept of ecosystem, a term describing the interdependence of species

Volo Bog Nature Preserve in Lake County, Illinois' best example of a bog ecosystem. It has zones of vegetation that encroach on a pond, filling it in. The pond is surrounded by a floating mat of herbs and shrubs encircled by a forest of Tamarack trees.

in the living world with one another and with their nonliving environment. Ecosystems can be recognized at any level, from the entire earth—the global ecosystem or biosphere—down to small communities such as glades and ponds. Although the term is most often used for natural ecosystems, man-made and managed environments such as cornfields and pine plantations are also ecosystems, although very simple ones. The flow of energy through food chains and webs and the recycling of nutrients are basic ecosystem principles that apply to all. At the bottom of the chains and webs are the plants that produce food, and above these are the organisms that feed on them and each other.

All ecosystems on earth, except some life around hot springs, get their energy from the sun. Plants use the light from the sun to produce stored chemical energy through photosynthesis, and heat from the sun provides the warmth needed by life. Except for the sun, earth's ecosystems get all they need from the earth itself. Understanding ecosystem functions and potential problems requires awareness of some of their characteristics such as diversity and stability and concepts such as biomass.

Large and diverse ecosystems are thought to be more stable than smaller or simpler ecosystems that have fewer species. This is because failure of a few species to contribute their function in a small or simple system can lead to near total ecosystem collapse. Such failure is less likely where many species and large areas are involved. An example of this is a pond ecosystem. Ponds are essentially "closed ecosystems" as far as their oxygen supply is concerned. Most of the oxygen needed by fish and other animals in the pond is produced right in the pond by plants, including microscopic algae. If light is cut off from the pond by ice and snow in winter or a dense growth of algae at the water's surface in summer, plants in the water are deprived of light and quit making oxygen, and most of the animals suffocate. Such impacts are less likely in large lakes or the ocean.

Biomass is the living or recently produced mass, usually expressed as dry weight of organic matter per acre, supported by an ecosystem annually. Most of this is vegetation, but it could include animals as well. In prairie stands, the production of biomass per year for a given tract of land is somewhat similar regardless of changes in vegetation structure resulting from fire. If the area is burned, old vegetation or biomass is removed, but the release of nutrients from the burned plants stimulates increased growth of the vegetation, restoring vegetative biomass to near its previous level by increasing its productivity that year. As for grassland animal biomass, voles and Henslow's Sparrows will decrease after the fire, but Deer Mice and Bobwhites will increase, in both cases due to changes to the structure of vegetation or habitat. The end result may be a similar biomass composed of different species.

Ecologists have noted that ecosystems are so diverse and complex that it is very difficult, if not impossible, to predict what basic changes such as climate change and transport of disease organisms by man might cause in the earth's ecosystem. Examples of possible changes are the worldwide "bleaching" or dieback of coral reefs that recently occurred when ocean temperatures raised just a fraction and the worldwide die-off of frogs and salamanders that may be tied to the spread of disease around the world by man. Neither was predicted. The coral decline is more serious to us because coral animals provide the habitat for the diverse worldwide reef ecosystem that contributes significantly to our oxygen supply. Frogs and salamanders are usually minor components of ecosystems, so their loss will probably be felt more at the species than ecosystem level.

Are there ecological thresholds we do not suspect that threaten our very survival? Can radiation slipping through a thinned ozone layer kill enough microscopic algae to deplete our oxygen supply? It is in our self-interest to be cautious in altering the biosphere—the ecosystem of the earth.

December 1993

~~~~~~~~~~~~~~~~~~~~~~~~~~~~~~~~

Ecological Management and Restoration

Once a wetland, prairie, or forest is acquired or controlled for preservation, the work of nature conservationists has only begun. Just letting Mother Nature "manage" a natural area by keeping human hands off seemed logical in the early days of natural area preservation, but it was not long until the fallacy of this approach was obvious. Shrubs and trees invaded and destroyed prairies, past drainage efforts altered soil moisture and the community dependent upon it, alien trees and weeds began replacing native vegetation, and altered peripheral areas showed little inclination to reseed themselves to natural communities.

Among the most rapid negative effect of protection without management is the succession or conversion of prairies to woodlands in the absence of fire. Frequent and widespread fires created and maintained our prairies prior to European settlement, and they have demonstrated they cannot survive without the continuation of periodic burning. In the absence of fire, grasses and flowers are replaced by shrubs and trees, and the prairie disappears in short order. Where fire has been excluded for decades, it alone may not restore the prairie, and selective cutting or deadening of shrubs and trees may be necessary.

The invasion of alien trees, shrubs, and herbs destroys the natural character of wetlands, forests, and prairies alike in the absence of management to control them. This management often includes the use of fire, cutting, and herbicides to control or eliminate unwanted exotic weeds. Restoring altered wetlands often involves filling drainage ditches and removing drain tiles that have been installed to convert wetland to agriculture. Reestablishing native vegetation involves seeding and transplanting of native species and the removal of plants and animals not native to the site. These activities have been underway for decades in Illinois by federal, state, county, and private conservationists, producing remarkable positive results.

Remember the next time you see smoke from a wildland fire that it may be breathing life into a declining prairie or savanna, and should you see workers cutting trees in a park or preserve do not jump to the conclusion that this is bad. The tree being cut may be a Common Buckthorn, at home in Europe but an aggressive weed here.

The creation of prairies by seeding and planting is a common practice in Illinois today, especially in schoolyards and parks, where they provide educational opportunities as well as scenic enhancement. The planting of forest trees for ecological restoration is also growing in popularity, with the Cache River Project in southern Illinois being a leading example.

I was recently impressed by the scale and progress of the restoration program at McHenry County Conservation District's Glacial Park. This three-thousand-acre tract of glacial landforms, forests, prairies, marshes, and streams is one of the largest and most diverse restorations I have seen. Fire has been introduced and is restoring degraded savanna, barrens, and prairie; exotic trees have been removed; seeding and nursery transplants have established barrens and prairie areas; and a variety of wetlands and streams are being restored. The district has its own nursery operation on the premises to provide plant materials for the revegetation program.

One of the most impressive aspects of the project is the wetland and stream restoration. It has involved the removal of literally miles of field tiles installed in the nineteenth and early twentieth centuries for internal soil drainage to convert wetland to cropland. Some fields had three different levels or depths of tile in the soil. Since no record exists of what tile is present and where it runs, restorationists have to start at the lower outlet of a tile and dig it upstream to the end, following all lateral tiles to their end as well. If drainage continues after removing a tile field, workers know they have another deeper system to locate and remove. Rather than just removing a hundred feet or so of tile to form a break in the drainage system, the complete tile system must be removed to prevent drying of hillside seeps and moist slopes drained by the laterals.

Once the tiles are removed, it is often necessary to reestablish a surface drainage stream. This is done as nearly as possible to the location of the original streams as shown on early maps and as described in oral histories taken from older residents of the area. The major stream restoration is yet to occur. Eventually, a channelized and straightened portion of Nippersink Creek within Glacial Park will be blocked off and the creek returned to its original meandering bed.

The future of our natural heritage is often dependent on the success of the ecological management and restoration implemented after land is set aside for preservation. It is not adequate to just protect an area and let nature take its course. We have already changed the species mix and other conditions in the state too much for this to work.

November 1996

AUTHOR'S NOTE.—*Glacial Park has been completed and is now open to the public.*

~~~~~~

Indicator Species

Natural ecosystems are those assemblages of interdependent plants and animals that comprise a natural community such as a forest, prairie, stream, or wetland. As ecologist Frank Egler has said, "Ecosystems are not only more complex than we think; they are more complex than we *can* think." In spite of the limitations this complexity imposes on managers, they need to manage and evaluate the quality of natural ecosystems. Measuring the change and health of an ecosystem through extensive ecological sampling of a broad range of organisms is the ideal. But often this is not possible. One way managers can do this is with indicator species.

By knowing which species are most sensitive to ecological deterioration or change and selecting from these the animals and plants that are most easily observed or censused, we can come up with a list of species that will indicate ecological health or condition. Ecologically sensitive animals that declare their presence by their calls or songs as well as visibility are especially valuable indicators. Birds and frogs fit into this category. Many birds are sensitive to the size and condition of forest, grassland, and wetland ecosystem blocks. Breeding bird censuses, based on bird calls along the same census route over many years, have proven the value of specific bird species as indicators of change. As our forests have become more fragmented, such long-term data show that long-distance migrant birds of the forest interior such as Wood Thrushes, Scarlet Tanagers, and Ovenbirds have declined drastically. Their loss reduces the diversity and alters the ecology of these ecosystems.

In using birds as indicator species, it has become necessary to realize that they migrate long distances and that shifts in their numbers may be related to changes in their wintering grounds as well as ecosystem changes in Illinois.

Frogs are amphibians and live much of their lives in and around water. Their skin readily absorbs chemicals and toxins from the environment, and their eggs lack protective shells. Because of this, they are exposed to a variety of potentially detrimental environmental factors. These characteristics make amphibians very sensitive to their environment, and together with calls that can be heard over great distances, they become ideal indicator species. A worldwide decline of amphibians is presently under way. It is probably due to local problems such as habitat pollution or destruction, the spread of diseases, and increased ultraviolet radiation resulting from thinning of the earth's ozone layer. Studies show some eggs of high-elevation frogs are being killed by exposure to increased ultraviolet radiation. Research into other possible causes is under way. Many people watch and count birds for recreation and study. The annual Christmas bird counts are examples. But many fewer people have caught on to the fascination of learning frog calls and driving a regular census route from year to year to detect changes in frog populations. We need more frog watchers and listeners.

Among the most sensitive species to aquatic ecosystem change are the freshwater mussels. In the process of filter feeding, they accumulate and concentrate many pollutants and disease organisms from the water. However, they are less than ideal indicator species because of the difficulty in finding and censusing them. Some mussels were extinct for decades before their loss was realized because their home at the bottom of rivers is so remote from ours. Nonetheless, their disappearance is an invaluable indication of ecosystem failure when it is detected.

Algae are another important indicator species. Abundant green filamentous algae waving in a stream's current or algal blooms that tinge the water of lakes and rivers greenish indicate pollution. This past summer, the Wabash River was running a murky greenish color, an indication of its polluted state.

Prairie ecologists regularly use disturbance-sensitive prairie plants as indicators of natural quality. Grazing and soil disturbance such as plowing can kill or reduce these indicators while leaving many more vigorous prairie plants in place. The absence or presence of these indicator species indicates the quality of the prairie and can tell us something about its past use and abuse. For example, the presence of Prairie Dropseed grass is a sure indicator of unplowed prairie sod since it does not survive plowing and is very slow to reestablish itself in disturbed prairies. The absence of Leadplant, gentians, and Compass Plant in a prairie indicate past grazing.

Indicator species help us read and interpret the health of the landscape and its many natural ecosystems. They are important tools in our struggle to protect and maintain these remnants of our natural heritage.

December 1995

AUTHOR'S NOTE.—*Most amphibian die-off through 2015 has been blamed on the human spread of disease.*

Macrosites

The buzzword in nature conservation in Illinois lately is macrosite. It refers to a much larger tract of land than the traditional natural area but is related in that macrosites are generally developed around core natural areas. Macrosites are also referred to as bioreserves by some conservationists, and their establishment and management involve relatively new conservation disciplines such as landscape ecology, landscape scale management, and the ecosystem approach to land management.

The shift in conservation concern toward macrosites began when ecologists realized that pristine and species-rich natural areas were often too small to guarantee survival of all of their important and characteristic plants and animals. Small area and isolated populations can lead to loss of genetic diversity and loss of reproductive success. Wide-ranging larger animals, such as bobcats and otters, and birds requiring the interior of forests for nesting, exhibit the need for larger areas. Population sizes of both plants and animals need to be large enough to prevent inbreeding, indicating that the larger the area (and population) the better the chance of avoiding genetic problems.

The shift to macrosites in conservation planning has caught on worldwide. I recently heard biologists from Russia, Costa Rica, and Australia talking about application of the approach in their lands. Typically, macrosites have one or more significant ecological features or natural areas, which are publicly owned and protected. Around these features is a mix of private and public land that enhances the value of the core features. These lands buffer the core feature and provide land for natural community restoration to enlarge the habitat.

A variety of land protection tools, from voluntary cooperation and incentive payments for private landowners through conservation easements to outright public land ownership, may be used to maintain natural values. The benefits of macrosites will accrue to landowners in the area as well as the public at large. It is anticipated that some macrosites will be passive recreational tourism destinations.

Macrosites in Illinois can be thousands to tens of thousands of acres. If they are to become a reality, they will have to have the co-operation of private landowners. Some will involve a variety of public agencies and private organizations. To be effective in conserving nature, macrosites in Illinois will almost always have to include some reforestation or prairie or wetland restoration since large unfrag-mented areas of these habitats do not exist.

One of the best examples of a macrosite in development in Illinois is the Cache River Wetlands Project in southern Illinois. This proj-ect aims to protect sixty thousand acres of wetlands and associated lowland forest. It is a joint effort between the State Department of Natural Resources, the US Fish and Wildlife Service, The Nature Conservancy, and Ducks Unlimited. The latter two are private non-governmental organizations. A local group called Citizens Commit-tee to Save the Cache helped start the protection effort. Federally funded agriculture programs are being used to reduce soil erosion in the watershed of the Cache River and to enhance forest management and reforestation on private land.

A major component of the Cache River effort is reforestation on publicly acquired acres through direct seeding of acorns and nuts collected by volunteer scout groups. Reforestation is handled by The Nature Conservancy rather than the government. The Illinois Department of Natural Resources is planning a visitor center that it would operate near a major highway to interpret the area and a public boat access. Access trails and parking will be provided by the Department of Natural Resources, US Fish and Wildlife Service, and The Nature Conservancy. The Cache River macrosite has much potential as a tourist destination.

The macrosite protection model with various private and public agencies and private landowners working together to conserve and restore a valuable natural resource can potentially be replicated at many sites across Illinois. Expect to hear more about macrosites in the future as we move away from managing single species and small tracts of land to concern for total landscapes. Macrosites are where much conservation of natural resources will be accomplished in coming decades.

November 1994

AUTHOR'S NOTE.—*The Department of Natural Resources has developed the Cache River Wetlands Center on Illinois Route 37, three miles south of Cypress, Illinois. The Nature Conservancy has acquired a large acreage of grazed prairie at Nachusa Grassland in Lee County and is restoring it with prairie restoration and ecological management.*

Volunteers Helping Nature

If I said I was going to write this column about nags, you might suspect I had slipped from nature writing to an interest in horse racing. But a nonequestrian definition for NAG is Natural Area Guardian, a volunteer who devotes some of his or her free time to maintaining nature preserves and restoring natural communities. NAGS are just one of several volunteer groups who are making significant contributions to nature conservation in Illinois. Many others are simply called volunteer stewards. Most are affiliated with nonprofit conservation organizations, but some are individually and privately organized. This essay is devoted to a better understanding of their contribution to our natural heritage and to giving them the recognition they deserve. Perhaps some readers will be moved to join one of these groups or even found a new one.

Most parks, preserves, and museums have volunteer support groups that help with preparation of displays, maintenance, and interpretive programs. And many preserves also have organizations that developed largely to promote their acquisition and preservation. But the groups I am recognizing here are the volunteer practitioners of natural land stewardship and restoration. They are the folks who conduct field management practices such as exotic weed control, prescribed burning, species and community monitoring, blocking wetland drainage, native seed gathering, and planting and restoring whole natural habitats.

Many of these groups provide assistance and support to professional managers, but others are more or less on their own. All receive instruction either in workshops or on the job, and most are following agency-approved policies and guidelines. The first group to organize was the NAGs, which started as the Lee County Natural Area Guardians in 1979. Wanting an affiliation with a legitimate conservation organization, they approached the local Soil and Water Conservation District. Finding a welcome home there, they were instrumental in amending Illinois law to establish themselves and other NAG groups as legally designated committees of County Soil and Water Conservation Districts. There are now NAG groups in twelve counties, and Lee County NAG president Deb Carey has made presentations on them to six southern Illinois counties that are considering establishing these volunteer programs. NAGs are dues-paying organizations that also do considerable fundraising for their districts as well as volunteering work time. One of their goals is to demonstrate that agriculture and environmentalism are compatible.

By far the largest of the citizen groups is the Volunteer Stewardship Network of Northern Illinois sponsored by The Nature Conservancy and the Illinois Nature Preserves Commission. After its founding in 1983, this stewardship group has grown to 4,000 members working on some 160 sites by early 1995. It is administered from The Nature Conservancy's Chicago office. Expanding on this successful model, The Nature Conservancy has added a Central Illinois Stewardship Network that is coordinated from their Peoria office. They manage and restore central Illinois natural areas as far south as Litchfield.

The southern chapter of The Illinois Native Plant Society in conjunction with The Nature Conservancy's Cache River office is working to organize a volunteer stewardship network in southern Illinois. One of the largest one-day uses of volunteers in Illinois is The Nature Conservancy's annual acorn harvest in support of the reforestation effort at the Cache River Joint Venture at the southern tip of the state. Max Hutchison of The Nature Conservancy's staff reports that this past fall some five hundred scouts collected a ton of acorns in a single day. That is one and a half pickup truckloads!

The appeal of actually doing something physical with your own hands to benefit struggling natural ecosystems is very fulfilling to many. In addition to the fresh air and exercise, it offers the benefit of seeing the result of your effort firsthand. Whatever their motivation, these volunteers are a major factor in the future of the natural heritage of Illinois. They already number far more than all of the employees of the Illinois Department of Natural Resources and continue to grow.

Even if you cannot join one of these groups, one thing that Illinois residents can do to help these volunteers is donate to the Wildlife Preservation Fund when completing your Illinois income tax return. This fund has provided small grants to many of these volunteer groups for work equipment and other support over the years. These groups deserve our help for all that they give to the conservation cause.

February 1995

The Fate of Prairie in Illinois

Only one hundredth of 1 percent of the high quality prairie that existed in Illinois at the time of European settlement remains today—just 2,352 acres out of an original twenty-one million! A little more is left if you consider degraded remnants such as over-grazed prairie pastures and prairies that have partially grown up into brush and trees. By any accounting, our prairies have suffered more losses as a percentage of original extent than any of our major natural communities.

Many readers will not be familiar with Illinois prairie since it is now so scarce. The term refers to upland vegetation dominated by grasses and forbs (wildflowers). This is in contrast with forests and wetlands, which are our other major natural communities. When we include rocky, grass-dominated hillside communities called glades, and barrens, which are a mixture of prairie grasses and shrubs, along with more typical, level, grassy plains, prairie probably occurred in every Illinois county at the time of European settlement. The predominance of prairie varied from region to region, with the least amount of prairie in the southern tip of the state.

The Grand Prairie region stretched from the area around Raymond in Montgomery County up to Joliet and then back westward to the Quad Cities. This area of very flat terrain was so dominated by prairie that the occasional groves of trees were individually named. If forest groves were named in your area, like Funk's Grove near Bloomington, chances are you live in the Grand Prairie. In areas adjacent to the Grand Prairie, prairies were smaller and existed as inclusions in the forest and were individually named. Elk Prairie near Carbondale, Looking Glass Prairie near Lebanon, Fox Prairie near Olney, and Carthage Prairie at Carthage are examples.

How could such widespread vegetation be so nearly completely destroyed in less than a century? The perfection of the steel plow by John Deere in the 1840s provides most of the answer. His plow was the first capable of breaking and turning under the heavy prairie sod. Remarkably, in the era when a team of horses provided the only power source, one man with a steel plow could convert an acre of virgin prairie to an acre of fertile crop land in a single day. Virtually all of Illinois' prairie disappeared in sixty years—before the age of mechanized farming. Prairies that were not plowed suffered other fates at the hands of humans. Some were used as pasture and were destroyed by grazing. Many grew up into forest or shrubs as the settlers fragmented the prairies and stopped or hindered the wide-ranging prairie wildfires. Fire is critical to the survival of prairie under Illinois' present moist climate.

Illinois' prairie heritage consists mostly of scraps of land that survived in areas too wet, sandy, rocky, or steep to cultivate or use. A few choice prairie remnants survive in pioneer cemeteries, within railroad rights of way, and in subdivisions that were abandoned around Chicago during the Depression. Government at all levels and private conservation organizations have done a good job of saving what remains of high quality original prairie, and attention is now turning to the restoration of disturbed prairies and the creation of prairies by planting.

The Department of Natural Resources is planting prairies on many sites in a continuing program that restores five hundred to six hundred acres per year with seed and plants produced at its Mason State Nursery. A major project by the department at Green River Fish and Wildlife Area in Lee County will result in a two-thousand-acre prairie and prairie-wetland complex, when planned work is completed.

Upland sandy prairie remnants and wet swales are being connected by four hundred acres of plantings on formerly cultivated land. Invading Silver Maple trees and exotic pines and shrubs are being removed. At Goose Lake Prairie State Natural Area near Morris, the department has restored degraded prairie by removing invading thorny shrubs and providing prescribed burning. It is now adding to the 1,500 acres of restored native prairie with 500 acres of prairie plantings. Some 250 acres have been planted and the remainder will be planted in the next two years. An effort to restore a bit of the original prairie of the Wabash Valley is under way by the Department of Natural Resources and the Lawrenceville-Vincennes Airport on airport land.

The Nature Conservancy and many volunteer helpers have done much prairie restoration and planting on Cook County Forest Preserve District lands around Chicago. Another of their major projects is Nachusa Grasslands east of Dixon. Here they have purchased a large acreage of upland pastured prairie remnants and are improving them with management and are connecting them with extensive plantings. The Fermi National Accelerator Laboratory at Batavia has done its share by planting about a thousand acres of prairie within the ring formed by its accelerator. The Department of Transportation and many forest preserve and conservation districts have planted prairies as well. In far southern Illinois, the Shawnee National Forest has embarked on a major program to restore prairies called "barrens" by the early settlers of this region. Their efforts include brush cutting and prescribed burning of degraded remnants primarily in southern Pope County.

All of the prairie restoration and planting work underway in Illinois is helping to bring back an important part of Illinois' natural heritage that was almost lost. Future generations will thank us for our efforts.

February 1993

AUTHOR'S NOTE.—*In 2015 the high quality prairie included in Illinois' Natural Areas Inventory had increased from 2,352 to 2,579 acres. Some of this is restored prairie. The Illinois Department of Natural Resources nursery continues to produce prairie forbs and grass for restoration and the Green River prairie restoration now includes 2000 acres. The Shawnee National Forest has begun large-scale landscape burning, which helps barren remnants, but has encountered citizen opposition to restoration work in some areas.*

~~~~~~~~~~~~~~~~~~

Mother Nature in Winter

While we throw another log on the fire or turn up the thermostat to deal with the cold of winter, Mother Nature lacks the luxury of such habitat manipulation. Her wild creatures have had to adapt to Illinois' cold winters through a broad range of strategies, everything from leaving the state to burying in mud. Let's examine some of the common ones.

Migration to areas of milder climate is an option mostly for some birds and bats, but a few insects such as the Monarch butterfly, some dragonflies, and some fish migrate as well. While the Monarchs appear to be seeking warmer climes, some migratory birds seem driven more by how far they have to go to find food than by a need for warm weather. Feathers are great insulators. Flocking, grain-feeding birds, such as the Common Grackle, mostly go south of the average permanent snow-cover line; soil probers, such as Woodcocks and sandpipers, go south of the soil-frost line; and nectar and flying-insect feeders end up in the subtropics or tropics. Migratory fish include the Northern Hogsucker that withdraws from the smaller, swifter streams it has ascended in spring to the quiet pools of larger rivers for the winter. The Skipjack Herring may even descend the Mississippi to the Gulf of Mexico. The end result for migratory species is an escape from some or all of the cold weather.

Most fish simply overwinter in deeper water far enough below the ice to escape freezing. Since water is densest and heaviest at about thirty-nine degrees Fahrenheit and sinks to the bottom at that temperature, in relatively still water the temperature never gets colder than that, except immediately adjacent to the water's surface or to ice. Fish are able to remain active all winter in this relatively warm water. Just imagine what it would do to aquatic ecology if water continued to get denser and heavier as it gets colder and ice sank!

Other cold-blooded vertebrates such as amphibians and reptiles mostly hibernate. Terrestrial forms such as snakes, tortoises, and some frogs, toads, and salamanders just burrow or den below the frost line in the soil to hibernate. Air-breathing aquatic turtles and amphibians mostly hibernate in mud or under debris on the bottom of streams and lakes where they absorb oxygen through their skin rather than breathing with their lungs.

Most mammals simply put on a thicker, warmer coat of fur and remain active all winter. Many "lie low" during extremely low temperatures but never hibernate. A few mammals, whose food supply is not adequate in winter, are true hibernators. They enter a state of reduced respiration, body temperature, and energy consumption supported by fat energy stored in their bodies. This is accomplished in caves and dens in soil that are free from freezing temperatures. Illinois' hibernating mammals include some bats, the Woodchuck, Franklin's Ground Squirrel, Thirteen-lined Ground Squirrel, Meadow Jumping Mouse, and a former resident, the Black Bear. The Armadillo, a recent immigrant to Illinois, is a mammal that lacks a warm fur coat as well as the ability to hibernate. It is a strong digger that excavates a den where it can withstand cold spells for a short time but has to get out for food on a regular basis.

Illinois' most abundant native animals, the insects, have a wide range of overwintering strategies. Many spend the winter beyond the frost line in the soil, rotten wood, or in water. Here they can remain active as larvae or adults. Of those wintering within the frost zone and out in the air, some, including many grasshoppers and butterflies survive the cold in the egg stage. Some have eggs laid out in the open, while others lay them under soil or debris or protect them in specially constructed egg cases. An example of the latter approach is the Praying Mantis, which attaches its elaborate egg case to a branch or twig. Still other insects such as the silk moths spin cocoons and spend the winter as pupae or partially transformed adults. The Wooly Worm spends the winter as a larva at least partly protected by its wooly coat. We see them on our roads in autumn as they search out protected sites under leaves or old boards where they curl up and "sleep" through the worst of winter. Many insects overwinter as adults that simply seek out protected sites during the coldest weather. When you see active insects, such as houseflies, after only a day or so of warm weather, you can be sure it was overwintering as an adult. The Mourning Cloak butterfly is another insect that overwinters as an adult. It can be found flitting about the forests of Illinois on the very first warm days of spring, often feeding on Sugar Maple sap before any wildflowers have opened.

Mother Nature has provided her creatures with migration, warm coats, and a variety of other strategies for dealing with Illinois' January cold. We mimic some of these solutions when we head for Florida or put on heavier clothes, but many are unique to wildlife.

January 1996

The Underground Lifestyle

When the heat of summer drives many wildlife species to search for shade and that cool spot down by the creek, some of the residents of one of Illinois' hottest habitats stay at home unfazed. Our sand prairies and unforested sand dunes are among the hottest environments in the Prairie State. They create a desert scape that heats to extremely high temperatures under summer's sun. The surface layer of sand heats to well above one hundred degrees Fahrenheit and reflects heat and light to the underside of the sparse vegetation. Three typical animals of these sandy natural habitats are insulated from this heat. They have adapted to the underground lifestyle referred to as fossorial by biologists. In contrast to animals such as Woodchucks that den in the ground but forage on the surface, fossorial animals pass most of their lives tunneling or pushing their way through soil. The Eastern Mole is Illinois' most common example.

Our sand areas are inhabited by three species of fossorial vertebrate animals, more than any other habitat in the state. And two of these are "sand swimmers" as opposed to burrowers. "Sand swimmers" plow through sand beneath the surface in search of food but without excavating a burrow. Our "sand swimmers" are Strecker's Chorus Frog and the Yellow Mud Turtle, and they feed mainly on worms and insects. Both species emerge in the spring to breed and lay eggs but soon thereafter dig into the relatively loose sand of our prairies and dunes where they spend the rest of the year. Their lifestyle is possible only because of the unique uncompacted nature of sand. More compact and heavy soils such as loam require burrowing for the underground lifestyle. While possessing thick muscular forelegs for plowing through sand, the Strecker's Chorus Frog lacks claws and is not be able to burrow in heavier soils. Illinois is not unique in having animals adapted to this habitat niche. Most large sand areas in temperate-to-warm climates around the world have "sand swimmers."

The other subterranean inhabitant of Illinois sand prairies is the Plains Pocket Gopher. This rodent spends virtually all of its life burrowing through sand and also inhabits heavier soils. It creates burrows as it searches for the roots that comprise the bulk of its food. It keeps its tunnels clear by pushing excavated soil up into mounds that are a giveaway to its presence.

This squirrel-sized mammal has large claws for digging and can close its mouth behind its incisor teeth so the teeth can be used in digging without getting dirt in its mouth. It has fur-lined "pockets" on either side of the mouth for storage of food. Another adaptation of the gopher to the underground life style is its short stubby tail with tactile hairs for feeling its way when backing down burrows. It spends virtually its entire life burrowing through soil and rarely comes to the surface. By the time summer temperatures reach one hundred degrees Fahrenheit at the desert-like surface of our sand prairies, these three subterranean dwellers are well beneath the heat in cool moist sand. Their adaptation to the fossorial lifestyle was doubtless driven by a variety of forces, possibly including escape of extreme summer heat.

July 1995

AUTHOR'S NOTE.—*Our Strecker's Chorus Frog is the subspecies described as the Illinois Chorus Frog, and our Yellow Mud Turtle is the subspecies named the Illinois Mud Turtle.*

Conserving Native Plants

Illinois has had a program to conserve its native plants since 1985. This program is housed in the Division of Natural Heritage of the Department of Natural Resources and includes cooperation with many public agencies and private organizations and individuals.

When considering what the major threats to our wild plants and native flora are, most of us immediately think of the bulldozer, plow, and dragline. While these threats of outright habitat destruction are obvious, the conservation of plants is far more complex than just saving some habitat for them. In addition, fire suppression, invasive exotic plants and animals, altered flood regimes, deer overpopulation, herbicide drifting from cropland, loss of pollinating insects, introduced plant diseases, genetic or inbreeding problems, and human harvest of plants for commercial markets are all threats to our native plants. Indeed, while much has been accomplished for habitat protection for wild plants through our nature preserves and parks, some natural communities were already gone before these preservation movements started saving habitats.

Among these "lost" habitats of Illinois are savannas, the prairies of the Wabash River lowlands, and the "barrens" or prairies of the southern tip of the state. For these communities, planting and restoring them from scattered surviving plants is the only answer. The Nature Conservancy, Shawnee National Forest, and Department of Natural Resources are all involved in efforts to do just that.

Leaving aside the acquisition and protection of natural habitats, the plant conservation program has concentrated on the other problems. Fire is critical to the survival of some natural communities and their plant species. Fire suppresses competing vegetation such as shrubs and trees of which some native plants are intolerant. It also helps prepare bare earth conditions needed for reproduction of some native plants. Since fire and civilization are largely incompatible, we now suppress wildland fires to the detriment of many native plants. Our loss of savannas and barrens is largely due to lack of fire. At least one native plant, Beard Grass, has disappeared from Illinois in the last twenty years due to fire suppression. The native plant conservation program supports and promotes the use of prescribed fire for maintenance of Illinois' native flora.

Exotic plants capable of invading and dominating natural communities crowd out and greatly reduce native plants, even in nature preserves. Exotic plants such as Japanese Honeysuckle, Wintercreeper, Purple Loosestrife, and Common Buckthorn literally crowd out native plants. To combat this threat, the native plant program proposed and administers the Illinois Exotic Weed Act. This law prohibits the sale and planting of Multiflora Rose, Japanese Honeysuckle, and Purple Loosestrife in Illinois.

The Grass Carp, an escaped vegetation-eating fish, is a threat to native aquatic plants. On a recent visit to the Cache River area of southern Illinois I learned that they had eaten virtually all of the Coontail, a once-common native plant in low- current parts of the river. They entered the Cache River during the flood of 1993. There does not appear to be any immediate solution to this threat to native aquatic plants.

The harvest of native plants from the wild for sale to the medicinal and nursery trade is a serious threat to a dozen or more native plants. These plants are often taken from private lands without the landowner's permission. Efforts by the plant conservation program to have laws enacted to prevent this have failed to pass the Illinois legislature.

Introduced plant diseases have taken their toll on native plants as well. The Chestnut Blight, Dutch Elm Disease, Butternut Canker, and Dogwood Anthracnose have greatly reduced native trees. Plant conservation efforts to date have centered on reintroduction of blight-resistant Chestnut trees and storing seed from Illinois' Butternuts to use in reestablishment in the state if a treatment for the canker is found.

In cooperation with the National Center for Plant Conservation, the Illinois plant conservation program maintains seeds of many extremely rare Illinois plants in long-term seed storage at the National Center for Genetic Resources Preservation in Colorado. Seed storage amounts to captive populations that contain the natural genetic variation of the species in Illinois that can be used to reintroduce the species if it is extirpated from the state. In this regard, rare plants are much easier and more economical to maintain in "captivity" than animals. No zoo required.

Methods of monitoring individual plants or populations of endangered plants from year to year were developed so that the cause of mortality for them might be determined. I and several District Heritage Biologists selected twelve critical species, including federally endangered species, such as Prairie Bush Clover and Mead's Milkweed, as well as Illinois endangered species, such as Yellow Wood and Small Whorled Pogonia Orchid, for monitoring. This program revealed the need for fire to scarify seed for three species before they would germinate. Other species were determined to be killed by insects, drought, and by fungal disease. This information was incorporated into management of the species.

Small Whorled Pogonia Orchid. Monitoring the only Illinois population of these orchids revealed that the larger of two surviving plants was dug up and eaten by an Eastern Chipmunk, and the last surviving plant appeared to die from effects of drought.

Public awareness and appreciation of native plants was promoted by production of educational posters, newsletters, and status reports on monitored populations of rare plants. This nature column is also a part of the native plant conservation program educational effort. Today, many classrooms in our schools have habitat posters and teachers have interpretive guides to what is taking place on them. After more than a decade of operation and cooperation with many other private and public conservationists, our native plants have benefitted considerably from this comprehensive conservation program.

July 1996

AUTHOR'S NOTE.—*Since 1997 there has been no staff botanist at the Department of Natural Resources to continue this program. When researchers from Purdue University sought the Illinois Butternut seeds that had been stored in a freezer for research into possible restoration of the species they discovered that the stored seed had been discarded. The newsletter that brought the plant conservation community together has been abandoned.*

Deer and Native Plants

The White-tailed Deer is Illinois' largest native wild mammal. Because it is very common and does not mind being around people, it is seen by everyone but inner city residents. Deer are not just of interest to hunters. Few who see wild deer fail to marvel at their beauty and grace, living reminders of a wild world that once was.

That such large wild animals live in our midst seems a miracle. But of course it is not a miracle at all, just the response of a very adaptable and successful animal to protection and management. With our abundant food crops to supplement wild foods and no predators to control their numbers, deer often become so abundant as to be a problem to just about everyone at one time or another.

Motorists have to dodge them or risk expensive repairs, farmers watch them eat valuable crops, orchardists and nursery operators lose trees as bucks scrape their antlers on trees and browse branches, and suburban homeowners suffer damage to valuable shrubbery and landscaping. Occasionally a deer crashes through a plate glass window that it cannot tell from the habitat it reflects. To top it all off, some carry deer ticks that can infect humans with Lyme Disease.

My problem with deer is different from most. I am concerned with the damage they do to natural areas and native plants. Plants are adapted to being eaten occasionally. After all, they are the base of the food chain for all of our natural and agricultural ecosystems. But browsing by uncontrolled deer populations has destroyed wildflowers and endangered plant species and forest tree reproduction in parts of Illinois. Natural forests and prairies that millions of dollars were spent to protect as living examples of our natural heritage have been destroyed or severely damaged by deer. Forests in urban northeastern

Illinois have been the hardest hit by deer because no gun hunting is allowed there.

I remember Cook County's Busse Woods Forest Preserve and the Ryerson Conservation Area in Lake County when they were carpeted with beautiful Large White Trilliums each spring, but no more. By the early 1980s, Busse Woods, near Schaumburg had lost all semblance of a wildflower display, and the deer had eaten every shrub and twig in their reach. Grasses and sedges, which are adapted to grazing, made up what little ground cover remained. The Department of Natural Resources established an urban deer control program at this site in 1983 under contract with the Illinois Natural History Survey and in cooperation with the Cook County Forest Preserve District. This deer population was reduced and is now maintained at about ten animals per square mile. After a decade the wildflowers, young trees, and shrubs are gradually coming back. You can still walk over tens of acres without seeing Large White Trillium, Maidenhair Fern, or Dutchman's Breeches. But this spring (1994) we actually saw Jack-in-the-pulpits and Large White Trilliums big enough to flower. A few years ago I doubted it would recover, but now I would guess the vegetation could be back close to natural in another thirty to forty years.

Deer-control programs are common in northeastern Illinois now with ten agencies controlling deer at twenty-four sites. In spite of this, biologists with the Department of Natural Resources and the Forest Preserve District get many calls from citizens needing help controlling deer damage. As the statewide deer herd has increased, damage has occurred to natural vegetation in other parts of the state as well. Special management hunts have been used to control deer there.

Dr. Roger Anderson of Illinois State University has studied which wildflowers the deer prefer most in Illinois' forests and prairies. Trilliums, which have a whorl of three leaves and a flower at the top of a leafless stalk, are one of their favorites. Trilliums lose all of their leaves and seeds in a single bite from a deer. They do not resprout after grazing in a given year but come back smaller each year until they die if the deer are not controlled. Dr. Anderson uses small trilliums or the absence of trilliums as indicators of deer damage in Illinois' forests. As damage increases, the loss of shrubs and saplings to browsing is visible from great distances. In prairies, Anderson has found that deer eat forbs or wildflowers, but unlike cattle they do not like grass. Deer have apparently eliminated the endangered Prairie

White-fringed Orchid from one prairie, while Illinois' only stand of the endangered Needle Rose is browsed so heavily by deer that it has not flowered in four years.

Deer are wonderful symbols of our wild heritage. As such, a healthy deer herd is important to the quality of life in Illinois. But harmony between deer and the natural world will be maintained only through concerned human stewardship.

June 1994

Green Trillium is limited to woodland habitats near the Mississippi River in Illinois and Missouri. It exhibits the whorl of three leaves and a single flower at the top of a stem that can be taken in a single bite by a deer.

AUTHOR'S NOTE.—*By 2015 the Needle Rose had been eliminated from Illinois by deer browsing. However, Busse Woods has continued to recover and now hosts an impressive display of wildflowers.*

~~~~~~~~~~~~~~~~~~~

Root Diggers

One of the threats to our native plant heritage is its exploitation for the market—the harvest of wild roots, herbs, and bark for profit. Ginseng is the native plant that immediately comes to mind when wild-root digging is discussed, but many other wild plants are harvested for their market value as well. Goldenseal, Culver's Root, Pale Coneflower, Seneca Snakeroot, Virginia Snakeroot, and Bloodroot are among the many native plants whose roots are dug. Some of the plants whose bark is harvested for market include Sassafras, Slippery Elm, Prickly Ash, Black Haw, and various sumacs. Among plants whose leaves or foliage are sold are Goldenseal, Round-headed Lespedeza, Black Walnut, and Witch Hazel.

These native botanicals are used in everything from herbal teas and vitamin supplements to toilet water and toothpaste. Ginseng is generally hailed as a cure-all and stimulant of the immune system as is Pale Coneflower (Echinacea). Sanguinaria extract from Bloodroot supposedly prevents tartar buildup on teeth and Culver's Root provides an effective laxative. Populations of Ginseng and Goldenseal in Illinois have declined drastically over the years due to this exploitation. Once among the most common woodland herbs, they are now difficult to find. Culver's Root and Pale Coneflower are important wildflowers or forbs in prairies and prairie restorations. Many prairie remnants and even some ornamental plantings have been raided and degraded by unscrupulous root diggers.

Ginseng is the only one of these plants with any legal protection. Illinois statute establishes an open season for harvest from the last Saturday in August through November 1 annually. Legal harvest of ginseng is restricted to the period when ripe seeds are available on the plants for harvesters to plant when digging. Hopefully enough diggers will plant the seeds to assure future populations. The sale of Ginseng is also prohibited prior to the open season to discourage commerce in early dug plants. Illinois law also makes it illegal for someone to dig Ginseng from the land of another without the landowner's permission.

None of the other harvested plants have any protection on private land other than the trespass laws. A landowner whose Goldenseal is taken by another has no recourse other than to pursue a trespass complaint. Past efforts by the Department of Natural Resources to have the General Assembly enact legislation to protect these plants on private lands have not been successful. On the other hand, all native plants in state parks, nature preserves, and other Department of Natural Resources administered lands are protected from taking. The same is true for many park district and forest preserve district lands. Harvest in the Shawnee National Forest is restricted to holders of special use permits, which carefully limit taking to protect sensitive species.

Except for Ginseng, there are no data on the number of plants taken for commerce in native botanicals each year. Approximately two thousand licensed Ginseng diggers harvest about six thousand pounds of dry Ginseng root annually in Illinois. Sample counts of roots per pound indicate that this amounts to about 1.6 million plants harvested each year. If harvest records indicate the need, ginseng harvest season can be closed to protect the species. To date this has not been necessary. It does not seem likely that harvest pressure is as severe on other species as it is on Ginseng because the price paid for them is much less. However, significant damage has been done to prairie remnants, and the population level of goldenseal is held at a greatly reduced level by this harvesting.

An important step in protecting Illinois' native plant heritage would be the enactment of a law prohibiting the taking of such plants from the property of another without the owner's written permission.

September 1995

AUTHOR'S NOTE.—*As of 2015 no law has been enacted to require landowner permission for persons to dig roots (except Ginseng) or to take other botanicals from the land of another.*

Floods and the Endangered False Aster

Recent (1993) floods on the Mississippi and Illinois Rivers have had varying effects on wild plants and animals. On one plant, the threatened Decurrent False Aster, the effects could be severe. This false aster is a perennial herb about five to six feet tall that grows only in lowlands along the Illinois River and along a small area of the Mississippi near its junction with the Illinois. Each plant has hundreds of white daisy-like flowers in late August and September.

Why it grows here and nowhere else in the world is somewhat of a mystery, but it seems to grow only in the alluvial and sandy soils associated with glaciation of the Illinois valley. It may require the texture of these soils or some trace element they contain. At any rate, the Decurrent False Aster only lives in river lowlands subject to flooding.

After a severe summer flood on the Illinois River in 1979, annual searches for this false aster failed to find any plants at all until 1982. For several years I feared it had become extinct. After a series of dry and average years its numbers recovered reaching a record high in the 1988 drought. With support from the US Fish and Wildlife Service and the US Army Corps of Engineers, Dr. Marian Smith and her students of Southern Illinois University at Edwardsville began studies of the biology of the Decurrent False Aster in an attempt to understand its limiting factors.

The findings of Dr. Smith and her students, and those of another researcher, provide insights into why flooding and particularly summer flooding can now be a disaster for this plant. Smith learned that this false aster tolerates immersion in water more than almost any plant that grows normally on land. She and her students studied a population that was completely inundated by water in an artificially flooded borrow pit. The plants thrived all summer under the water and some even flowered under water! Through greenhouse studies and field observations, these researchers also learned that this plant requires full direct sun to live and grow. It cannot grow in the shade of woods or even in dense weeds. Dr. Jerry Baskin of the University of Kentucky studied the germination of this false aster's seeds. He discovered that unlike most seeds, the seeds of this particular plant

Decurrent False Aster, which grows in lowland sunny habitats adjacent to the Illinois River and along the Mississippi River near the mouth of the Illinois. Why it has such a restricted range is a mystery.

must be exposed to light before they will germinate. Seeds just a few millimeters under the soil's surface will not germinate no matter how ideal the soil moisture and temperature may be.

So why should a plant that can grow submerged in water, which lived happily in the Illinois River valley before the arrival of Europeans, be devastated by floods now? The answer lies in how conditions have changed along the river and in Illinois over the last 175 years. Before settlement, the Illinois River was noted for its clarity of water. Runoff from the prairies and forests that covered the state was clear and gradual. The current was so sluggish that it did not even scour mud from the riverbank, and there were no tugboats to churn mud from the river's bottom.

Today runoff from the crop fields that replaced our prairies is rapid and carries much soil and silt with it. This muddies the river water, especially at flood time. These floodwaters lay down a thick deposit of silt and mud over everything when they recede. Levees now prevent flooding of much of the "floodplain" so that flooding in the remaining unprotected wildlands is deeper and more frequent than in presettlement times.

These changes affect the Decurrent False Aster in several ways. In spite of their tolerance for flooding by clear water, the muddy water of our floods today cuts off light to the plants. The flooding can kill many plants by denying them light. The fact that our floods are more frequent and deeper because of the levees adds to the potential of floods to kill them. Also, the silt deposited by present-day floods buries their seeds under thick layers of mud. This silt cuts light off to the seeds preventing them from germinating.

In short, we have turned a river ecosystem that was home to a unique plant into one that barely supports it. Each major flood event brings with it the possibility of extinction. How the flood of 1993 treats the Decurrent False Aster will probably not be known until 1994. At this writing the Illinois River has not flooded as badly as the Mississippi, so the prognosis is fair. In any event, the species will not be lost completely as I have its seeds stored in a freezer as a hedge against disaster. But where do I plant them?

July 1993

AUTHOR'S NOTE.—*At this writing in 2015 the Decurrent False Aster survives in the Illinois River valley.*

Meredosia Lake, a typical bottomland lake of the Illinois River floodplain near the town of Meredosia. Decurrent False Aster is seen growing on the lake's open sunny shore.

The 1993 Flood's Impacts on Plants

While the impact of the great Mississippi River flood of 1993 on Illinois' native plants and animals will be best assessed next spring and summer, preliminary observations give us some hint of what lies ahead. One of the biggest fears of naturalists is that the flooding killed many trees, shrubs, and other plants. Significant death of such vegetation would change habitats for most wildlife and could require decades to recover. In the case of old virgin forests, centuries would be required to replace ancient trees.

The US Forest Service has compiled information on the effects of flooding on different tree species. They classify trees into four categories: very tolerant of flooding, such as Bald Cypress; tolerant, such as Silver Maple and Pin Oak; somewhat tolerant, such as Bur Oak; and intolerant, such as Black Walnut. Armed with this information, Department of Natural Resources botanists decided to visit some key forests this December in hopes of determining probable flooding impacts. Two very high quality virgin forests were among the many forests flooded in the summer of 1993. These are Horseshoe Lake Nature Preserve near Cairo and Long Island Forest near Quincy. The latter forest is part of the Mark Twain National Wildlife Refuge and is located on Long Island in the Mississippi River north of Quincy. Department botanist Bill McClain and Dr. John Ebinger of Eastern Illinois University visited it.

This forest apparently stood flooded to a depth of ten to fifteen feet most of the summer, causing grape vines and shrubs to sprout roots at the water's surface in an effort to get oxygen. These roots now dangle high overhead as a reminder of the water's summer level. It appears that most of the Hackberry trees, some of the Silver Maples, and many of the shrubs and groundcover herbs are dead. Hackberry is listed as tolerant of flooding by the Forest Service so if it has died, many other less tolerant species may be dead as well. The condition of all species is not easily told in winter.

Horseshoe Lake Nature Preserve is a virgin forest of oak, American Beech, Sweet Gum, and Bald Cypress within Horseshoe Lake State Fish and Wildlife Area at the southern tip of Illinois. It flooded early in the summer when a levee broke and remained flooded until fall. Since beech is an upland tree that is presumed intolerant of flooding, I visited this forest in December to check on it and other possibly vulnerable species.

Flooding here had only been about two to three feet deep, and some of the highest ridges may not have flooded at all. Even so, many beeches had been flooded at least to shallow depths. It appeared that the beech trees and most others were still alive. However, some of the beautiful little Red Buckeye trees that compose the shrub layer had died. Some of the Red Buckeyes with dead trunks and branches had recently sprouted from the base of the plant, indicating that some still had live roots. A few buckeye seeds also had sprouted. Starting growth in the fall is atypical and was apparently due to flood effects or the warm autumn. Last September I noticed many oaks turning prematurely brown in lower flooded parts of the Horseshoe Lake State Fish and Wildlife Area and along the nearby Cache River. Many forests in the Horseshoe Lake vicinity may have fared worse than the relatively high elevation nature preserve.

Another plant seriously impacted by the flood is the threatened Decurrent False Aster. In the whole world, this herb grows only in lowlands along the Illinois River and along the Mississippi near the mouth of the Illinois. When I made my annual census in September of 1993, only ten populations remained of the twenty-eight that existed in the fall of 1992, and some of these were greatly reduced in size. Downstream from Peoria, where the flood was deepest, only two small populations were found, and apparently all Missouri populations perished. Even where levees held at East St. Louis and Beardstown, seepage water inundated and killed most plants.

Just how many trees are dead or will die later from the flood's effects? Will "dead" shrubs and herbs sprout from their roots? Will the threatened Decurrent False Aster come back from seed remaining in the soil? The final answer to these questions will have to wait at least until next spring and summer. In the meantime, these winter observations indicate that plant mortality is probably significant but not as bad as had been feared in some places.

As the spring of 1994 spread northward across Illinois, a sad story of destruction unfolded. North of Quincy at the village of Meyer, Illinois' only known population of Blue Violet was inundated last summer when a levee broke. When Department of Natural Resources botanists visited the area in mid-April, not a single living Blue Violet could be found. Other species of violets were seen, indicating that they should have been visible if they had survived. It appears that the flood and perhaps the cleanup that followed were fatal to this little wildflower. Its loss is special since it means that one of the state's twenty-two kinds of native violets, our state flower, may no longer grow here.

In late April I visited the virgin forest of Horseshoe Lake Nature Preserve near Cairo to assess the damage to the ancient beech and other trees there. As my visit last December indicated, some of the trees had survived, but the destruction I found now was far greater than I had anticipated. I found the area flooded because the nearby Len Small levee that had been repaired over the winter had been breached again by recent floods. Some two thousand feet of the new levee had been washed away, flooding the preserve for the second year in a row. These floodwaters made assessment of last summer's flood impact difficult, but they will probably not compound the 1993 flood impact greatly unless they remain high into this growing season.

As I started counting the giant old American Beech trees my heart began to sink. Of thirty-five old beeches that stood there in the spring of 1993, seventeen had been killed by the flooding, and three others had been blown over. The wind damage was also probably flood related as the saturated soil made the trees easier to topple. Many other kinds of trees had died as well. Sugar Maple, Hackberry, Basket Oak, Box Elder, Black Walnut, and American Elm were among the casualties, as were smaller trees such as Red Buckeye and Paw Paw. On the positive side, live specimens of all of these species still existed, usually on slightly higher ground than the dead ones. Most of the beautiful Red Buckeyes had survived, and a rare wildflower known as Dwarf Phacelia was still present.

As I made my way to the only Cucumber Magnolia tree known in this forest, I was saddened to see that it appeared to lack leaves. Closer examination revealed that dwarf leaves had emerged on two branches high in its canopy. It still held a spark of life! The flooding kept me from reaching the site of the endangered Nuttall's Oak. It may have survived because it is more tolerant to flooding than trees such as beech, but only a later visit this summer will tell. The loss of twenty out of thirty-five ancient American Beech trees in a single year underscores the unique nature of the 1993 flood. These trees had stood 150 to 200 years before this flood, indicating that such a flood had not occurred over this long time span.

The uniqueness of the 1993 flood lies in the time it occurred and its duration. The normal floods that Horseshoe Lake Nature Preserve's forest and the entire Mississippi River floodplain are adapted to, occur in late winter and early spring. The Mississippi River has flooded at more or less regular intervals over the years at this season. The damaging character of the 1993 flood is that it came during the summer growing season and lasted for months. These waters deprived the tree roots of air at a time when they need it most.

Many of the beeches produced a large crop of nuts last summer as a last gasp before dying. Only time will tell if these will lead to a new generation in the future.

February 1994 and May 1994

AUTHOR'S NOTE.—*Follow-up visits revealed that the Cucumber Magnolia had died and eliminated this species from the preserve, but a large Nuttall's Oak survived.*

Fire Suppression

Of the natural phenomena greeting the settlers of Illinois, the annual fires of autumn were the most frequently mentioned in early descriptions of the state. The second most frequent observation was how quickly the prairie grew up into forest when the annual fires were stopped. The above conclusion was reached by John White and his associates at Ecological Services in Urbana after completing an exhaustive study of historical descriptions of the state. Fire shaped the early landscape of Illinois more than any other force, and today wildfire is a rarity, almost totally suppressed by man. My goal here is to explain the ecological effects of fire suppression to help the reader understand the implications of the loss of fire on our landscape and wildlife.

As John White noted, the first striking result of fire suppression was the rapid sprouting of trees where only prairie seemed to grow. This also happened in savannas, which are mixtures of prairie and scattered trees. Most of these rapidly growing trees were probably young oak "grubs" that had been established for years but were kept burned down to the ground by the annual fires. Although their tops were small they had developed large root systems, which were protected from the fire. When fires stopped, trees rapidly shot up from these preexisting root systems. Of course some trees seeded in as well.

The loss of prairie to fire suppression continues today. Hill prairies on steep dry bluffs resisted conversion to forest for the longest period after fires were stopped. However, travelers along highways that parallel Illinois' river bluffs can view the ongoing loss of hill prairies as they first get a few shrubs and trees in them and finally grow into forest. Prairie remnants are also disappearing along railroad tracks since the replacement of steam locomotives, which released sparks that started fires, with diesel engines and the advent of herbicides to control vegetation along railroads instead of fire.

Presettlement fires burned the forests as well as the prairies and shaped the forests we have today. Illinois' oak–hickory forest owes its existence to these fires. Both adult and young oaks and hickories are resistant to fire relative to other kinds of trees. In sites protected from the most severe fires by firebreaks such as rivers and steep slopes, these trees with thick fire-resistant bark flourished. In some of the most protected sites, fire-sensitive trees such as Sugar Maple and American Beech existed, but they were severely limited in area because their thin bark made them easily killed by the annual fires. Today, Sugar Maple is spreading rapidly and replacing oaks and hickories in forests throughout Illinois. While this major change in our forests is slower than the loss of prairie, it is a major impact whose full effects will be felt in decades to come. The replacement of nut- and acorn-producing hickories and oaks with maples will have a major impact on the food available to forest wildlife.

In prairie and other grassy habitats such as old fields, fire suppression adversely affects the habitat of wildlife such as Bobwhite Quail and Deer Mice and favors voles and other animals that prefer dense old grass for food and cover. Bobwhites, especially their young, need to get their feet on the ground to find food and escape danger. They do not do well walking on top of old dead grasses, and invariably decline in numbers without fire. In the southeast, where Bobwhites are managed for hunting, they are known as the firebird.

At present, Illinois has apparently lost at least one native species, Beard Grass, to fire suppression. This grass of barrens or prairie-like habitats in the Shawnee Hills was last seen in Illinois in the late

1970s before its open grassy habitat grew up completely into forest. Beginning in 1989, the Shawnee National Forest began rehabilitating the habitat with tree removal and reintroduction of fire in the hope that seed of the grass remained in the soil. In spite of this effort, the grass has not returned.

There is no question that severe and large-scale landscape fires are not compatible with most of present-day Illinois. There is also no question that the resulting fire suppression is causing major changes to our natural heritage. Nature preserve managers are applying prescribed fire to managed prairies, savannas, and fire-dependent woodlands, so we will continue to have examples of these natural communities. Foresters are also working on ways to maintain oak and hickory in the face of increasing Sugar Maple in Illinois' forests. One thing is certain, fire suppression and its impact on nature will be mitigated only by our stewardship of the land.

August 1993

AUTHOR'S NOTE.—*Efforts are under way to perpetuate oak–hickory forest through prescribed burning on many public lands in Illinois.*

Conducting a Prairie Burn

This column has described many of the natural wonders of Illinois over the past year, but this time let's take a look at one of many tasks being undertaken to save that natural heritage for the future. Join me as we follow a Natural Heritage Biologist on a hypothetical prescribed burn of a prairie in late March or early April. These biologists are practitioners of the relatively new science of conservation biology. Prescribing and conducting controlled burns to simulate natural prairie fires is just one of the ways they promote the conservation of Illinois' natural heritage. They work for Illinoisans and their heritage through the Department of Natural Resources, Division of Natural Heritage.

It is eight o'clock on a Monday morning when we join Bill (our fictitious biologist) on the road to a prairie burn. His small pickup is loaded with fire-control gear as he listens to the NOAA all-weather station on his radio. Monday is normally an office day for Heritage

Biologists, but little is normal during burning season. Bill was on the phone Sunday evening pulling together a burn crew of twelve so he could take advantage of ideal burning weather forecast for today.

After filling half a dozen backpack sprayers with water, he heads for the prairie. He arrives at nine, about an hour before the rest of the crew. As fire boss, with complete responsibility for the burn, he wants to check the firebreak he constructed last week. Leaves may have blown onto it, or a dead tree may have fallen across it. After checking the break, he goes out into the prairie to determine the moisture level in the grass and makes sure all is clear in the area to be burned. At ten o'clock his crew arrives. Most are staff of nearby conservation areas and parks, but a wildlife biologist and forester are also here as are two volunteer stewards. Bill lays a map of the burn area on the hood of his truck and explains the plan for the burn. The wind is about ten miles per hour from the west, so the fire will be set as a backfire along the firebreak on the east side. Backfires burn into the wind and thus are slow moving and easy to manage. They are used to widen the break so that wind-driven fires will not jump them.

Bill selects two experienced crew members to handle setting the fire with drip torches. Drip torches are canisters filled with a mixture of diesel fuel and gasoline. They drip fire when lit and allow the rapid and easy setting of fire. Each torch bearer will have a two-way radio and so will Bill. The burn is large and in hilly terrain, so radios are necessary for the fire boss to keep track of conditions on all sides of the fire. A check of the weather radio indicates that the relative humidity is still 55 percent, too high for effective burning. A heavy dew the night before is not drying fast either, and it is decided to wait until 11:30 before starting the burn. Bill knows that the wind will get stronger later in the day, but judges that it will still be within acceptable parameters. After safety, his first concern is that the fire achieves the planned ecological results. The best way to assure this is to wait until the humidity drops below 50 percent and the fuel is dryer.

Two of the crew members are new at burning, so Bill takes this waiting time to explain the workings of the fire-control equipment to them. The backpack sprayer is the best portable tool for controlling grass fire. Fully loaded with five gallons of water, it weighs fifty pounds. It throws a stream of water, much like a small version of a garden hose, that can put out a prairie fire when directed to the base of its flames. Rakes are used to construct firebreaks and also to put out fire in the woods. Burning leaves are raked into the adjacent burnt-out area by a firefighter as he moves along the burning edge of the fire. Flappers are squares of rubberized fabric attached to a long handle. They extinguish fire by smothering it and are effective at controlling slow-moving back fires in grass as well as leaves in forest.

As eleven thirty comes, the crew begins igniting the fire at a common point on the east side. The torchbearers proceed to set fire along the break in opposite directions. Other crew members space themselves at intervals along the break to make sure the fire does not jump it. Once the fire has burned some distance out from the break, they move along to watch more newly set areas. After a check by radio determines that the back fire has safely widened the break on the downwind side of the burn and that everyone is clear of the area, Bill gives the OK to begin setting the head fire. Head fires run with the wind, and one in heavy prairie fuel like this is an awesome sight. The roar of vast amounts of oxygen being consumed adds to the spectacle. Bill and the crew watch as the firestorm dies in its tracks as it runs out of fuel.

At one o'clock in the afternoon it is time to break out the sandwiches and soda. After lunch break, the crew goes out to extinguish any burning material that has not gone out on its own. A standing dead tree near the fire line has caught fire, and Bill brings in a chain saw and fells it into the burned-out area. Backpacks are used to drown the

Prescribed burn under way in sparse sand prairie vegetation of Mason County, Illinois.

last embers of this and other fires. After a check of the fire's ecological effects and taking note of weather conditions and other site data needed to complete the postburn report, Bill heads home. The sense of accomplishment he feels is a bonus his job offers that the uninitiated may find hard to appreciate. But Bill is not surprised by the number of volunteers he has seen quitting their jobs to study conservation biology. Nature conservation is an emotional experience as well as a profession.

May 1993

Prescribed Fire in the Woods

As Indian summer progresses, the frosts deaden vegetation, and the warm days cure the grasses and fallen leaves into fuel for fire. One of the trademarks of warm Indian summer days in late October and early November is haze. Today this haze may reflect humidity and a somewhat stagnant atmosphere, but in earlier times smoke from man-ignited wildland fires contributed to Indian summer's haze as well. While prairie burning has become an accepted natural-area management practice over the past twenty years, burning in our forests is only now gaining acceptance. Clearly, severe fire can damage and destroy valuable timber, but an increasing number of nature conservationists are turning to prescribed fire in forests to achieve a variety of benefits in managed natural areas.

Many of our oak–hickory forests are changing to Sugar Maple forests through vegetation succession in the absence of fire. Fire that once killed young maples and opened up the forest canopy so young oaks could grow to maturity has been excluded from most Illinois woodlands since the 1930s. I recently interviewed Henry Eilers, a retired Litchfield nurseryman, about his experience burning in the woods of Montgomery County. Henry is the steward for the city of Litchfield and The Nature Conservancy, with management responsibility for the city's 245-acre Shoal Creek Barrens natural area.

Starting in 1989 and continuing through 1995, Henry and his twenty-five to thirty volunteer assistants have burned portions of this upland forest and adjacent grassy habitat annually. The effect of these fires on wildflowers has been spectacular. "Flowering plants of the beautiful Purple Coneflower and Shooting-star increased 1,000 fold," reports Henry. Showy Orchid, a delicate, moist forest wildflower, increased from just a few plants to become a common species. This was totally unexpected as it was thought that mostly dry forest plants would benefit and that the orchid was delicate and might be damaged by the fire. Other wildflowers that increased greatly are Whorled Milkweed, Yellow Coneflower, and False Boneset. The endangered Buffalo Clover appeared as if by magic after the first burn. Its hard seeds had been waiting in the soil seed bank for fire to scarify them so they could germinate. Buffalo Clover is now a typical plant of this forest, indicating that the rarity and endangered status of this plant in Illinois today may be a result of fire suppression.

The response of animals to fire at Shoal Creek is also notable says Eilers. Butterflies have increased greatly with the burning, including striking species such as the Falcate Orangetip and the Great Spangled Fritillary. Henry points out that over the seven years of their management, any given area of forest has burned three to four times. They never burn all of the area in a single year out of respect for insects that may be locally injured by fire. Henry's experience indicates that where an Illinois woods is being managed for natural diversity and beauty rather than timber production, prescribed fire is a key tool of the steward.

The Shoal Creek Barrens does not have any of the exotic garlic mustard that is overrunning the wildflowers in many forests in the north half of Illinois. If it did, his fire management would doubtless have reduced this problem. Garlic mustard is a biennial plant with an overwintering green rosette of leaves that can be killed by fire during the fall and winter. Management by the Department of Natural Resources in a scrub oak forest in Mason County has shown that fire can be an effective means of controlling this weed.

Always mindful that severe wildfire can damage forests, managers are increasingly aware of the great good carefully applied fire can do for Illinois' forests. Where management's goal is maintenance or restoration of biological diversity or perpetuation of oak woodlands, fire has an important role to play. From Chicagoland to Peoria and down to the Shawnee National Forest, more and more, managers are turning to fire as a tool in forest management. If you see smoke rising from a forest this fall through next spring, you may be seeing the evidence of conservationists at work.

October 1995

AUTHOR'S NOTE.—*The Shawnee National Forest has implemented a program of large landscape-management burning in selected areas of its forest.*

~~~~~~~~~~~~~~~~~~~~~~~~~~~~~~

Fire and Wildflowers

Last fall I wrote a column on "Fire in the Woods" in which I recounted the positive experience a group of volunteers and the city of Litchfield had in using fire to manage the city's Shoal Creek Barrens woodland for natural diversity. Much wildland management is aimed at producing some product for human harvest or consumption such as timber or game animals, but the goal of the Litchfield group was enhancement of the habitat for all of the native plants and animals that make the woods their home.

Last fall they conducted a large burn on the east shore of Lake Lou Yaeger, and this spring the chief steward of the woods, Henry Eilers, invited me to visit and see the profusion of wildflowers that resulted. Eilers says the goal of their November fire was a natural fall burn of the east shore area. On our visit we noted small areas scattered throughout the woods that remained unburned, where fuel was thin or damp. By chance, one larger two-to-three-acre area had also not burned. This mosaic of unburned and burned areas is typical of fall-burned woodlands and accounts for the survival of insects and other fire-sensitive wildlife in wildfire areas. These natural fire-free refuges supplement the planned unburned habitat that the stewards designated before the fire.

The first thing to catch the visitor's eye in the burned woodland this April is the carpet of spring beauties and other wildflowers and the greener appearance of the groundcover grasses and sedges. While nearby unburned woodlands are brown with old leaves, the groundcover of the burned woods is green. This is both because the brown leaves impart their color to the unburned landscape and also because they insulate the soil against the warming rays of the sun. The faster warming of the soil in burned woods stimulates an abundance of new green growth far ahead of the unburned woods.

I found no evidence of the fire killing or damaging mature trees, but many seedlings, sprouts, and shrubs were killed back to ground level, giving the forest understory an open appearance. Trees that one supposes might be fire sensitive, such as Ohio Buckeye and Eastern Red Cedar, have come through without notable damage. I was amazed to see moist woodland wildflowers, such as Virginia Bluebell, Great Bellwort, and Downy Yellow Violet, blooming abundantly and unscathed by the fall burn. A fire in the spring would probably not be so easily withstood by these forest beauties. Dry habitat woodland wildflowers, such as Spring Beauty, Bird-foot Violet, Shooting-star, Pussy-toes, and Violet Oxalis, thrive in the burned areas. Some steep, south-facing slopes that support savanna remnants with prairie wildflowers, such as Hoary Puccoon and Golden Alexanders, abound in brilliant color. These communities are stimulated to abundant flowering and seed set while getting relief from the encroachment of invading shrubs and small trees.

The management goal of the Shoal Creek Woods stewards is to return the area to the mix of oak–hickory forest, savanna, and scattered prairie openings that it was before fire suppression began in the 1930s. This lack of fire started the trend—that plant ecologists call vegetative succession—away from oak and hickory toward dominance of the forest by Sugar Maple. Sugar Maple produces little food for wildlife compared to the acorns and nuts of oak and hickory. Without fire to control it, the maple eliminates oak and hickory reproduction by producing dense shade that kills or suppresses their seedlings, while its own shade-tolerant seedlings thrive. In addition to the elimination of oaks and hickories, the dense maple shade virtually eliminates wildflowers and other groundcover vegetation after maple leaves come out in the spring. This reduces the diversity of plant and animal life (biodiversity) that the woods supports.

The reintroduction of fire helps return the vegetation to its original condition by killing the fire-sensitive Sugar Maple seedlings and saplings to the benefit of young oaks. Larger Sugar Maple trees that have gotten too large for the fire to control are girdled by the stewards to speed up the restoration process. While fire created the original forest and savanna community, restoring it with fire alone might take centuries. With modern management techniques, the restoration should be accomplished in decades rather than centuries.

May 1996

~~~~~~

Wetland Creation

Wetlands are important wildlife habitat, purifiers of water, retention areas for floodwaters, and scenic wonders. Many have been drained in Illinois, but restorationists are starting to put a few back. This summer (1995), I viewed a prairie pothole wetland that was created at Prairie Ridge State Natural Area in 1994. Prairie Ridge is Illinois' Prairie Chicken sanctuary, in Jasper County. Prairie potholes are shallow and treeless with open water surrounded by wetland herbs that grade into surrounding prairie vegetation. You often cannot see they are there until you walk up to them. These wetlands are very productive of resident wildlife and provide important habitat for migrating shorebirds, wading birds, and waterfowl.

The difference between pond construction and prairie pothole construction centers on site selection, construction method, and depth of water. Of course, there is considerable difference in management as well. The four-acre pothole in question was constructed in a nearly level upland grassland area with a gently sloping but adequate watershed to supply it. Excavation was by a scraper that was able to deepen and shape it a few inches at a time. The shoreline was constructed with smooth arching curves and undulations that mimic a natural pothole pond. To add additional shoreline habitat, a sinuous narrow island was designed into the wetland. Maximum water depth is about four feet, and no permanent fish population is desired.

The shallows and shore area between water and land have much to do with the value of a wetland to wildlife. The more gradual it is, the broader the emergent vegetation zone is for nesting and the more mudflat-shorebird habitat is created by lowering the water at the proper season. It also increases wading-bird foraging habitat. A water control structure at the berm that functions to dam the wetland's water flow allows lowering the water in small increments as well as totally draining it. The shore area was both seeded and planted with wetland herbaceous plants. The planting stock was nursery-reared at the Department of Natural Resource's Mason State Nursery. Aggressive plants that tend to "take over" and create monoculture vegetation, such as Cattail, were avoided. The end result is a shallow wetland with abundant shoreline, which is fringed with native, emergent aquatic plants.

Site superintendent Scott Simpson advises that in its first spring five broods of Mallards used the wetland for rearing and fledging young. When I saw the area in early August its shore was host to Killdeers, Mallards, a Great Blue Heron, and a flock of those small gray "sandpipers" that defy identification by all but dedicated birders. District Heritage Biologist Terry Esker commented on how fast aquatic turtles, water snakes, and Muskrats found the area. In less than a year all of these immigrants had taken up residence.

Scott Simpson's management plan consists of holding water high in the spring, to provide emergent vegetation and maximum water area for nesting and foraging birds, and then drawing down the water in late summer to provide habitat for migrating shore birds. The creation of this wetland was a cooperative venture between public and private agencies. The Department of Natural Resources provided the land, plant materials, and some labor, and the US Fish and Wildlife Service provided a challenge grant of $2,500, which was used to contract the earth moving. The Isaac Walton League contributed $400 for the pipe and water-control structure, and the federal Natural Resources Conservation Service provided engineering, field surveys, and design specifications. Three more prairie wetlands were constructed at Prairie Ridge this summer using $13,000 in donated "marsh money" from Ducks Unlimited, and one more is scheduled for the Marion County Prairie Chicken Sanctuary this autumn. Other major wetland restoration efforts are under way along the Cache River in southern Illinois and along the Des Plaines River in northeastern Illinois.

Wetland restoration and creation is a growing endeavor as conservationists strive to compensate for past and current wetland losses by direct action. If the efforts I have seen at the Prairie Chicken Sanctuary are any indication, Illinois' wetland wildlife is in for a big boost as more people catch on to the potential of wetland restoration.

September 1995

AUTHOR'S NOTE.—*As of 2015, no compilation of acreage of restored wetlands in Illinois is available. An* Illinois Wetland Restoration and Creation Guide *(Special Publication 19) is now available from the Illinois Natural History Survey in Champaign.*

Stream Conservation

Illinois streams have suffered greatly at the hands of civilization. Silt from cropland and pollution from cities, fields, and factories have taken a great toll on the stream life that Illinois inherited from Native Americans just two hundred years ago. Anyone who fishes streams in the state or studies their ecology realizes that much of Illinois' stream heritage still remains in special places that have somehow survived relatively intact. Conservationists interested in managing and protecting Illinois' stream heritage realized that these remnants and their resources needed to be identified as the first step to their protection and wise use.

To document these special rivers and creeks, the state's Department of Natural Resources joined the Illinois Environmental Protection Agency in 1984 to develop a biological streams–characterization procedure based on fishery and water-quality data. By 1989 this program had evaluated 478 streams, identifying twenty-four excellent-quality stream segments. Three watersheds stood out for the nature and extent of the quality stream segments within their basins. These were the Kishwaukee in northern Illinois and the Mackinaw and Vermilion (of the Wabash) in central Illinois. Lusk Creek and Big Creek, both direct tributaries of the Ohio River in southern Illinois, were also rated Class A streams, as were many scattered stream segments across Illinois. Expanding on this work in 1992, the Illinois Natural History Survey added consideration of endangered and threatened species—mussels, crayfish, and vascular plants—to identify the stream segments supporting the greatest biological diversity. Their work included the large bordering rivers as well as internal streams. These two analyses give Illinois a valuable database for stream-habitat protection and management.

Some of the larger rivers with high quality and biological significance include portions of the Rock, Kankakee, Fox, Vermilion (Wabash drainage), Wabash, Ohio, and Mississippi. Examples of medium-sized stream segments are portions of the Apple, Kishwaukee, Mackinaw, Middle Fork, Embarrass, Kaskaskia, and Cache. Many smaller streams such as Big Creek in Hardin County, Orchard Creek

107

in Alexander County, Ramsey Creek in Fayette County, and the Little Vermilion River are also examples of important refugia of Illinois' stream heritage.

But stream protection is a difficult proposition. Streams cross the property of numerous landowners, and protection requires the cooperation of many people. Past efforts to establish a system of protected wild and scenic rivers in Illinois by legislative designation have failed. Now, a variety of public and private conservation interests have decided to try a new cooperative private-landowner approach to stream protection. They plan to select specific streams or stream segments of important heritage value and meet with each individual landowner along them. The basic assumption is that a majority of landowners will want to cooperate in the enhancement of their land and that of their neighbors. Each owner will have to contribute something to the whole, but in turn will benefit from cleaner water, better fishing, and reduced flooding from the actions of others upstream. It is a true community approach to protecting a common natural resource with neighbor helping neighbor.

In addition to advice on actions landowners can take to enhance streams on their land, the contact person will provide information on available programs to help accomplish these actions. For example, with an approved plan, the Department of Natural Resources can provide planting stock for establishment of shade and filter strips. The principal landowner stewardship tasks for maintaining and restoring stream biological diversity are: controlling soil erosion in the watershed and bank erosion along the stream; maintaining shading trees and filter strips of vegetation along the banks; and keeping livestock out of streams. Controlling water pollution is important too, but is generally accomplished by government regulation.

At present, The Nature Conservancy, a private conservation organization, is contacting landowners along the Mackinaw River, while the Department of Natural Resources is working on segments of the Little Vermilion River and the Embarrass River. A joint private and local government group led by the Open Lands Project of Chicago is undertaking a similar approach on the Kishwaukee River.

Only time will tell if cooperative private stewardship will significantly improve the survival of Illinois' stream heritage. I think the chances are good that it will.

September 1994

AUTHOR'S NOTE.—*In 2015 this program is no longer continuing. The program settled on protecting the North Fork of the Vermilion River as its initial effort. Conservation easements were purchased and are held by the Vermilion County Soil and Water Conservation District. The easements are helping protect the stream.*

Silent Spring Again

During the cold winter months, naturalists have traditionally taken solace in the sureness of the coming spring. Anticipation of the annual wildflower display and the songs of returning warblers, thrushes, and other migrant birds helps us through the dreary season. But in recent years, fewer and fewer birds have returned from their winter home in the tropics to Illinois. Like the bird die-off due to pesticides in the 1960s, we are now experiencing a second "silent spring" and quiet summer as well.

While some of the problem is surely tied to what is happening on their wintering grounds, Scott Robinson and Jeffrey Brawn of the Illinois Natural History Survey have found that much of the trouble is right here in Illinois. The problem is a failure to raise young under conditions now prevailing in our nesting habitat. The birds showing the greatest decline are not the common overwintering birds and short-distance migrants, such as the Northern Cardinal and Robin. These birds are either always here or arrive early and can stay later in the summer. If their first brood of young fails to survive they generally renest. The birds that have declined or disappeared from many of our woods are long-distance migrants that have only a short time to nest before they have to head south again. These include the thrushes, warblers, vireos, flycatchers, and tanagers—some of our most beautiful and colorful birds. They are also some of our best songsters.

Who can say that we have not lost greatly when the song of the Wood Thrush no longer greets us on our woodland trails, and the red flash of a Summer Tanager is only a memory. Many of these long-distance migrants nest in the interior of our forests, away from the edge and often on or near the ground. Biologists refer to these birds as "forest interior species" and the species collectively as "neotropical migrants." Their failure to reproduce in today's Illinois is due to nest failure caused by predation and nest parasitism.

Predation involves the destruction of nests by predators that eat the eggs and young. While it is not always possible to tell what animal has destroyed a nest, it appears that raccoons are the most important predator of nests near the ground. Skunks and other animals doubtless also take their share. Blue Jays are thought to be one of the primary predators of higher nests. Nest parasitism is by Brown-headed Cowbirds. This native bird makes no nest of its own, but lays its eggs in those of other species. The young Cowbirds hatch earlier than the eggs of the host species and are generally larger than the young of the parasitized species. Therefore, young Cowbirds more readily grow to maturity, often leaving the juveniles of the "host" bird to starve.

Since Raccoons, Blue Jays, and Cowbirds are native wildlife that used to live in harmony with our forest interior birds, what has gone wrong? Scott Robinson and others believe that the main culprit is the way we have fragmented our forests. Most Illinois forests are mere scraps of what they once were. Virtually none are large.

Predators such as Raccoons, Blue Jays, and foxes hunt along the edges of forests but not deep in their interior. But because of the way our forests have been cut up and dissected, most wooded habitat is close to an edge now. This newly created forest-edge habitat has increased predator numbers while eliminating the safe-nesting habitat far from the edge needed by interior birds. A big increase in the backyard feeding of birds is also thought to have contributed to an increase in the Blue Jay population.

The Cowbird problem is also related to forest fragmentation. Cowbirds feed near grazing animals or on other open grassy ground and search for nests to parasitize in adjacent grasslands and along the edges of forests. Before settlement, Cowbirds would forage near Bison, but now farm livestock substitutes for Bison, and Cowbirds have also adapted to feeding in any grassland or weedy growth near forest fragments. Once limited to the edge of large forests, Cowbirds are now able to find and parasitize nests nearly throughout the small woodlots that comprise most of Illinois' present forest habitat. Bird studies of thirteen forests scattered around Illinois conducted by the Illinois Natural History Survey showed that 80 to 100 percent of Wood Thrush nests were parasitized by Cowbirds, and 50 to 90 percent of these nests were destroyed by predators. This does not leave enough young to replace the adults that die through the year.

The Illinois Natural History Survey study concludes that many of the forest interior birds Illinois has each summer are surplus birds from the larger forests in Indiana and Missouri. They emigrate here in search of habitat, only to attempt to reproduce and fail. Since most forestland in Illinois is privately owned, this is a problem with no easy solution. What is needed is reforestation to enlarge and connect remnant forests and some control on Cowbird numbers. Barring this, the future of many of our songbirds is not bright.

December 1992

AUTHOR'S NOTE.—*Blue Jays have been reduced in numbers by West Nile Virus.*

Birds' Need for Space

How many kinds of nesting birds you have in your woods or fields depends a lot on the size of your habitat area. Some birds need more space than others. Many Illinois birds are sensitive to the size of a habitat block and do not nest where the habitat is too small. These are called area-sensitive species. Both forest and grassland birds can be classified as low, moderate, and high in sensitivity to habitat size.

Among forest birds, the Northern Cardinal belongs to the low-sensitivity group, along with the Blue Jay, Catbird, Common Grackle, and American Robin. These birds can live in small forest stands. The moderate forest group includes such species as the Wood Thrush, Hairy Woodpecker, Red-eyed Vireo, and White-breasted Nuthatch. Some of the birds most sensitive to forest size are the Least Flycatcher, the Ovenbird, the Hooded Warbler, and the Broad-winged Hawk. They successfully live only in large forest tracts.

If you have a ten-acre woods, you can expect to have chickadees, Northern Cardinals, and Catbirds, but the probability of having a nesting Scarlet Tanager or Wood Thrush is only about 20 percent. The chance of such a small woods harboring nesting Pileated Woodpeckers and Ovenbirds is near zero. If you enlarge the woods to one hundred acres, you have a 70 percent chance of attracting breeding Wood Thrushes and Scarlet Tanagers, and your odds on Ovenbirds go up to 30 percent. At one thousand acres, expect a forest to have 75 percent of the most area-sensitive forest birds normally nesting in its region and 95 percent of the moderately sensitive species. Many birds in the low-sensitivity group are common around our homes and familiar to everyone. The American Robin and Common Grackle can make do with a single backyard tree. But if you want to see a Yellow-throated Vireo, Cerulean Warbler, or Pileated Woodpecker at nesting time, better head for the big woods.

Area sensitivity involves a lot of factors including predators, nest parasites such as Cowbirds, foraging requirements, and sensitivity to disturbance. Birds that nest in grasslands exhibit a sensitivity to area or size similar to forest birds. Examples of low-sensitivity grassland birds that can get by on small patches of grass are Northern Bobwhite, Red-winged Blackbird, Goldfinch, and Dickcissel. Many of these can nest successfully in grassy borders of fields or even on roadsides. Moderately sensitive birds include the Eastern Meadowlark, Grasshopper Sparrow, and Sedge Wren. On average, a ten-acre grassland can be expected to support breeding populations of 20 percent of the species in this group, while a one hundred-acre tract could house 60 percent of them. Grassland birds highly sensitive to habitat area include Northern Harrier, Upland Sandpiper, Prairie Chicken, Bobolink, and Henslow's Sparrow among others. The probability of a one-thousand-acre grassland containing a species of this group is just 60 percent.

Factors other than size are also important to grassland nesters. Scott Simpson, site superintendent of Prairie Ridge State Natural Area, reports that until all fence rows were cleared of trees and tall shrubs near his grassland nesting habitat, it was rare to see Northern Harriers and Short-eared Owls nesting there. Use of the sanctuaries for nesting by these birds has increased greatly since removal of all trees and brush from the edges of grasslands. These sensitive nesters apparently like to think they are in the middle of a vast open prairie.

Landowners wishing to help area-sensitive birds should keep a few points in mind. If you have woods broken up by a narrow ridgetop field, or if you have two nearby-but-separated woodlots, consider

Young Short-eared Owl lying alone in prairie grass where its mother has placed it. She scatters the hatchlings from her ground nest, which reduces the chance that a predator will get them all.

reforesting to fill in the narrow field or to connect the two woods into one larger forest. Prairie restorationists and pasture managers can help area-sensitive birds by eliminating trees around their grasslands and by making grass stands as large as possible.

August 1993

Counting Breeding Birds

Bird counts are popular with Illinoisans. Statewide counts like the Christmas bird counts and spring bird counts provide long-term information on overwintering and migrant bird numbers, but censuses of breeding-season birds are also very important to managers. The 1996 breeding bird censuses have just been completed. Each June, Department of Natural Resources biologists and a host of volunteers head to Illinois' fields, forests, and wetlands to monitor the birds that nest and rear young in the Prairie State. While the best time to see the most kinds of birds here is during the spring and fall migrations, many migrant species just pass through and are not dependent on the state's habitats to rear their young.

Once the last of the spring migrants pass through in May, birds seen in Illinois in June are reasonably assumed to be nesting or attempting to nest here. Counts made in June provide the most reliable measure of our breeding-bird population trends. Two statewide censuses of breeding birds that are completed annually in June are the breeding-bird surveys and the colonial-waterbird surveys. Our breeding-bird surveys are part of a national program established by the US Fish and Wildlife Service in 1966 and have been conducted in Illinois each year since then. The program consists of eighty-one randomly located 24.5 mile low-traffic roadway routes. Each route is driven in June. The surveyor starts one half hour before sunrise and counts all the birds seen or heard in a three-minute period at the starting point and subsequent stops at each half-mile interval.

The observer must be an expert birder, capable of identifying birds by both sight and song or call. As many as twenty routes may be driven by state biologists each year, but the majority are surveyed by volunteers. Department of Natural Resources bird biologist Vern Kleen of the Natural Heritage Division, helps coordinate the program in Illinois by finding qualified volunteers where needed. He also runs several of the routes himself. Data sheets are returned by surveyors directly to the US Fish and Wildlife Service at Laurel, Maryland. They compile the total annual statistics and a state report, which is sent to Vern Kleen the following winter.

If you have seen someone standing next to their car with binoculars and listening early on a June morning, you have probably witnessed a bird census in progress. Data generated from this program have been used to document dramatic changes in bird populations, such as the statewide decline in grassland nesting birds and the decline of birds nesting in the interior of large forest tracts. They also document the improvement in grassland bird numbers resulting from the federal Conservation Reserve Program, which pays farmers to control soil erosion with grass or forest plantings. These surveys tell us that we have a problem with too little grassland bird habitat and that forest fragmentation is a management problem that needs to be addressed.

The statewide colonial-waterbird surveys are mostly conducted by state Natural Heritage Biologists with some help from volunteers.

This Department of Natural Resources program began in 1983. It involves checking the active status of known heron rookeries and counting the number of nests occupied by each species annually. Colonial herons, egrets, and cormorants are censused by this program. Vern Kleen surveys many rookeries from the air at the end of May, with one flight each along the major rivers and lakes of northern and southern Illinois. For about 75 percent of our sixty known rookeries, this is the only count that is done. District Heritage Biologists and a few volunteers census northeastern Illinois and other scattered rookeries from the ground, mostly during June. Ground visits to rookeries are limited to a single visit each year, as entering them in this manner is very disruptive to the birds.

There is always some movement of nesting birds from year to year, and this change in location of nesting colonies is mostly detected by aerial surveys. Two new large rookeries were found in southern Illinois this year (1996), and another was located at the Savanna Army Depot in northwestern Illinois. A large colony of six hundred nesting pairs of Great Blue Herons at Rend Lake in 1995 have abandoned those nests this year. These birds may have contributed to the two new rookeries found in southern Illinois.

Keeping track of these colonial nesters is important to their conservation. With nearly all of the birds of these species nesting in just sixty locations in the state, knowing where they are is critical to protecting this important part of our feathered heritage.

July 1996

The Decline of Grassland Birds

Much has been written about the problems and decline of warblers and other songbirds that nest in our forests and migrate to the tropics for the winter. They have suffered from loss and fragmentation of forests and Cowbird parasitism of their nests. But a serious decline in our grassland birds has received much less attention by the media.

Illinois' grassland birds are the species that originally nested in our prairies and other open grassy habitats. Meadowlarks, Bobolinks, Dickcissels, and of course the Prairie Chicken are classic examples.

While a few, such as the Sharp-tailed Grouse, Whooping Crane, and Swallow-tailed Kite, were eliminated from the state with the loss of its expansive prairies, most Illinois grassland birds survived by turning to hayfields and pastures for habitat. The Prairie Chicken increased dramatically in the mid-1800s, as it took advantage of increased food from farming, while still having some prairie and pastures for nesting and roosting. The Horned Lark and Vesper Sparrow also increased because of their ability to nest in nearly bare, cultivated land.

When the first detailed survey of grassland bird numbers in Illinois was completed in 1909, Prairie Chickens, Dickcissels, and Henslow's Sparrows had declined significantly since 1850 accounts. In 1909, the most abundant breeding bird in Illinois grasslands was the Bobolink, with an estimated statewide population of 1.2 million, followed in order by Meadowlark, Dickcissel, Red-winged Blackbird, and Grasshopper Sparrow. Remarkably, the Dickcissel ranked third in spite of significant declines, but the Prairie Chicken comprised less than 1 percent of grassland birds found.

A second statewide bird census was completed in 1958 by Richard and Jean Graber of the Illinois Natural History Survey. In spite of the fact that the Prairie Chicken was essentially gone and a few other species were becoming rare, they found that grassland birds had essentially held their own over the previous fifty years. The Red-winged Blackbird had more than tripled in numbers to become the most commonly encountered bird in Illinois grasslands. The Bobolink increased to 1.9 million birds but still dropped to third place in abundance behind the meadowlarks. These were followed by Dickcissel and Savanna Sparrow.

Around 1960, a major change began taking place in Illinois agriculture. Small diversified farms with a mixture of pasture and hayfields for livestock began converting to intensive corn and soybean production without livestock. The Grabers estimated the loss of grassland habitat as a result of this shift at 50 percent per decade from 1960 through 1980 and conducted bird censuses in 1978 and 1979 that demonstrated a greater than 90 percent decline in most grassland birds in just twenty years!

Dr. Jim Herkert, now with the Illinois Endangered Species Protection Board, studied Illinois grassland bird population levels in the late 1980s up to the present and quantified this decline in more

116

detail. His 1987 to 1989 census work indicated the kinds of birds living in our grassland habitats changed little from 1958 to 1989. Four of the five most abundant birds were the same both years. However, the numbers of birds had declined drastically. In 1967, the US Fish and Wildlife Service began a nationwide program of breeding-bird surveys that included Illinois. Recognizing that significant declines had probably occurred prior to 1967, Herkert further analyzed the grassland-bird decline from 1967 to 1989 using breeding-bird survey data. Over this twenty-two year period, Bobolinks declined 90.4 percent, Meadowlarks 67 percent, Savanna Sparrows 58.9 percent, Grasshopper Sparrows 56 percent, and Field Sparrows 52.6 percent. Herkert estimates that Bobolinks declined from 1.9 million nesting birds in 1958 to less than twenty thousand in 1995.

Herkert quantified habitat changes and looked at changes in farming practices in an effort to explain these declines. The acreage in hay in Illinois declined from 2.1 million acres in 1960 to 1.1 million in 1994. He also found that farmers presently cut hay earlier in the season than formerly, which can be a disaster for nesting grassland birds. The acreage in pasture has declined from 6.2 million acres in 1906 to just 1.5 million acres in 1992. He also noted the smaller size of hayfields and pastures, which reduces the number of grassland species they can benefit.

One bright spot is the Conservation Reserve Program, initiated by the 1985 federal farm bill. Through this program, over eight hundred thousand acres of grass cover has been established in Illinois on marginal and highly erodible farmland. Herkert points out that this has significantly helped Dickcissels, Henslow's Sparrows, and Grasshopper Sparrows over the past ten years. Another bright spot is the number of prairies being planted and restored. He points out that these are intensively used by grassland birds and cites the large number of species using Illinois' Prairie Chicken sanctuaries in addition to the Prairie Chickens themselves.

March 1996

AUTHOR'S NOTE.—*Grassland acreage in the Conservation Reserve Program has declined as set-aside acreage was brought back into crop production in response to the increased price of corn. Grassland birds continue to decline.*

Male Dickcissel perched on a prairie grass stem in Illinois while defending its nesting territory. Wintering in grasslands of Venezuela and nesting in temperate prairies of North America, it remains one of our most common grassland birds.

~~~~~~~~~~~~~~~~~~

Frogs in Trouble

Frogs, and their amphibian relatives the salamanders, are dying off around the globe. This decline has now started to affect Illinois as well. I first heard about the troubles of frogs and other amphibians in April of 1990, when my family and I were watching a slide show at our lodge at the Monteverde Cloud Forest Reserve in Costa Rica. After showing beautiful pictures of the Golden Toad, a frog found only at Monteverde, our speaker mentioned that only a few had been seen in 1988, and, in spite of intensive searches, only a single male had been found in 1989. None showed up at the breeding ponds in 1990. The speaker casually mentioned that it was suspected to be related to a recently recognized worldwide die-off of frogs and other amphibians. At this point I recalled having heard a few years before that Cricket Frogs had all but disappeared from our neighboring

118

state of Wisconsin. These once common creatures had been placed on the endangered species list in that state in the late 1980s. At a subsequent scientific meeting, I heard of the recent disappearance of formerly abundant toads from high-mountain habitats in the Andes of Ecuador. These toads apparently disappeared in the late 1980s, about the same time as the Golden Toad decline. It was also reported that a high-elevation salamander on another mountain in Costa Rica had recently been found to be missing.

Amphibians are especially vulnerable to environmental pollution and changes. Their moist skins readily absorb contaminants and let them enter the animal. The skins of some species are so effective at absorption that they have lost their lungs and now breathe with their skin. They also lay eggs that lack protective shells and which are often exposed to direct solar radiation. If there is an "indicator species" of environmental degradation among the backboned animals, amphibians fit the bill.

An international conference on the amphibian problem was held in August 1990 in New Orleans. There was a consensus among the scientists that this die-off was real and worldwide. They think that several factors may be causing the decline simultaneously. The extinctions on high mountains in the tropics and elsewhere, far from obvious human pollution, may be caused by global environmental changes. On the other hand, some die-offs are associated with dense human populations and associated pollution and habitat destruction. It appears that a variety of causes exist. Global changes may include thinning of the ozone layer of the atmosphere and air pollution. Ozone thinning leads to increased ultraviolet radiation, which could be killing amphibian eggs or adults. This effect would be most pronounced at higher elevations and high latitudes, which is right where some of the losses have been noted. The decline that has been detected in Illinois is in northern and northeastern Illinois. Ray Pauley of the Brookfield Zoo points out that both amphibian and reptile populations have been steadily deteriorating in the Chicago region over the past two decades due to a variety of human impacts. The Cricket Frog, among other species, has disappeared from wetlands, where it was common in the early 1970s. Many of these losses are readily attributed to pollution, human-caused mortality, and habitat destruction.

If a decline due to global environmental deterioration exists in Illinois, it would be difficult to detect because of the general decline under way due to local human impacts. However, the Cricket Frog's decline in Wisconsin may indicate broader environmental changes. No decline in amphibians has yet been documented in central and southern Illinois. Concerned naturalists are setting up frog-call censuses to monitor these possible indicators of the health of our environment. Our friends the frogs may be giving us our first warning of changes that could lead to reduced crops or public health threats in Illinois.

On a global basis, amphibians seem to be warning us that we are capable of altering the entire earth environment in a way that prevents survival of all its creatures. An international task force is studying the amphibian die-off. Hopefully, we will understand this problem in time to save most of our amphibian heritage.

September 1992

AUTHOR'S NOTE.—*In 2015 it appears that the human spread of diseases caused much of the worldwide decline in amphibians. No amphibian species have been extirpated from Illinois, and some species have expanded their ranges in southern Illinois.*

CHAPTER 5

PROBLEM EXOTIC SPECIES AND DISEASES AFFECTING ILLINOIS

This chapter includes essays on the conservation problems caused by the introduction of exotic plants, animals, and diseases into Illinois. These articles cover issues of great importance to the conservation of the state's natural heritage but are presented separately from the other conservation essays so they can be read together and in context.

~~~~~~~~~~~~~~~~~~~~~~~~~

Invasive Exotic Animals

Illinois is home to many animals that are not native, but were introduced by the actions of man and have found our state to their liking. This essay is a companion piece to one that follows on exotic plants. Let's explore the impact that alien animals are having in Illinois.

Agricultural interests are quick to point to Corn Rootworm and the Alfalfa Weevil as examples of exotics that cause serious crop damage, while public health officials lament the arrival of the Asian Tiger Mosquito and its superior ability to spread disease. Exotics that threaten human health and comfort like killer bees, Fire Ants, and Tiger Mosquitoes get most of the press, but alien animals threaten Illinois' natural heritage more than they do us. Naturalists think first of the exotic animals they see displacing native species and seriously altering natural habitats. These are the animals discussed here.

High on the list of alien animals that alter natural habitats the most in Illinois are the Carp and the Gypsy Moth. Carp "root" in the bottom of streams and lakes, muddying the waters, to the detriment of native plants and animals. They have long been established throughout Illinois. Gypsy Moth caterpillars can eat all of the leaves in a forest and eventually can kill many trees by multiple defoliations. These pests are restricted to northeastern Illinois for the present.

Several birds are chief among the aliens displacing native species. The European Starling and House Sparrow head this list. While pests of farmers and urban areas, their impact on nature is serious as well. Both are aggressive and nest in holes. Many native birds that nest in holes in trees and similar sites have been displaced by them. Most everyone has heard of the plight of the Eastern Bluebird, but it is not as generally known that Cliff Swallows have disappeared from most of Illinois because House Sparrows throw them out of their intricate nest structures, which they plaster to cliffs and bridges. I have seen starlings forcing birds as large as Hooded Mergansers and as small as Tree Swallows from their nest holes in trees and snags.

Other exotic birds include the Gray Partridge and Ring-necked Pheasant, which have been introduced as game species. As valuable as they are to hunters, the pheasant has a serious impact on our few remaining Prairie Chickens. Pheasants often lay their eggs in the nests of Prairie Chickens. Since pheasant eggs have a shorter incubation time than the eggs of Prairie Chickens, they hatch first. The mother Prairie Chicken waits a short time after the pheasants hatch and then leaves her unhatched eggs to die as she begins rearing the young pheasants.

One of the potentially most detrimental introduced animals to date is the Zebra Mussel. This mussel was introduced into the Great Lakes near Detroit from Europe in the mid-1980s. By the summer of 1991 it was abundant in the Illinois waters of Lake Michigan, and the same summer was first detected in the Illinois and Mississippi Rivers. It has now spread on the Mississippi as far north as northern Wisconsin and as far south as one hundred miles from the river's mouth in Louisiana. Unlike native mussels, which anchor themselves by partially burying in the bottom of a stream or pond, Zebra Mussels anchor themselves by attaching to hard surfaces with threads. Among the objects to which they seem to like to attach are Illinois' native mussels. They attach in such large numbers that they can kill the native species.

Dr. Doug Blodgett of the Illinois Natural History Survey reports that sampling devices pulled from the Illinois River near Grafton this summer (1993) had densities of ninety thousand Zebra Mussels per square meter. They average a little less than half an inch long with the largest Illinois specimen measuring an inch and a half. In the St. Clair River near Detroit, where this exotic mussel first appeared, the native mussel population on the Canadian side of the river was completely killed out in just five years. Blodgett and his fellow researchers found the first mortality of Illinois mussels near Grafton this summer. The Zebra Mussels crowded into the slight opening of the native mussels and forced their shells open as they grew at rates of up to a tenth of an inch in two weeks. This forcing open of the shell prevents normal water flow through the native mussel and both smothers and starves it.

Exotic animals have had a big impact on nature in Illinois. Many conservationists are concerned and are working on this problem, but new species are coming in all the time. Congress's Office of Technology Assessment is scheduled to release a study this fall on this problem and actions the nation can take to counter it. Unless controls are placed on introductions, it seems likely that Illinois will lose more and more of its natural heritage in the future.

September 1992

AUTHOR'S NOTE.—*Zebra Mussel populations have declined some after peaking in the mid-1990s without decimating Illinois' native mussels.*

~~~~~~~~~~~~~~~~~~~~~~~~~~~~~~~~~~~~

Invasive Exotic Plants

Long plagued by habitat destruction due to human activity, Illinois' natural heritage today faces an ever-growing threat from aggressive alien plants. These are not the weeds of croplands and roadsides that make up 30 percent of our spontaneous flora, but rather the relatively few weeds that are capable of thriving in undisturbed natural forests, prairies, and wetlands.

Most of these are perennials, and many are woody shrubs, trees, and vines. Unlike the crop weeds that mostly got here accidentally, these wildland weeds have largely been introduced on purpose as ornamental plantings and for conservation purposes. These serious exotic weeds are capable of changing a natural community with hundreds of kinds of wildflowers and wildlife food plants into a stand of one aggressive weed of little value to animals or humans. Because

Illinois has developed and disturbed its land more intensively than most states, Illinois is at the forefront of this growing national crisis. The exotic weed problem in Illinois is probably surpassed only by Hawaii and Florida.

Residents in the north half of Illinois are probably wondering what that white flower is that they can see growing in such dense stands in the woods and thickets this past spring. It is a biennial herb called Garlic Mustard, which is literally exploding across the landscape. It is a member of the mustard family and smells like garlic or onion when its leaves are crushed. It is rapidly invading the forests of northern Illinois and converting beautiful, diverse, and rich wildflower areas into weed patches. Whether it will eventually invade southern Illinois' forests is unknown at this time. Examples of other serious exotic weeds include Japanese Honeysuckle and Wintercreeper vines in southern Illinois, Purple Loosestrife in northern Illinois wetlands, and Crown Vetch and Amur Honeysuckle throughout the state. The Department of Natural Resources has compiled a list of thirty-six exotic plants that are serious problems in wildlands in at least some parts of the state. However, the "critical" list of severe pest plants includes just fifteen species.

What can we do to save Illinois' wildlands from becoming one giant weed patch? For starters, the state has passed a law outlawing the sale and planting of Multiflora Rose, Japanese Honeysuckle, and Purple Loosestrife in Illinois. Unfortunately, commercial nursery interests have killed efforts to legislate an expansion of the list of banned pests. Some serious wildland weeds are also still promoted for conservation and landscaping purposes.

Preserve managers around Illinois are combating exotic weeds on managed natural areas by cutting, pulling, burning, and herbiciding where appropriate. With the exception of Purple Loosestrife in some wetlands and Garlic Mustard in some forests, it seems most natural areas can be saved with a lot of work and at considerable cost. But the same cannot be said about the rest of Illinois. Will future naturalists in the state see a landscape dotted with small, pristine preserves in a landscape otherwise dominated by alien weeds? If the United States does not develop and implement a program to prevent the introduction of new exotic wildland weeds and to control those that are already here, this is exactly the future we face.

Stopping the introduction of new exotic weeds is a matter of policy and regulation. We have extensive regulations to prevent the introduction of agricultural pests. These regulations need to be expanded to include wildland weeds as well. The reason exotic weeds are so out of control in Illinois is that they were introduced into North America without the plant diseases and insect pests that control their numbers where they originated. Introducing these natural controls in America is a process called biological control. It requires considerable research and development to assure that the controls do not become pests themselves. If nature is to be saved, biological controls seem to be the only answer for the fifteen worst weeds in Illinois. The development of biological controls is done only by government since there is no profit motivation. Once the control agents are released, they spread naturally throughout the range of the pest and control it at no cost to the landowner or public.

The development of biological controls is accomplished in the United States only by the US Department of Agriculture. Their program has been reduced significantly over the past several years to the benefit of no one except possibly the herbicide industry. To date, Congress has not seen fit to fund this research for conservation purposes, just agricultural weeds. Biological control work presently underway on Purple Loosestrife is being done by the US Department of Agriculture but is funded by various states and the US Fish and Wildlife Service.

The congressional Office of Technology Assessment is issuing a report to Congress this summer on the exotics problem. The future of Illinois' natural heritage depends on Congress's taking action to regulate imports and fund biological control research and development.

June 1993

AUTHOR'S NOTE.—*Since this was written, twenty-five species have been added to the prohibited list of the Illinois Exotic Weed Act. The list can be found on the Internet. Illinois had a significant role in development of the successful biocontrol of Purple Loosestrife when funding for the needed research was obtained by Congressman Sidney Yates of Evanston. The federal Animal and Plant Health Inspection Service now screens introduced species for potential wildland invasive exotics.*

～～～～～～～～～～～～～～～～

Planting Ethics

It is seed- and plant-catalog time again—that season when home-owners start thinking of landscaping and planting for the spring and summer ahead. Readers of my essays are generally interested in nature, so this one is dedicated to some environmental factors that homeowners should consider when selecting plant materials. The plants you buy for landscaping can have a definite impact on nature in your area.

Anyone who has farmed, gardened, or cared for a lawn knows the tremendous problem weeds can be. Fewer realize that natural communities, such as forests, prairies, and wetlands, are increasingly subject to weed problems as well. The Department of Natural Re-sources, Natural Heritage Division spent $253,000 for exotic-species control in the nature preserves and natural areas they manage over the ten years that ended in 1993. And this figure just covers staff sal-aries, not herbicide, equipment, and travel expenses. Invasive exotic weeds are fast becoming one of the primary threats to survival of Illinois' natural heritage.

The use of problem wildland weeds in landscaping is a major source of their infestation of new areas. This is where you can help. As you shop for plant materials through your catalogs and at the nursery, keep in mind that many problem exotic weeds are available for sale in spite of their damaging potential for nature. Since government has not been able to regulate them, it is up to the concerned citizen to recognize them and avoid purchasing and planting them. One problem with nursery stock is that various names are used for the same plant, and you cannot always tell what you are buying. Purple Wintercreeper, Wintercreeper, and Trailing Euonymus could all be nursery tag names for what botanists know by the Latin name *Euonymus fortunei*. Even though some people just hate Latin names, they are necessary sometimes to tell what you are buying. Because of this, I will be using them and writing them in italics.

Crown Vetch (*Coronilla varia*) and Purple Loosestrife (*Lythrum salicaria*) are the two plants on my do-not-plant list that are not woody.

The former is a sprawling mat-forming plant that smothers anything in its path. It is planted as seed and, once established, is literally impossible to get rid of. The loosestrife is sold as a potted flowering plant but should not be encountered in Illinois outlets, since it is illegal to sell or plant in the state. Be alert for it in catalogs. The two legal vines to avoid are the evergreen groundcover Wintercreeper (*Euonymus fortunei*) and the Round-leaved Bittersweet vine (*Celastrus orbiculatus*). Japanese or Hall's Honeysuckle vine (*Lonicera japonica*) is illegal to sell or plant in Illinois, but may be in some catalogs. The largest group to be aware of is the shrubs. The only one of these that is outlawed in Illinois is Multiflora Rose (*Rosa multiflora*). The worst of the legal shrubs is Amur Honeysuckle (*Lonicera maackii*). It can invade and destroy the shrub layer of any upland forest and is spread widely by birds that eat its berries and pass its seeds. Other bad shrubs are Autumn Olive (*Elaeagnus umbellata*), Winged Wahoo or Burning Bush (*Euonymus alatus*), and Tatarian Honeysuckle (*Lonicera tatarica*).

The most serious of the trees to avoid are small trees that might be considered large shrubs by some. Tall Hedge or Smooth Buckthorn (*Rhamnus frangula*) is the worst of these. It is spread by birds and readily invades and degrades wetlands in northern Illinois and a variety of wooded habitats elsewhere. Common Buckthorn (*Rhamnus catharticus*) is a small tree with shining leaves that has replaced the sapling layer of most northeastern Illinois forests. We can slow its spread to other regions by refusing to plant it.

My final no-no is Amur or Flame Maple (*Acer ginnala*). Unlike most maples that have a single trunk, this species has multiple trunks and resembles a shrub when young. Older specimens reach fifteen to twenty feet in height. You can tell it is a maple by the shape of its leaves and fruit. The leaves also give it its flame designation; they turn bright red in the fall.

So when you get ready to plant this spring, think of the wildflowers and wildlife out there depending on diverse natural habitats for their needs. Choosing the wrong plants for landscaping can turn their home into a monoculture of exotic weeds that will not support them and could cause serious weed problems for you and your neighbors. One way to be sure your plants are safe is to choose native species.

March 1995

AUTHOR'S NOTE.—*All plants mentioned in this essay have been added to the list of plants prohibited from sale or planting in Illinois under the Illinois Exotic Weed Act except Crown Vetch, Burning Bush, Wintercreeper, and Flame Maple.*

Exotic Tree Diseases

Plant diseases imported from other lands are threatening many native trees in the eastern United States. If the trend continues, the forest heritage of Illinois could be severely damaged. The earliest exotic disease infestation in the United States was the Chestnut Blight that wiped out the stately American Chestnut in the early twentieth century. It was imported at New York from Asia with nursery stock in 1904 and spread from there at a rate of twenty-four miles per year. Virtually all wild trees of this species were dead by 1950. Illinois' only native Chestnut stand, an eighty-acre tract overlooking the Ohio River east of Olmsted, succumbed by 1941, when botanist G. H. Boewe found only stump sprouts surviving. It has not been seen there since.

Dutch Elm Disease was next to hit our forest trees. Introduced from Europe at Cleveland, Ohio, in 1930, this fungus spread rapidly. By 1979, 75 percent of American elms in the northeastern states were dead. Many elms had died in forests in the north half of Illinois by 1980. In the last few years I have seen many elms dying in the southern tip of Illinois. American elm is now absent from many northern Illinois forests.

Butternut Canker is the current menace. Butternut is a smaller relative of Black Walnut that grows as scattered stands of trees throughout Illinois. Illinois' Butternut trees are dying at a rapid rate because of a fungus disease called Butternut Canker that was first recognized in southwestern Wisconsin in 1967. Its area of origin is unknown. Unlike Chestnut, which sprouts from the root crown, Butternuts do not sprout after being killed by this fungus. Whole stands, including seedlings, are killed outright. The Department of Natural Resources placed Butternut seed from throughout Illinois in long-term storage in 1992 to serve as a sample of the original genetic diversity of Illinois' trees. These seed are available for propagation and reestablishment of the species in Illinois should a cure for the disease be found.

The most prominent disease that is about to invade Illinois forests is Dogwood Anthracnose, an introduced fungal disease that attacks Flowering Dogwood trees. Flowering Dogwood is a beautiful and important native member of our forests in the southern two-thirds of the state and is planted as an ornamental statewide. Dogwood Anthracnose first appeared in the eastern United States at New York City in 1978. It rapidly spread through the Appalachian forests and reached northern Georgia by 1987. In some infested areas 80 percent of the dogwoods have died. The disease has now begun a slow spread westward toward Illinois. In 1993 it suddenly appeared in Indiana with sixteen cases found in twelve counties scattered throughout that state. A confirmed case in Marshall County, Kentucky, is the closest to Illinois to date. It seems almost certain to show up this spring in Illinois. Dogwoods with this disease will have brown spots on blighted leaves and dead leaves and twigs. Brown spots may appear on the flowers as well. Researchers have recently discovered a few dogwoods that appear to be resistant to the disease, so there is at least hope of developing a variety that can withstand this fungus. Beech bark disease is well established in the eastern states as far south as Tennessee. It has killed up to half of the American beech trees in some areas but has not been detected close to Illinois yet.

North America faces a special challenge in keeping out forest pests at the present time. The depletion of our forests has generated economic pressures for importation of raw logs from other continents. A whole host of new pests would probably come with the logs. The US Forest Service recently completed studies of potential pests that might be brought into the country if logs are imported from Siberia, New Zealand, and Chile. Their conclusion is that serious economic and ecological consequences would likely result from such imports. The problems we see today in Illinois may be a harbinger of things to come.

The US Forest Service compiled a list of over three hundred pest insects and diseases of native trees that have been introduced into the United States. Just how many of them will become problems in Illinois is uncertain.

April 1994

AUTHOR'S NOTE.—*Butternut seeds stored by the Department of Natural Resources had been discarded before researchers from Purdue University sought the seeds for developing a canker-resistant strain of the species.*

~~~~~~~~~~~~~~~~~~~~~~~~~~~~~~~

Flowering Dogwood in Peril

A fungus disease that kills flowering dogwood trees has just been confirmed from the forests of Illinois. It may pose a threat to the continued survival of this common and beautiful native tree of Illinois woodlands.

As I was conducting a plant survey of the Department of Natural Resources' Dean Hills Nature Preserve this spring (1995), I noticed several dead and dying dogwoods. The preserve is northeast of Vandalia in Fayette County. Many of the smaller trees six feet tall and under were completely dead, while taller trees had dead lower limbs but some live upper limbs. Some of the trees that were mostly dead had scattered new leaves on their trunks where leaves normally do not grow. These symptoms resembled what I had read about Dogwood Anthracnose, an exotic fungal disease that was apparently introduced into the United States from Asia in the late 1970s. It rapidly spread up and down the eastern states from its introduction site at New York, killing most of the flowering dogwoods in forested habitats, especially in the cooler, moister mountains.

Fearing the worst, I collected samples of sick leaves and sent them to Dr. Weidong Chen, plant pathologist at the Illinois Natural History Survey in Champaign. He cultured the samples and confirmed the culprit as *Discula destructiva*, the Dogwood Anthracnose fungus. Dr. Chen says that the disease was widespread in both Indiana and Missouri last summer (1994), and was probably here also but not detected.

As I continued my fieldwork, I found plants from Hardin, Franklin, Massac, Lawrence, and St. Clair Counties that appear to be dying from the same disease. At this writing, these samples are being cultured to confirm the disease. It appears that Dogwood Anthracnose may already occur throughout the native range of flowering dogwood in Illinois, which is roughly the southern two-thirds of the state.

While cherished as an ornamental tree, the flowering dogwood is also a very common and important component of Illinois' upland forests. Its fruits are relished by birds, squirrels, and Eastern Chipmunks, and its flowers herald the arrival of spring to all.

The disease's spread west to our area was slower than its rampage up and down the Appalachians. This was at least partly because of our hotter, drier summers. It does not do well if the temperature reaches ninety-five degrees, and, like most fungus, it likes moisture and high humidity. My observations to date indicate that the disease will be most severe and deadly in Illinois in cool, wet springs, such as the state has just experienced. Under such conditions many of the younger trees will die, cutting off reproduction and replacement of older trees. Over time, this failure to reproduce could eliminate Flowering Dogwood from many woods or at least cool, moist habitats, such as ravines and north-facing slopes. This is what has happened in the eastern states.

Trees in dry, exposed forests and fields and ornamental yard trees survive the disease better. The hot sun and air movement associated with open lawns lower humidity around yard trees and retard the growth of the fungus. For this reason, you may not notice a problem with "your" dogwood, while those in the nearby woods are dying. During dry spells that could stress yard dogwoods, be sure to water them, as a weakened and stressed tree is less able to fend off the disease. Avoid overhead watering. It will help if you can open up your yard and improve air circulation around your tree, thus lowering the humidity.

To measure and monitor the impact of the disease at Dean Hills Nature Preserve, Department of Natural Resources staff and Dr. John Ebinger of Eastern Illinois University established twenty vegetation-monitoring plots, including a total of one half acre of the infected forest in August of 1995. The same plots were resampled in September of 1996. The goal of the study is to determine the rate of mortality in the native dogwoods and eventually determine what trees replace them if the dogwoods die out. The results of this year's sampling are not encouraging.

Among dogwoods greater than knee-height (saplings and larger), there were 244 healthy plants in the plots in 1995 and only ten in 1996. The number of sick and dying dogwoods of this size increased from eighty-three in 1995 to 239 in 1996. The fate of seedlings less than knee height was similar. The 451 healthy seedlings seen in 1995 were represented by just twelve healthy seedlings in 1996. The number of infected and dying seedlings rose from thirty-five in 1995 to 278 in 1996. Standing and fallen dead dogwoods were common in the plots this past September. There were seventy-eight fewer live dogwoods of the sapling and larger class and 196 fewer live seedlings. A total of 274 dogwoods, 33 percent of those present in the plots, had died in one year's time! Clearly, the disease has spread rapidly in this population with deadly results.

Earlier, I had hoped that the disease would be most virulent in the more moist ravines and less deadly on the dry ridge tops where the humidity is lower and the fungus might not be able to spread and grow as well. This has not been the case. Some plots were placed in ravines and others on ridge tops. The spread and mortality from the disease is the same in both forest habitat types.

The appearance of the infected forest has been greatly altered with the death of so many dogwoods. What had been woods with a lush, leafy understory of small trees is now an open woods with few understory leaves to block your view. At first glance it appears that the understory has been killed or set back by fire. Only on closer inspection is it apparent that the alteration is caused by disease and involves the death of just a single very abundant species. Projecting our current observations into the future, it may be as few as five years before all of the dogwoods are gone from Dean Hills.

Although I have not made any extensive surveys for this disease in Illinois, I have seen plants that appear to be infected with it scattered throughout the range of flowering dogwood in Illinois. The future of this valuable native tree in the wild seems bleak in Illinois at present. It seems that it may suffer the same fate that befell the state's native chestnuts and elms, victims of alien diseases brought in by the trade in plant materials from other continents. Only improved screening of imports will prevent the repetition of this tragedy in the future.

June 1995 and November 1996

AUTHOR'S NOTE.—*In spite of the impacts described here, at this writing in 2015, Flowering Dogwood is still common in Illinois' forests. Some trees have had their lower limbs killed by the fungus with upper limbs healthy, but many trees seem healthy.*

Biocontrol of Invasive Exotic Plants

Exotic plants like Purple Loosestrife and Amur Honeysuckle are serious degraders of wildlife habitat and natural communities in Illinois. Wildlife and natural area managers spend a lot of time and money battling exotic plants with costly herbicides. A new and better approach is becoming available.

A large part of the reason that these alien pest weeds are so successful in Illinois is that they were introduced to the area without the insects and diseases that control them in their native land. The process of introducing these control organisms (usually insects) to control pest weeds is called biological control or biocontrol for short. The technique can also be used to control exotic pest animals, such as insects, but here we are just considering plants.

The goal of biocontrol of exotic weeds is to reduce the problem-plant impacts so it is no longer a pest. Sometimes complete eradication is achieved, but leaving a small controlled population of the weed is ideal. This assures that the control insect will survive and guard against the return of the weed. Control agents typically can eat or attack only a single species of plant and will starve to death if none of the weed remains. The advantage of biocontrol over chemicals is that once developed and in place, it continues to control the pest indefinitely across the whole landscape at no additional cost or effort. Control with herbicides, where possible, requires investment in chemicals and labor almost annually and solves the problem only on small, managed parts of the landscape, leaving most wildlife habitat untreated.

Biocontrol is developed by government rather than private industry, because there is great benefit to the public and wildlife but no profit in a "product" that goes wild and spreads across the land on its own. In the United States, biocontrol has been the responsibility of the US Department of Agriculture, as most of it has been aimed at crop pests and agricultural weeds. Except for range weeds out west, the USDA has not dealt with wildland weeds until recently. Development of biocontrol for a weed with insects costs about a million dollars and takes about nine years. Studies have shown it to be very cost effective, with benefits far outweighing costs.

One concern about introducing new insects as control agents is that they might become new pests themselves. This is not as big a threat as one would suspect because insects can often eat only a single kind of plant or a few closely related plants. This is because plants contain poisonous chemicals and other defenses that keep bugs from eating them. Only a relatively few insects overcome these defenses and those that do often cannot deal with the chemicals and defenses of other plant species.

The first step in developing biocontrol is sending someone to the land where the target weed originated or contracting with scientists there to determine what insects attack the plant in its native range. The most promising control insects are identified and moved into cages in the laboratory in the country where they are native. There they are offered nontarget plants from the United States that they might feed on in addition to the target weed once they are introduced here. These are starvation tests, assuring that the insects will starve to death before they will eat desirable crops or native plants in their new home. Sometimes insects are allowed into the United States under quarantine to conduct or expand starvation tests, because it is easier to get test plants here. Also, procedures are developed here for culturing the control insects in large numbers for release. After research proves that the control insect will impact only the target weed, approval for release of the insect is obtained from the government's Animal and Plant Health Inspection Service.

The first releases are generally studies to monitor the released insects under caged conditions in the habitat of the pest plant. Climatic differences here relative to their area of origin might prevent overwintering or reproduction in the United States. Close observation is needed to determine why a control insect fails if it fails. If these studies indicate that the control insect is viable and likely to succeed, releases are made into the wild.

Illinois played a lead role in implementing the research protocol for Purple Loosestrife, a serious weed of wetlands across the northern United States. At the request of Illinois conservationists, Congressman Sidney Yates of Evanston inserted funds into the Interior Department budget to do the research. In 1991, test releases of two European leaf-eating beetles that cleared the protocol were made in Minnesota for control of Purple Loosestrife. These tests showed the beetles to be effective at damaging the loosestrife and capable of reproducing and overwintering in North America. Results are not always so positive. For example, in early December it was announced that a weevil brought into Florida from Australia to save the Everglades from the Melaleuca tree refuses to lay eggs there. Another insect is being sought now as the Everglades continues to lose an estimated fifty acres daily to the Melaleuca tree.

The Illinois Department of Natural Resources released the leaf beetles, proven to control Purple Loosestrife in Minnesota, into Illinois in the spring of 1994. With funding from the Department of Natural Resources and three county agencies, Illinois joined six other Midwestern states in a federally coordinated effort to get the beetles established in 1994.

Surveys in the spring of 1995 reveal that the first Illinois releases survived the winter and laid eggs this spring, and many of the eggs hatched. However, the small size of the populations left the larvae (caterpillars) vulnerable to predation by Ladybug Beetles, spiders, and other predators. It's a jungle out there in the insect world, and leaf beetle larvae are apparently tasty! Hopefully, some caterpillars will make it, but it is apparent that a larger stocking program is needed for the program to succeed in a timely fashion. The Illinois Natural History Survey, with funding from the US Army Corps of Engineers, is now rearing the leaf beetles and root weevils, which have also been approved, for release in larger numbers in Illinois. They are also researching release techniques to maximize survival and breeding success of these control agents.

Five supplemental releases and two new releases of leaf beetles were made in northeastern Illinois in late June of 1995 along with the first five releases of root weevils. The new releases seem to have been more successful than the 1994 releases because improved release cages were used, and the insects had been held and fed for a longer period than were those released in 1994. Additional releases are planned for later this summer, but no estimate is available on when control might be achieved. Some guess that reduction in loosestrife might be visible in ten years.

Illinois' program is just one part of a nationwide effort. Purple Loosestrife is a problem from the Atlantic to the Pacific. The earliest releases were made in New York, Minnesota, and Washington state.

I expect Minnesota to be the first state in the Midwest to succeed in reducing the loosestrife pest with biocontrol. Minnesota has established good populations of leaf beetles and root weevils in the wild.

Over the last eight years, the Illinois Department of Natural Resources, Division of Natural Heritage has spent over $28,000 battling Purple Loosestrife with herbicides in preserves and other wetlands. This expenditure is in lightly infested areas where efforts continue to try to keep it out. Control efforts have ceased in many wetlands where the battle with herbicides is deemed to have been lost. In these areas, the only hope of salvaging the considerable public investment in natural habitat is the biocontrol program.

December 1993 and July 1995

AUTHOR'S NOTE.—*As of 2015, Purple Loosestrife has been effectively controlled in Illinois by this biocontrol program.*

~~~~~~~~~~~~~~~~~~~~~~~~~~~~~~~~~~~~~~~

Garlic Mustard

A major destructive biological invasion is under way in northern and central Illinois forests. The Garlic Mustard herb of Europe has become established in the state and is rapidly spreading and smothering our native wildflowers. Motorists and hikers in these parts of Illinois could scarcely miss this "new" weed this spring as it appeared in many parks, roadsides, private forests, and preserves. It converts diverse stands of ferns, trilliums, bluebells, and Jack-in-the-pulpit into dense growths of tall white-flowering weeds. It also takes over roadsides and other idle areas that have some shade.

Southern Illinois naturalists cannot afford to feel safe from this scourge. Apparently, it will be just a matter of time until it reaches the beauty spots in the southern part of the state as well. A two-acre patch was found near One Horse Gap in Pope County this spring, and another invasion is under way at Horseshoe Lake north of Cairo.

As its name implies, the invader is a member of the mustard family with the unique feature of an onion odor when crushed. It is one to three feet tall with four-petaled white flowers at the top. The quarter-inch-diameter flowers appear in May and are soon replaced by pods one to two inches long, which split to release seeds in late July.

Its coarsely toothed heart-shaped leaves are alternate up the stems. A single seed introduced into an area starts a new population as the plant pollinates itself and is self-fertile. The short life span of this biennial allows for rapid reproduction and spread.

Conservation biologists battle it on managed preserves and natural areas with herbicides and fire. But its rapid spread defies some efforts, and even where successful it is little consolation to protect relatively small, managed areas when the rest of the forest landscape is converting to this weed. In my entire career in nature conservation, I have never felt as helpless as when viewing the ravages of this weed invasion and realizing that on the total landscape scale, there is nothing we can do. It brings home the reality of our helplessness in the face of a collapsing ecosystem. As the life support system for our woodland ferns and wildflowers crashes, one has to wonder if we could do any more if our own life support system were in trouble.

I believe the only hope for Garlic Mustard control lies in biological control—the carefully researched importation and release of the diseases and insects that control it in its European homeland. I searched long and hard for Garlic Mustard while on a visit to Europe and found it to be very rare. I finally found one plant in Switzerland, and it was a pitiful sight. Coated in a powdery mildew fungus, its leaves were full of holes from insects or disease. However, reuniting this terrible weed with these diseases and pests is not an easy task. Many crops, such as beets, turnips, and radishes, are its relatives and could potentially be harmed by these controlling agents. For this reason, research to bring in European control agents would be costly, and funding has not been available. Unlike chemical controls, biocontrols have no profit potential once developed and released and are developed only by government.

With funding from the Department of Natural Resources, Dr. Weidong Chen of the Illinois Natural History Survey in Champaign is studying existing diseases that affect Garlic Mustard in Illinois. Since these diseases are already established in the wild in Illinois, extensive testing against crop plants and intensive protocols for introducing new pathogens are not relevant. His goal is to test their impact on Garlic Mustard and determine whether they can be used in combination with one another to help gain control of this pest. Harvard University's E. O. Wilson recently told viewers of PBS's *Web of Life* TV program that invasive alien species are second only to habitat conversion as a cause of loss of biodiversity. Considering the "explosion" of Garlic Mustard in Illinois this spring, I could not agree more.

June 1995

AUTHOR'S NOTE.—*As of March 2015, biocontrol has not been developed for Garlic Mustard. It continues to be a serious threat to woodland wildflower communities and has spread more widely in southern Illinois.*

The Introduced Zebra Mussel

At the far southern tip of Illinois, a community of forty million animals waits for death from smothering and starvation. The condemned are native mussels in a huge colony or "bed" at the bottom of the Ohio River stretching from a mile to four-and-a-half miles downstream from Olmsted, Illinois. They share their impending fate with other millions of mussels in the reach of the Ohio from Paducah, Kentucky, to Cairo, Illinois.

Mussels native to Illinois are slowly being smothered and starved by a dense coating of alien Zebra Mussels that developed in the river this summer (1994). The introduced Zebras literally coat the bottom of the river in most places, especially mussel beds. The larval Zebra Mussels can swim and seek out native mussels (along with other hard objects) on the river bottom to attach to. The larvae attach to the mussel by strong cordlike strands and begin rapid growth into a mussel up to one inch long. Hundreds can attach to a single native mussel and block water flow into and out of the animal, which is its method of breathing and feeding. Some Zebras also get inside native mussels and as they grow they pry them open so far that they can no longer breathe or feed. The end result is a slow death for countless millions of animals.

The Zebra Mussel was introduced into the Great Lakes from Europe in 1985 or 1986. Areas near the initial infestation are now devoid of native mussels. Zebra Mussels spread rapidly in the lower Great Lakes and into the Mississippi River drainage, helped in this regard by their habit of attaching to anything hard, including barges and pleasure boats. The first record of Zebras in the Ohio River was a few that were found at the Olmsted mussel bed in October 1991 by Corps of Engineers biologists monitoring the bed as part of the new dam construction just upstream. According to Mike Turner of the Louisville Corps, they found no Zebras here in 1992 and only a few in 1993. But their population has exploded in 1994.

Turner and his colleagues found densities of four thousand to eight thousand Zebra Mussels per square meter virtually all over the bottom of the Ohio this summer, and they seem to be continuing to increase. Hundreds could be found attached to single native mussels. In areas where the bottom is mud and no hard surface exists, the Zebras can attach to one another until they bridge over the area and form a living carpet, which serves as a substrate for even more Zebras.

The current outbreak on the lower Ohio is the first in an area with a rich and diverse mussel fauna, including endangered species. Historically, this reach of the river has supported six species that are currently federally listed as endangered and still supports one of these and possibly two others. But it is not just the fate of endangered species that worries conservationists and naturalists, but the entire big river mussel fauna. The Olmsted mussel bed currently contains twenty-three known species of native mussels, and several others occur within the river reach currently under siege.

The conservation community is just gearing up to deal with this crisis. As I recently stood with Turner on the lock of Dam 53 near Olmsted, he showed me a collection of mussels that had been cleaned of Zebras and were being kept alive in mesh bags in the river. He has an even bigger sample from the area "in captivity" at Louisville, Kentucky. As we looked down through the clear waters at the dense coating of Zebras attached to the walls of the lock we spotted half a dozen Goldeye fish plucking and eating them. What a pitiful contribution to the control of billions of Zebras! It was at this point that I realized the great clarity of the water. I grew up along the Ohio and had never seen it so clear. The vast number of Zebra Mussels, filter feeders themselves, had filtered so much of the river's water that they had increased its clarity!

As biologists and managers consider actions to save the mussels, the Corps of Engineers has contractors out sampling and retaining mussels from this area. These collections can form the core of a captive protected population, if that is one of the conservation actions eventually undertaken. Most critical are actions to save the big river mussels like Ebony Shell, Butterfly, and Elephant's Ear. Many mussel species living in the Ohio also live in creeks and small rivers that Zebras are not expected to reach for years. But those restricted to the large river habitat may be in immediate danger of extinction.

After native mussels on the Illinois River declined about 20 percent one year after a 1993 Zebra Mussel infestation, it was anticipated that similar declines would be seen on the lower Ohio in the summer of 1995. However, sampling by the Army Corps of Engineers and the Tennessee Valley Authority at the Olmsted mussel bed in late July of 1995 found no significant mortality of native mussels. The native mussels were still covered with Zebra Mussels, and the Zebras had grown much larger than they were in 1994, but little evidence of Zebra-induced mortality was found.

Barry Payne of the Corps of Engineers says that they anticipated a decline similar to that experienced on the Illinois River in 1994, so were pleasantly surprised not to find one. Another optimistic finding was no evidence of reproduction by the Zebra Mussels. No young Zebras were seen, just old individuals over a year old. On the downside, Payne notes that even though their project is not monitoring aquatic snails at Olmsted, general observation of river snails there indicate that they have declined to only about a third of the number present when monitoring began in the mid-1980s. Zebras attach to these inch- long (or less) snails in such numbers that they create what Payne calls "snail balls." These are clusters of Zebras with a snail at the center. While the Zebras apparently do not kill the snails outright, they keep them from breeding and thus reproducing. With relatively short life spans of three to four years, the snails have already declined significantly because they cannot replace their numbers.

The situation on the Illinois River this summer (1995) differs considerably. After a decline in Zebra Mussel numbers in 1994, the Illinois River Zebras are on the increase this summer with a new cohort of young. Sampling by the Illinois Natural History Survey in early June revealed sixty million free-floating Zebra Mussel larvae passing Havana, Illinois, each second! Preliminary observations by Doug Blodgett of the survey indicate a significant decline in native mussel numbers in their Illinois River study areas this year over last. He also notes that they have suffered significant losses of aquatic snails as has occurred on the Ohio. Speculation as to why the Illinois River

Varicose Rocksnail in the Ohio River with a load of Zebra Mussels attached to it, making it barely visible. Its head and antennae appear at the lower edge of the Zebra Mussel "ball."

native mussels have been impacted more than the Ohio River mussels centers on the size of the rivers and their flow rates. The Illinois flows slower and is smaller and shallower than the Ohio. It has periods of higher temperature and low dissolved oxygen in the summer that the Ohio probably does not experience. Heat and oxygen depletion can stress native mussels and probably kills some of those that are already stressed by being covered with Zebra Mussels.

Given the unsure future of native mussels in our rivers, several efforts are continuing to maintain populations of big river mussel species in habitats protected from Zebra Mussels. A joint federal–state effort moved a population of upper Mississippi River mussels into a fish hatchery at Genoa, Wisconsin, this spring. In addition, all of the mussels obtained in the Army Corps of Engineers July sampling on the lower Ohio were also cleaned of Zebras and moved to the corps' holding area near Louisville, Kentucky.

One can only speculate what the future holds for native mussels and snails in the lower Ohio. It now seems that the snails are in the most immediate danger of extirpation, but relatively little attention is being given to them by conservationists. As regards the mussels, the big question on the Ohio is whether the native mussels there can sustain themselves indefinitely with loads of Zebra Mussels on their backs. Even bigger questions are whether future "waves" of young Zebras are coming to the Ohio and what their impact might be.

In 1996, I accompanied Drew Miller and Barry Payne of the US Army Corps of Engineers on their annual monitoring of the Ohio River Olmsted mussel bed. The results of my observations there are promising for the mussels. As in 1995, we again saw no evidence of native mussel mortality and noted many fewer Zebras attached to the native mussels. I only saw one mussel with as many as eight to ten Zebras attached, and many native mussels had no Zebras on them at all. However, the Ohio River aquatic snails, often called periwinkles by local folk, have not fared as well. While the Corps of Engineers has not specifically studied these snails, their fourteen years of monitoring the Olmsted mussel bed yielded twenty to twenty-five snails from each quarter-meter-square sample of bottom gravel until the Zebras arrived in 1994. By 1995 the snails were reduced to a third of their former abundance. Surviving snails were covered with Zebra Mussels and struggled to move with this load on their shells. Now, in 1996, they are gone. No snails were found in the ten samples I helped process, and Miller said they had seen none the prior day either.

The two dominant snails in this lower Ohio River fauna are the Armored Rocksnail and the Varicose Rocksnail. Both have shells shaped like tiny cones less than an inch long. The former is armored with blunt spines around the head end of the shell, while the other is covered with rows of wart-like bumps on its sides. These animals are restricted to the Ohio River below its falls at Louisville, Kentucky, the lower Wabash River, and the Green River of Kentucky. As far as I know, the Wabash and Green Rivers have not been invaded by Zebra Mussels, and presumably these snails are safe there for the time being.

While we saw no evidence of mussel mortality at Olmsted, my observations near Metropolis indicate that some of the smaller native mussels have been killed in the Ohio. Here I found dead shells of the little Fawnsfoot Mussel covered with Zebra Mussel threads. They appeared to have been killed by Zebras. These were among the first mussels killed by Zebras in the Illinois River and so far seem to be the only mussel casualties in the Ohio River downstream from Paducah.

Elsewhere, some Zebra Mussel populations continue to increase. Department of Natural Resources fisheries biologist Les Frankland says that Zebra Mussel numbers are higher in the Ohio River at Shawneetown than he has ever seen. Natural History Survey biologist Doug Blodgett advises that while Zebra Mussel numbers remain low in the Illinois River, they are increasing rapidly on the upper Mississippi River. High mortality of a variety of native mussels has occurred on the upper Ohio River between Ohio and West Virginia. There, a captive rearing operation is under way in a fish hatchery to save native mussel stock for reintroduction if Zebra levels decline.

The Zebra Mussel invasion to date is a mixed bag of impacts on our native fauna. Aquatic snails have been hit hardest, followed by small mussel species. Zebra Mussel numbers seem to decline after reaching a peak early in the invasion of a river. If future peaks and population levels continue to decline, the threat to native mussels may not be as great as once feared. If future populations are denser than past infestations, native mussels will surely suffer. Current information indicates that aquatic snails need more conservation attention than they have had in the past.

October 1994, August 1995, and September 1996

AUTHOR'S NOTE.—*As of September 2015 there is still no evidence of significant native mussel mortality due to Zebra Mussels in the Lower Ohio River. All of the native aquatic snail species still survive in the lower Ohio but with lower numbers of some species compared to the period before the Zebra Mussels arrived.*

CHAPTER 6

ANIMALS OF ILLINOIS

The essays in this chapter relate to the natural history of animals in Illinois. Subjects include their ecology, ranges, population trends, diversity, and other interesting facts.

~~~~~~~~~~~~~~~~~~~~~~~~~~~~~~~~~

Interesting Animal Ranges in Illinois

Illinoisans have probably noticed wildlife species that occur in one part of Illinois but not another. For example, mockingbirds are common and conspicuous in southern Illinois, but become local in our central counties and are rare in the northeast and absent from the northwest. Their beautiful songs call our attention to their presence and also their absence. Many other wildlife species reach the limits of their ranges in Illinois, but this may be less noticeable because they are more secretive or inconspicuous.

The factors controlling species distribution can vary with the animal group. Bird distribution is often controlled by climate (as with mockingbirds) or by habitat availability. Habitat is mostly tied to natural vegetation, which reflects climate, moisture, soil, and landforms. Nonflying animals such as mammals, amphibians, and reptiles can have their ranges limited by a variety of factors such as barriers to their movement, climate, soil types, and availability of habitat. Habitat changes brought on by farming and other human uses of the land have affected the range of many species. Our actions have opened up the landscape, making it more like the drier habitats of the plains of the west. Both Coyotes and Badgers have found this new landscape to their liking. They have greatly expanded their ranges in Illinois in the last two decades in response to this habitat change.

The Crayfish Frog is limited in Illinois by soils. It lives in crayfish holes in the heavy clay soils of south-central and western Illinois. The north edge of their range ends abruptly at the Shelbyville moraine, which marks the northern edge of these soils. Blanding's Turtle, on the other hand, seems limited to former wet prairie areas north of the Shelbyville moraine. Its distribution is related to areas of extensive wet prairie associated with youthful soils without an abundance of clay. The Strecker's Chorus Frog and the Yellow Mud Turtle both live only in sandy soils in which they burrow part of the year. They are restricted to sandy areas along the Illinois and Mississippi Rivers.

As one might expect, our rivers are barriers to movement of some animals. Perhaps the most striking example of this is the Plains Pocket Gopher. This rodent lives essentially all of its life underground. Like a mole, it forms extensive burrows, and very rarely comes up to the surface. An animal like this would not be expected to swim a large river, and apparently they do not. They are a western mammal that ranges in Illinois from the East St. Louis area all along the south and east side of the Illinois and Kankakee Rivers to Indiana. They occur primarily in the loose sandy soils found near these rivers. Pocket Gophers are generally distributed west of the Mississippi, but they managed to cross this river only at St. Louis. They have not been able to cross the Illinois River, which creates a large gap in their Illinois range between the Illinois and Mississippi due to the barrier of these rivers. It does not appear that the gophers swam the river at St. Louis, but rather that the river changed course sometime between six thousand and twenty-five hundred years ago and stranded some of them on the Illinois side. Many animals have not had the Mississippi's help in crossing. The Spotted Skunk, Coal Skink, and Three-toed Box Turtle range right up to the west side of the river but have never become established in Illinois.

One other factor to consider in the range of animals is time. The Eastern Chipmunk is absent from the eastern Shawnee Hills of southern Illinois. It appears that this little member of the squirrel family is spreading from north to south and just has not yet had time to reach Pope, Massac, and Hardin Counties. In 1977, chipmunks reached a friend's farm northeast of Vienna in Johnson County as they continued their expansion to the east. In time they should reach all of Illinois.

As one can see, a variety of factors account for the variation in wild-life populations we find today in different parts of the Prairie State.

October 1992

AUTHOR'S NOTE.—*In 2015, the Chipmunk reached western Massac County.*

Spring Migration and the Value of Birds

Naturalists in Illinois look forward each spring to the first two weeks of May, the period of greatest birdlife diversity in Illinois as waves of migrating birds pass through the state. For this brief period, it is possible to find over two hundred kinds of birds in a single day in a single county. While short-range migrants like Red-winged Blackbirds and American Robins return in March and April, the birds that winter in the tropics of Central and South America usually arrive in our state at this time. Thrushes, warblers, vireos, and shorebirds are among the tropical migrants reaching Illinois in early May. Many of these birds are just passing through Illinois to nest in the boreal forest or the tundra beyond. The chance to see these species is short-lived, although you get a second chance to see them passing through to the south in the fall.

The spring migration is special to bird enthusiasts though, because migrants and residents alike are in colorful breeding plumage and are singing to attract mates. Fall migrants have drab plumage and are more close-mouthed. Since bird songs are important aids to identifying small songbirds high in the forest canopy, one can locate more species in Illinois in the spring than at any other season.

In 1971, the Illinois Audubon Society began annual spring bird counts to document the number of species and individual birds in Illinois on a single day in each county. This effort continues today as a cooperative venture between the state's bird-watchers and the Department of Natural Resources. Nineteen ninety-five's spring bird count day is Saturday, May 6. On this day about fifteen hundred birders will be out all across Illinois looking and listening for all the species they can find. Every county will have at least one bird-watcher afield, but some counties have several teams totaling up to forty or fifty people searching designated geographic areas and habitat blocks. Of course, the more pairs of eyes and ears there are, the more birds they will find.

The spring count record is held by Lake County birders who documented 206 species of birds in that county on a single spring bird count day. The record for southern Illinois is 176 species in Union County. The difference in count results reflects the size of the search team perhaps as much as the number of bird species present. By way of comparison, single-day bird counts in Illinois near Christmas regularly find only forty to one hundred species. The greatest number of birds found on a single day by one party of birders staying together is 175. This record was set by five birders in May of 1994 in central Illinois, but they were not limited to a single county.

So take the time in the next couple of weeks to listen to that warbler or thrush singing above and to peer up toward the treetops for a glimpse of a colorful bird. It is the best chance you will have to see some species all year. And as you watch the songbirds flit through the tree canopy in search of insects for food, consider the recent study by foresters at the Morton Arboretum and the University of Missouri. They determined that not only are these birds beautiful for us to watch and listen to, they are also important to the growth of commercial forests. After caging small oak trees to exclude birds but allowing insects to enter, these foresters studied the difference in growth rate of these bird-deprived trees with those open to foraging by birds and a third set of trees kept free of insects by spraying with insecticides.

At the end of two growing seasons, the caged trees that were deprived of the benefit of insect removal by birds showed significantly less growth than noncaged or sprayed trees. Comparison of bird feeding to remove insects versus sprayed trees showed no significant difference between the two. Thus the birds that enrich our lives with their song and beauty also benefit forest growth significantly by their predation on caterpillars and other foliage-eating insects. Not only is their insect control effective, it is just as effective as costly insecticide spraying and is much more environmentally sound.

The next time someone critical of the value of nature says "what good is that bird," we can point out their contribution toward lumber production as well as their aesthetic enhancement of our lives.

May 1, 1995

~~~~~~~~~~~~~~~~~~~~~~~~~~~~~~~~~~~~~~~

Of Beaks and Birds

Ever since the dinosaurs invented the gizzard method of chewing and passed it along to the birds, our feathered friends have had little use for teeth. And with birds' jaws freed from the chore of chewing, Mother Nature converted their jaws into that unique structure called the beak. Except for the Platypus's bill, beaks have no parallel in the mammal world and few in nature today. Turtles have them and some dinosaurs had them but, of course, they are extinct. Being free of most tasks other than procuring food, the beak has changed shape to meet the needs of various birds as they have adapted to many ecological niches.

In spite of the fact that birds use their beaks for defense, courting, nest building, feeding young, and the excavation of nest cavities, most of its evolution was driven by adaptation to capture or obtain food. As you watch birds at your feeders and in your yard, take a minute to check out their beaks. They can tell you a lot about the species' feeding habits and lifestyles. If you can get out to the marsh and other habitats, you will see even more diversity. The beaks of our birds have been modified to feed on a variety of the bird world's great food groups: seeds, insects, fruits, flesh, fish, tubers, leaves, worms, and nectar.

Perhaps the most common beak type to observe in action in Illinois is that of the seedeater. Sparrows, finches, and our state bird, the Northern Cardinal, have this type. Anyone who feeds the birds can see lots of seedeaters in his or her yard close-up. The beaks of seedeaters are thick vertically with sharp edges used to crack and cut the husks off seed to get at the nut inside. The thickness of their beaks gives seedeaters the strength they need. Watch a Cardinal remove the husk of a sunflower seed. Pigeons and doves are seedeaters with long, thin beaks designed for picking up grain that is swallowed whole.

Beaks designed for feeding on insects are also common and come in two types: sharp and pointed; and broad and gaping. The pointed types are common to wood warblers, nuthatches, chickadees, and woodpeckers. The woodpecker uses its beak to dig into dead wood and under bark for insects and their larvae, while the others reach among bark, buds, and leaves for the same. A few woodpeckers use their beaks to dig in ant mounds and eat ants, while others drill holes in bark to reach and drink a tree's sap. The Brown Creeper has a curved and pointed beak that helps it get insects from beneath bark that the other birds might miss. The gaping type of insect beak is possessed by birds who take insects on the wing. Swallows, swifts, and flycatchers are typical, and the Whip-poor-will and Nighthawk are the extreme examples. Many of these have "whiskers" around the beak to help guide the insects into the mouth.

Beaks for catching fish are long and mostly pointed. Herons and kingfishers are examples of birds with this type of fishing beak. Some use their beaks to spear fish, but most just grasp them. Mergansers, the fish-eating ducks, have serrated beaks to help hold fish, and the pelican's beak forms a dip net for catching them. This group swallows fish whole.

Flesh-eating birds like hawks, owls, and eagles have a sharply hooked beak for ripping meat from prey that is not swallowed whole. Vultures and shrikes, which feed on carrion and "ripened" meat, have less sharply hooked beaks. Some hook-beaked birds are vegetarian. The crossbill uses its beak to pry open pine cones for their seeds, and parrots use theirs to tear fleshy fruits for consumption and to get at seeds.

Sandpipers and other shorebirds have long thin beaks for probing for worms and other subterranean animals. The woodcock has the ultimate worm probe, which it uses to extract earthworms from moist soil. Ducks have broad beaks with internal grooves for sifting small food items from mud and water. The Northern Shoveler is the most extreme of these, but the Mallard is probably the easiest to observe.

Many birds have generalist beaks and eat a wide variety of animal and plant foods. Turkeys, crows, grackles, and jays are some of these. They have beaks roughly resembling the chicken. Many birds eat fleshy fruits at one season or another, and most have generalist beaks. But the Cedar Waxwing is more adapted to fruit eating. Its beak opens especially wide to accommodate a variety of large fruits. Remarkably, Cedar Waxwings often turn to catching flying insects on the wing during summer. Their gaping beaks function in this regard like a flycatcher's.

Only a few of our birds eat lots of leaves and green plant parts. The ruffed grouse feeds on plant buds but does not have an obvious beak adaptation. Geese eat lots of fresh greens and do have a distinctive beak. Perhaps it represents the "grazing beak." One of the most distinctive beaks commonly seen in Illinois is the hummingbird's. It is long and thin for reaching deep into flowers for nectar. Amazingly, hummingbirds are also able to catch insects in flight with this very thin beak. The next time you watch birds, take time to notice their beaks and the distinctive roles they play in the bird's life.

July 1994

Feeding Feathered Friends

If you are like me, you feed birds, especially in the cold winter months. You like to watch them and you get a good feeling by "helping" them. If you participate in this form of wildlife management, you have lots of company. One in every five American households feeds wild birds in winter. Feeding seed is most common, since most of the birds that winter in Illinois are seedeaters. But woodpeckers, chickadees, and titmice like suet, and some fruit eaters, such as mockingbirds and waxwings, relish fruit, including raisins.

But this essay is not about how to feed birds, but rather what effect it has on them. Does it help them or hurt them? And what should the concerned bird-feeding citizen know to optimize benefit to the birds while enjoying them. Studies in Wisconsin indicate that the overall effect of feeding wild birds in the winter is slightly positive for the birds, but it is good to keep in mind that negative impacts are possible.

Stanley Temple and his students at the University of Wisconsin studied marked chickadees to determine that feeding did indeed increase overwinter survival of birds with access to bird feeders versus unfed chickadees in natural habitat. Over a three-year study, they found that 69 percent of chickadees with access to feeders survived the winter as compared to only 37 percent of those without supplemental food. This significant difference was due to how well they survived periods of especially cold and severe winter weather. Those with supplemental feeding did much better during these periods of high energy demand. So if you feed birds, be sure to have adequate food available during the coldest periods if you want to help them the most. During periods of normal winter weather there was no difference in survival between fed and unfed chickadees.

The biggest threat to birds from our feeding activity is disease that is spread at the feeder. The bacterial infection Salmonella is the most common of these killers, but internal parasite infections such as Trichomoniasis, a fungal infection called Apergillosis, and the viral infections Avian Pox and Avian Mange can all be associated with feeders. All of these diseases except Aspergillosis and mange are spread from the feeding or perching surface. Birds ingest these diseases with food contaminated by sick individuals, especially on platform-type feeders.

The best defense against these diseases is the design of your feeder and keeping it clean. Use feeders that have a perch adjacent to a feeding surface that the birds cannot sit on while feeding. Any feeder should be washed at least annually with a weak bleach solution, and platform feeders should be washed several times a season. The best defense against spreading the fungus Aspergillosis is not feeding moldy grain. Using several scattered feeders to lower bird concentrations is about all you can do to prevent transmission of the mites that cause mange.

If you see sick or dying birds around your feeder, clean it and move it to another location in the yard if this is possible. Again, in Wisconsin, a study of 624 feeder sites over a single winter found that 16 percent had at least one bird death from disease or unknown causes. This indicates the need to be alert to this possible problem. Other possible negative impacts on birds from feeding include attracting predators like cats or hawks, which then prey on the birds, and mortality from collisions with windows in your house. While occasional incidents occur, they are not significant at the population level.

One suspected negative impact of feeding birds, which has not been studied to my knowledge, is increased predation on nestling songbirds by Blue Jays. Just like chickadees, Blue Jays probably survive the winter in greater numbers because of the extra food provided by feeders. One item in the jay's summer diet is baby birds it snatches from nests. There has been a documented increase in nest predation of forest-nesting migrant birds. Some ornithologists suspect that increased jay populations resulting from bird feeding may be contributing to this nestling loss. All things considered, feeding helps wild birds.

The Illinois Department of Natural Resources has produced a thirty-three-page booklet called *Wood Projects for Illinois Wildlife*. It contains a section on attracting and feeding wildlife along with plans for constructing feeders. This guide is available for download from the DNR website (*www.dnr.state.il.us/publications*).

February 1995

AUTHOR'S NOTE.—*The reduction in the Blue Jay population since the spread of West Nile Virus has probably reduced predation by jays.*

~~~~~~~~~~~~~~~~~~~~~~~~~~~~~~~~~~~~

Eagles in Illinois

Illinoisans now have the chance to see the nation's symbol, the Bald Eagle, year-round. This was not the case just thirty years ago when the state's nesting population had been eliminated by the insecticide DDT. This pesticide prevented Illinois' eagles from reproducing. After banning DDT in the 1960s, the return of nesting eagles to Illinois was a slow process, but the wait has been worth it. Now in 1994, Bald Eagles are once again nesting in the Prairie State.

Bald eagles are fish eaters and nest mainly near large bodies of water. The first nest of the post-DDT era in Illinois was built at Crab Orchard National Wildlife Refuge in southern Illinois in 1973. It was occupied by nesting birds in 1974 before the nest tree blew down in a storm. It was not until 1978 that the returning bald eagles were successful at rearing young again in Illinois. A nest near the Mississippi River in Alexander County north of Cairo produced two young that year. Other eagles began nest construction along the Mississippi in Jo Daviess County the same year, and similar activity continued at Crab Orchard. From 1980 through 1987, Crab Orchard Refuge fledged one to two eagles annually except for 1985 when the nest tree blew down. These were the only known young eagles produced in the state during these years.

Eight young were produced from four nests in 1988, including two from one nest in Carroll County and one from a nest in Jo Daviess County. This was the first successful return of nesting bald eagles in northern Illinois. By the early 1990s nesting activity was scattered all along the Mississippi River and had spread to the Ohio River and a short way up the Wabash. Nesting also began along the Illinois River and at several large reservoirs in the southern half of the state. In 1992 thirteen counties had eagle nests with eight successful nests

Bald Eagle, which has just won a fight with another male of its species for nesting rights with a female. He is calling as he returns to perch next to her.

producing sixteen young. In 1993 fifteen counties had nests with six successful nests producing twelve young. The number of nests increases each year.

The Illinois Endangered Species Protection Board and the Department of Natural Resources' Natural Heritage Division have monitored the recovery of nesting eagles in Illinois over the years. Their data indicate that windstorms are the chief natural threat to eagle nests in the state. Human disturbance is the main factor leading to nest abandonment and failure. Nesting eagles simply need to be left alone. Now that bald eagles are again established as breeding residents of the Prairie State, we can all help them by not approaching their nests.

While eagles are present in Illinois in the summer, the best time to see them is still in winter when the more numerous birds that breed in the lake states to the north migrate to Illinois. Some wintering eagles congregate below dams where the current prevents freeze-up and allows them to catch fish. Others fly to southern Illinois where some water remains unfrozen all winter. Here they fish along the rivers and lakes or feed on geese and other waterfowl, especially in the wildlife refuges.

Good places to go eagle watching in winter are below the Mississippi River dams at the Quad Cities and downstream from there. Dam 15 at Rock Island and 19 at Hamilton/Keokuk are exceptional viewing spots. If the river is unfrozen, eagles can be seen along the Great River Road west of Alton and at Pere Marquette State Park. On the Illinois River check out the area near Havana and Dixon Mounds Museum. In southern Illinois, look for them at Crab Orchard National Wildlife Refuge, Union County, Mermet Lake, and Horseshoe Lake State Fish and Wildlife Areas and along the Ohio River in Pope County. For information on special eagle-viewing events with guides and special programs, check out the state of Illinois website: *http://www.illinois.gov/gov/eagles/Pages/EagleWatching.aspx*.

Don't let cabin fever get you this winter. Plan an outing to see our national symbol right here in the state of Illinois.

January 1994

Cormorant Comeback

In recent years, Illinoisans have been seeing more and more Double-crested Cormorants in the state. While once an endangered species in Illinois, they now seem well on the way to recovery.

These large black waterbirds are about the size of a small goose and can be mistaken for waterfowl at a distance. Flocks of them fly in lines much like geese, but their habit of sailing from time to time and their dark color and relatively long tail serve to distinguish them from waterfowl. At close range their long bill with a hook at the end and their orange throat are good identification characters. The fact that all four toes on its foot are connected by a single web is a clincher if you have a bird in hand.

Cormorants are first cousins of the pelicans and are even more closely related to the Anhinga or snakebird of the southern states. Of the five kinds of cormorants in the United States, all are restricted to coastal areas except the Double-crested. It winters in coastal areas, but many move inland in spring to nest along freshwater lakes and large rivers. The Double-crested feeds almost exclusively on fish, and it is becoming a common sight to see them diving for fish in the waters of our large rivers and lakes. They often take large fish and bring them to the surface to swallow head first and whole.

Like herons with which they sometimes nest, cormorants are colonial nesters, building nests of sticks in trees. Their colonial nesting habit makes it relatively easy to locate and count the number of nesting cormorants in Illinois. Nineteenth-century accounts of the birds of Illinois listed the Double-crested Cormorant only as a migrant in Illinois. The birds seen here supposedly had nested in the lake regions of the upper Midwest. But there are also old nesting records from along the major rivers of Illinois, and the species has probably always been present in the state as a nesting species.

By 1974 only twelve cormorant nests were known in Illinois. These were in two trees along the Mississippi River at Thomson in northwestern Illinois' Carroll County. Like the Bald Eagle and many other fish-eating birds, our cormorants had apparently suffered reproductive failure due to DDT insecticide in the environment. The Double-crested Cormorant was listed as an endangered species by the Illinois Nature Preserves Commission in 1971. It was subsequently listed as endangered by the Illinois Endangered Species Protection Board with its first official list of Illinois' endangered and threatened species in 1978.

As with many other species that were threatened by pesticides, cormorants began recovering after the banning of these polluting chemicals. After 1974 they continued to nest along the upper Mississippi River near Thomson, where the number of nests in Carroll County increased to twenty-five by 1979. In 1981 there were forty-nine nests on the upper Mississippi and the discovery of two nests on the upper Illinois River indicated that the recovering population was spreading to new breeding territory. The Mississippi River population increased to 103 nests in 1983, and the cormorants spread to establish five colonies totaling 124 nests in 1989. The new populations included colonies near lakes in northeastern Illinois and along the middle Illinois River. The nest numbers reached 466 at five colonies in 1993, prompting the Endangered Species Board to change the cormorant's status in Illinois from endangered to threatened in 1994.

During the summer of 1995, six colonies were found. Two of these are on the upper Mississippi, two on lakes in northeastern Illinois, one along the middle Illinois River, and one at Carlyle Lake in southern Illinois. The nest total was 676. Department of Natural Resources bird specialist Vern Kleen says that he thinks more colonies and nests are out there, but were not found. With Double-crested Cormorants nesting nearly statewide in increasing numbers, it seems only a matter of time before it is removed from the threatened species list. This recovery is a living tribute to the value of taking action to clean up our environment.

A benefit of their return is the ease with which these interesting birds can now be viewed. One can hardly visit Carlyle Lake or drive by Rend Lake on Interstate 57 without seeing several cormorants flying or feeding. The same is true along waterways near other nesting locations. Keep an eye out for them this fall. They should be easy to find until freeze-up of our lakes and rivers.

December 1995

AUTHOR'S NOTE.—*The Double-crested Cormorant has increased in numbers and has been removed from the Illinois threatened species list.*

Swallows

The swallows are back! Mother Nature's most graceful flying machines once again grace our airways as they sweep and soar to gather their insect food on the wing. The beauty of their flight separates swallows from other birds in my mind. Their aerodynamic bodies sail smoothly through the air in pursuit of insects, often near or over water, which adds to their mystique. After a winter spent mostly in South America, the return of Illinois' six kinds of swallows is an annual rite of spring dear to the heart of those longing for the warm days of spring and summer.

The first arrival of pioneering early migrant swallows varies from year to year somewhat dependent on the weather and species. These earliest travelers usually show up in March or early April in southern Illinois and just a few days later farther north. The earliest arrivals are Tree Swallows, which winter in our southern states, and

Rough-winged Swallows, which winter in Mexico and Central America. But true to the old saying "one swallow doesn't make a summer," it is not until our four South American wintering swallows return that we can be sure that spring is really here. The belief that swallows return on or near the same date, as at California's San Juan Capistrano Mission, is not all myth. Ornithologists Richard and Jean Graber report a Pope County Barn Swallow colony that consistently returned between April 11 and 13. A twenty-five-year record of arrivals at Liberty in Adams County had a Barn Swallow colony returning usually between April 13 and 17.

Purple Martin, Tree Swallow, Rough-winged Swallow, Barn Swallow, Cliff Swallow, and Bank Swallow are Illinois' regular resident members of the swallow tribe. All are known to nest statewide. The more western Violet-green Swallow has strayed into Illinois in the past but only very rarely. Our swallows are mostly gregarious, often nesting and feeding in flocks. The Purple Martin and Tree Swallow are tree-cavity nesters; the Bank Swallow and Rough-winged Swallows dig dens in banks; and Cliff and Barn Swallows attach mud-based nests to cliffs and buildings. The Rough-winged, Barn, and Tree Swallows are most likely to nest alone or in small numbers. Martins rarely have to search for cavities today as Martin houses are erected in such numbers that nesting in a natural cavity is a rarity. They have become our most urban swallows. Tree Swallows on the other hand like cavities or nest boxes near or over water and often nest in natural cavities. The Barn Swallow often builds its nest support ledge of mud under the eaves of barns and other buildings in rural areas.

While Purple Martins live in our towns and cities, they feed high above our homes largely out of sight. In contrast, barn swallows skim along the ground of lawns, pastures, and barnyards, in rural areas. They live closer to humans than other swallows. Barn Swallows are fascinating and graceful to watch. Their slim bodies, narrow curved wings, and forked tail give them a windswept appearance that seems perfectly designed for effortless flight. They delight in flying teasingly close to the cats that reside around farmsteads and will come within a few feet of people.

Some swallows have benefitted from human presence. Purple Martins, Tree Swallows, and Barn Swallows are surely more abundant today because of their adaptation to nest boxes and our buildings. Cliff Swallows had also adapted to plastering their mud houses under the eaves of barns until the arrival of the House Sparrow from Europe. House Sparrows invade Cliff Swallow nests, and, unlike the larger Purple Martin, they are unable to evict them. Cliff Swallows have retreated to remote cliffs above streams, the undersides of bridges, and the superstructure of dams, where the barnyard and urban-centered sparrows are scarce. I have also seen tree swallows forced from their nest hole by European Starlings. All told, our introduction of alien birds has probably impacted our native swallows more than any other native birds, except possibly the Bluebird. Bank Swallows have never moved in close to humans, preferring to build their colonies of two-to-three-foot-deep nest tunnels in remote vertical banks of soil. Their nesting sites are usually above water on a riverbank isolated from human habitation.

Swallows, especially those going to South America, are early migrants in the fall. They gather in large flocks in August, with most departing by the end of September. They need plenty of time to make the trip as they migrate during the day, feeding on the wing as they go. Unlike many night-migrating songbirds that head straight for South America over the Gulf of Mexico from our southern shores, swallows follow the roundabout route of the west shore of the Gulf and Caribbean.

Take time to observe the swallows this summer, and enjoy the sight of one of nature's most exquisite and graceful flying machines.

May 1996

AUTHOR'S NOTE.—*The House Sparrow has declined greatly in numbers since this was written, to the benefit of the Cliff Swallow.*

~~~~~~~~~~~~~~~~~~~~~~~~~~

Prairie Chicken Crisis

Illinois' native Prairie Chickens are on the verge of extinction! In the spring of 1992, after three decades of habitat protection and management efforts to save our last two flocks, the birds are failing to reproduce because of inbreeding caused by their low numbers. A preservation drama is unfolding as conservationists struggle to save these two flocks, the symbols of our prairie heritage, in Jasper and Marion Counties of southeastern Illinois. The predawn cackling of

Prairie Chicken cock "booming" on a lek at Illinois' Prairie Ridge State Natural Area. His display is aimed at attracting a female for mating.

arriving birds and the "booming" of Prairie Chicken cocks as they strut to attract hens for mating are among the wildest and most moving natural phenomena to be seen and heard in the Prairie State. To lose this heritage without the ultimate struggle to save them is unacceptable to conservationists.

The first efforts to save Illinois' Prairie Chickens began about 1962 when the loss of their habitat to row crop agriculture prompted the establishment of a system of sanctuaries to provide nesting and roosting cover. This initial sanctuary system was acquired by private conservation groups with management and monitoring of the birds provided by the Illinois Natural History Survey. Later the Department of Natural Resources purchased additional sanctuaries and assumed management of the lands while research on the flock continued by the Natural History Survey.

Over the following decades the Prairie Chicken numbers had their ups and downs attributable to weather conditions, nest parasitism, predation, and a natural cycle of abundance. However, studies showed a continuing decline in egg fertility and egg success over the years. Unsuccessful eggs develop or partially develop chicks that never hatch. This fertility and reproductive decline was accompanied by a reduction in the overall population size. All-time low populations in the two flocks in 1990 were attributed to this reduced ability to produce young. Genetic defects caused by inbreeding and low population size were the likely cause of this reproductive failure.

A plan was implemented to swap single clutches of eggs between the two Illinois flocks that summer as a first step to overcome the inbreeding problem. Genes that may have been lost in one flock might still survive in the other. This strategy was successful in producing young, as the hens at both Jasper and Marion Counties hatched broods from the swapped eggs. However, genetic studies were undertaken of both of the state's flocks, and comparisons were made to Prairie Chickens from Oklahoma, Kansas, Nebraska, and South Dakota. The studies showed that both Illinois flocks had low genetic diversity compared to healthy flocks elsewhere. Swapping between our flocks would not solve the problem; new genes were needed from elsewhere to overcome the inbreeding.

In August 1992 Illinois obtained fifteen hen Prairie Chickens from Minnesota. They were released at the Jasper County sanctuary in August when they were molting to minimize their flying away before getting used to their new surroundings. Each new hen was equipped with a radio transmitter so it could be located. By the beginning of the 1993 breeding season in March, five of the new birds had been killed. One of these had been lost when it flew into a power line on a foggy day.

The surviving ten birds remained in the sanctuary area until mid-March when six dispersed from the area. Prairie chickens are strong fliers and some seem to disperse in search of other Prairie Chickens as the breeding season starts. A brief search found one of them forty miles to the north and others somewhat closer, but no effort was made to capture and return them. This dispersal behavior is probably a natural mechanism that assures mixing of genes and prevents inbreeding. However, it is one reason why it is very difficult to establish new Prairie Chicken flocks by simple introduction. Of course it is also causing problems in efforts to introduce new genes into Illinois' flock.

The remaining four hens mated with Illinois cocks and are now setting on eggs. Conservation biologists at the Natural History Survey and the University of Illinois will be monitoring the genetic profile of our flocks—including any new offspring these introduced hens produce. This will help assess whether the genetic diversity of Illinois' Prairie Chickens is, in fact, increasing.

Plans call for continuing the program this summer by bringing in fifteen more hens and ten cocks from Minnesota. Counting the four remaining 1992 Minnesota birds, the 1993 Jasper County population is estimated at just twenty-eight Prairie Chickens; the Marion County flock is estimated at thirty; and a single male was found booming off the sanctuaries in Clay County. With an estimated sixty birds in the breeding population, this magnificent symbol of Illinois' prairie heritage remains perilously close to extirpation.

The four remaining Minnesota hens nested in the spring of 1993. Two of these nests were destroyed by predators and a third was abandoned by its hen. A single nest bearing the new genes hatched seventeen chicks, but observations indicated most if not all of them died. Realizing that a more intensive effort would be needed if the Illinois flocks are to be saved, eight cocks and four additional hens from Minnesota were introduced at Jasper County in August of 1993.

At the beginning of the 1994 breeding season there were eighteen cocks on the Marion County booming grounds compared to fifteen a year ago, but just seven at Jasper County compared to fourteen in 1993. The total populations are estimated to be double the number of booming cocks. The seven in Jasper County included five Illinois birds and two from Minnesota. The decline at Jasper County may have been due to storm- related mortality last summer that missed Marion County. Heavy rains at Jasper County caused local severe flooding that could have destroyed nests and young. Hailstorms can also be deadly to both young and old Prairie Chickens, but none were noted last summer.

In late March and early April this year (1994) ninety-six Kansas Prairie Chickens were released at the Jasper County sanctuaries. These included fifty hens and forty-six cocks. Thirteen of the Kansas cocks joined the residents on the booming ground, more than doubling the male breeding population there. Apparently, many of the Kansas birds dispersed after release, which is typical. However, the small resident population attracted and held enough birds that the release significantly increased the reproducing population. A sample of the released Minnesota and Kansas Prairie Chickens was fitted with radio transmitters to assess the success of the releases. As of this writing in early May, eight of twenty-three radioed Kansas hens remain on and near the sanctuaries and three of six Kansas cocks. If these percentages are representative of this year's transplanted birds as a whole, over 40 percent of the new birds have entered the breeding population.

One radioed Minnesota cock that was released in Jasper County in 1993 showed up at Marion County this spring, a movement of about thirty-eight air miles. It is possible that some of the dispersed Kansas birds might find their way to this population as well. Since the Kansas and Minnesota birds are from genetically diverse populations, managers and researchers from the Department of Natural Resources and the Illinois Natural History Survey feel the current effort will introduce new genes into the Illinois flock. Monitoring the radioed hens will facilitate the determination of their nesting and rearing success. At this time, two more years of introductions are anticipated. Now that some new birds are out there, Mother Nature has to cooperate. Last year's effort shows how a severe summer storm can alter nesting success.

In spring 1995 at least part of Illinois' Prairie Chicken flock seems to have turned the corner on its precipitous decline. After three years of introduction of Prairie Chickens from Minnesota and Kansas to overcome inbreeding problems, the population curve is creeping up. By late March 1995, the low resonating "whoo-whoo-ooo" of Prairie Chicken cocks booming on our Prairie Chicken sanctuaries signaled the arrival of census time. These annual booming-ground displays provide biologists their best opportunity to count the breeding birds there, which constitute Illinois' entire population.

Recent counts at the thirteen-hundred-acre Jasper County sanctuary (now named Prairie Ridge State Natural Area) show that the population is up to forty cocks this spring compared to only seven in the spring of 1994. Jasper County has been the site of new releases of birds in 1992, 1993, and 1994. A total of 123 birds were released. The Prairie Chicken flock at the 760-acre Marion County Sanctuary has not received stocking of new birds and declined from eighteen booming cocks last spring to twelve this year. The population turnaround at Jasper County has apparently averted the impending extinction of that flock. The addition of genetically diverse new blood into the flock may have reduced the inbreeding problems as well. The fertility of eggs checked by the Illinois Natural History Survey in Jasper County in 1994 was 99 percent, and 94 percent of the eggs hatched.

The Illinois Natural History Survey has followed the fate of past releases by tagging some with radio transmitters. Their work reveals just how dangerous life is for Prairie Chickens in Illinois. Of thirteen radio-tagged hens at Jasper County last spring, three were found dead before nesting season on private land adjacent to the sanctuary. One of these may have been killed by farming activity, and the cause of death of the others is not known. The remaining ten attempted to nest, but three of these failed to hatch their eggs. One of these nests was found and destroyed by predators before it could hatch. Another hen was killed by a raptor (hawk) before she completed laying her eggs. The third hen was killed on her nest by farm equipment when she nested on farmland off the sanctuaries. Of the remaining seven hens that hatched eggs, two lost their broods to unknown causes such as weather or predators. Two more of the hens were found dead during the brood-rearing period, one killed by a mammalian predator. Only three hens were still with their young by summer's end—just three of the ten present at the start of nesting season. Life and motherhood are truly dangerous for these birds as it is for all wildlife.

Other factors that have killed Prairie Chickens that were being radio-tracked over the past three years include one instance of a broken neck from flying into a power line and another that may have died from hitting a fence. Although high, these mortality rates are typical for game-bird species such as Prairie Chickens. The fact that the population is increasing in spite of them is encouraging.

Nineteen ninety-five will be the fourth year of a planned five-year population- augmentation effort under an interagency plan of the Department of Natural Resources, the Illinois Natural History Survey, the Illinois Nature Preserves Commission, and The Nature Conservancy. This Illinois Prairie Chicken recovery plan calls for importing more Prairie Chickens in 1995 and 1996. Another hundred birds will be trapped in Kansas and released in Jasper County this April. Thanks to these efforts, the future of the Prairie Chicken in Illinois looks better today than it did just five years ago.

This Prairie Chicken rescue project is made possible by a mix of game and nongame wildlife resources. The Minnesota birds were obtained in exchange for Illinois wild turkeys and our help with a research project there, while trapping and transporting the Kansas birds was helped by citizen income tax "check-off" contributions to the Illinois Wildlife Preservation Fund.

June 1993, May 1994, and April 1995

AUTHOR'S NOTE.—*In the spring of 2015 the Illinois Prairie Chicken flock contained forty booming cocks at Prairie Ridge State Natural Area in Jasper County (many of which were imported from Kansas) and twenty-seven native cocks at the Marion County sanctuary.*

~~~~~~~~~~~~~~~~~~~~~~~~~~~

The Armadillos Are Coming!

As my family and I walked toward the crafts fair on the courthouse lawn at Golconda last fall (1991), a local friend, Coy Stallions, hailed us from across the street. "Ever see a southern Illinois Armadillo?" he asked. Admitting that I hadn't, he directed us to the local Conservation Police Officer's front yard, where, sure enough, there lay a road-killed Armadillo. Now, of all the mammals that Dr. Donald Hoffmeister lists as possible future mammal finds in Illinois in his new *Mammals of Illinois* book, Armadillos aren't among them. So what was this critter doing here?

I asked around and learned that another road-killed Armadillo had been recorded in adjacent Hardin County a few years ago, and remembered reading in a Union County paper about an Armadillo spotted ambling along a roadside south of Anna back in the late 1970s. All of this raised the question in my mind whether the Armadillo could be establishing itself as a new member of Illinois' fauna.

Before proceeding, let's take a closer look at this wanderer from South America that is sometimes called a pig in armor or possum on the half shell. The Armadillo is a mammal, but unlike most of its kin, sports a heavy, bony shell rather than a fur coat. It eats mostly ants and other insects with an occasional worm or other small animal. It has no teeth except for primitive peg-like molars, but has sharp claws that it uses to dig its den and to uncover food. It does not hibernate, so must find food regularly even in cold weather. It gives birth to four young each year that are always identical quadruplets!

Armadillos are heavy and are reported to cross small streams by simply walking on the bottom. They can hold their breath for up to six minutes, an adaptation no doubt to help them as they root in the soil for food. Remarkably, if they need to they can gulp enough air into their digestive system to become buoyant and swim.

Armadillos were unknown in the United States outside the lower Rio Grande valley of Texas as recently as 1870. With human settlement and the reduction of predators, they began a constant northward migration that continues today. By 1925 they had reached southeastern Oklahoma and Louisiana. Soon thereafter they crossed the Mississippi and spread throughout Florida and the southeast. At present they range from the south edge of Nebraska, across southern Missouri, to the Mississippi River. East of the Mississippi they are known only as far north as Memphis, Tennessee.

Armadillos are sensitive to cold, staying in their den during the coldest weather but having to emerge to hunt for food after only a few days. They are reportedly killed by cold along the north edge of their range during very cold winters. Armadillos probably range so far north in the plains because the rapidly moving air masses there keep cold spells relatively short. The farther east one goes the farther south the Armadillo range is. To see how close they range to Illinois in Missouri, I called Paul Nelson of the Missouri State Park system. He advised that they had a road-killed Armadillo at Meramec State Park in 1991. This is barely forty miles southwest of St. Louis and just thirty-six miles from the Illinois state line. I was unable to determine how close they come to Illinois farther south in the Ozarks.

Being weak swimmers, it seems unlikely that Armadillos will cross the barriers of the Ohio and Mississippi Rivers on their own to establish themselves in Illinois. But this probably will not be necessary. Humans seem willing to help them. This is apparently how the Golconda Armadillo arrived. I learned later that some crew members of a barge from the south released the animal near Golconda as the barge was nosed in to bank to pick up workers. Pet and captive releases such as this first established them in Florida and will probably be the source of any populations that become established in Illinois. It seems only a matter of time before enough Armadillos are present to get a start. It remains to be seen if our winters are mild enough for them to survive long term.

August 1992

AUTHOR'S NOTE.—*As of 2015 a population of Armadillos has become established in the southern tip of Illinois. They are most abundant in counties along the Mississippi River.*

~~~~~~~~~~~~~~~~~~~~

River Otters in Illinois

The playful River Otter is one of nature's most interesting mammals, but your chance of seeing one in Illinois is not good. Even though they are large at about twenty pounds, they are both rare and secretive. If you have seen one, chances are that it was near a stream, lake, or other wetland.

Otters are supremely adapted to life in and around water, having webbed feet, small ears that can be closed to keep water out, and a thick tail that tapers to the tip giving the animal a streamlined shape. These adaptations and a dense brown fur that insulates it from cold water suit it well to swimming in pursuit of fish. While fish are its favorite food, they will also eat muskrats, birds, frogs, and even mussels.

Originally occurring throughout Illinois, by the beginning of the twentieth century, otters survived only at the southern tip of the state. They also disappeared from most of Illinois' bordering states, hanging on only in northern Wisconsin and southeast Missouri. By the mid-twentieth century, Minnesota otters expanded their range down the Mississippi River so that by the 1970s Illinois had its largest population along the Mississippi—from the Wisconsin state line south to northern Rock Island County. Southern Illinois River Otters have held on throughout this century, especially in the Cache River basin, but at relatively low numbers. They are presently less numerous than the northwestern Illinois otter population. Elsewhere in Illinois, otters show up from time to time, but these are interpreted as wide-ranging individuals rather than established breeding populations.

In spite of legal protection from harvest since 1929, Illinois otters have not expanded to establish breeding populations in most parts of the state. Poor water quality and deteriorating habitat for much of the twentieth century are thought to be part of the reason recovery has been slow. But these two parameters have improved markedly over the past two decades, and the time seems right to help the otters return. Similar situations exist in adjacent states. In 1982 both Missouri and Kentucky began releasing otters, and Iowa joined them in 1985. Illinois started introducing otters in 1994 as did Indiana in 1995.

Illinois' introduction program is guided by the Illinois River Otter Recovery Plan, a document prepared by the Department of Natural Resources and the Illinois Endangered Species Board and issued by the department's Division of Wildlife Resources. The goals of Illinois' recovery plan are the reestablishment of otters in suitable habitats, monitoring otter populations, and conserving key habitats to ensure long-term viability of the species in Illinois. Recovery planning is based on habitat units within seven stream watersheds. Current reproducing populations are restricted to two of the seven watersheds.

Our first two reintroductions were fifty otters into the Wabash River basin unit in January of 1994. Three additional releases totaling fifty-seven otters were set free in the same unit in 1995. The first releases into the Kaskaskia River watershed were twenty-four animals also released in 1995. Releases planned for 1996 include fifty more into the Kaskaskia River unit and sixty-two into Illinois River watershed streams, including the Mackinaw, Spoon, and La Moine Rivers. Illinois River watershed numbers could be increased if private donations allow. The Vermilion County Conservation District plans to release thirteen otters to the Vermilion River this spring. Only nine of 131 otters released to date have been found dead, while twenty-eight sightings of live otters have been reported from the release watersheds since the introductions began. These sightings compare to only seven such sightings in the decade before the releases.

One of the remarkable things about the River Otter reintroduction program is the diversity of funding sources used to acquire the otters. All come from a Louisiana supplier, but some were obtained first by Kentucky and then traded to Illinois for Wild Turkeys. Other funds have come from the Furbearer Fund, the Wildlife Preservation Fund, and private donations. The funds for the Wildlife Preservation Fund come from donations through the check-off on the Illinois state income tax form. In 1995, $8,100 of these funds supported the purchase of otters and $10,000 is scheduled for use by the project in the spring of 1996. Residents of the state can help restore Illinois' wildlife heritage by donating to this fund at tax preparation time.

January 1996

AUTHOR'S NOTE.—*As of 2015, River Otters are established throughout Illinois.*

～～～～～～～～～～～～～～～

Squirrels

Illinois' seven members of the squirrel family are among the most familiar native mammals in the state. This is because many are abundant and all but one are active by day. And tree squirrels have literally moved into town with us! Unlike nighttime foragers, such as Raccoons, Opossums, and Skunks, which few of us have seen in the wild, a tree squirrel feeding in a forest, park, or yard is a familiar sight. The diversity in our squirrel family members includes three tree squirrels, two ground squirrels, the Southern Flying Squirrel, the Eastern Chipmunk, and the Woodchuck.

Two of the tree squirrels, the Gray Squirrel and Fox Squirrel, are statewide in distribution and are abundant enough to support sport hunting. However, the tiny Red Squirrel is a northern animal that is restricted in Illinois to a small area centered on eastern Kankakee County. Tree squirrels are active throughout the year and are as important to the forest as the forest is to them. Their habit of burying acorns and nuts for winter food literally plants the forest's trees of the future.

In the wild, Gray Squirrels are animals of the dense forest, while the reddish Fox Squirrels prefer open woodland and small tracts of trees. Red Squirrels prefer pine plantations but do well in deciduous forest as well. The large, unbroken, bottomland forests of southern Illinois often have only Grays, but throughout most of Illinois both Gray and Fox Squirrels can be found together in both forests and cities. The larger tree squirrels have few effective natural predators. I once watched a Red-tailed Hawk pluck a Gray Squirrel from the end of a branch and descend to the forest floor with it in its talons. They landed out of sight just over a slight rise. After waiting in silence for nearly ten minutes I walked toward them and the hawk flew off and the squirrel ran away. Catching a squirrel is apparently easier for the hawk than killing or even blinding it.

Before the vast forests of the east were fragmented, Gray Squirrels regularly reached such numbers that they exhausted the local food supply and migrated in large swarms in search of food. They would even swim large rivers. Gray Squirrels were such pests that laws were passed requiring settlers to kill them. It is hard to believe that an animal with such a reputation would be purposely introduced into another land, but our Gray Squirrel was introduced into England and is now a pest there. Red Squirrels are a tiny version of their large cousins and are about intermediate in color between them. The best place to see one in Illinois is the city park in Momence.

Our last tree-inhabiting squirrel is the little Southern Flying Squirrel. With the aid of skin folds between its front and hind legs, it glides from tree to tree. It is common throughout the state, but most Illinoisans have never seen it because it is only active at night. It is seen by day only when disturbed and scared from its den in a hollow tree or limb.

Chipmunks live on the forest floor and are found scattered throughout Illinois. They are absent from bottomland forests because their dens would flood there. They are absent from many upland forests as well for unknown reasons. My observations indicate that areas without rock outcrops and small naturally fragmented forests often lack them. However, the entire eastern half of Illinois' Shawnee Hills is also without Chipmunks. I grew up roaming the forests of Massac and Pope Counties in this region and was unaware that Illinois even had Chipmunks until I visited bluff areas along the Cache River in Johnson County. Chipmunks are poor diggers, so they establish dens in rock crevices and stumps where the need to dig is minimized. Unlike our other ground-denning squirrels, they do not hibernate.

The Woodchuck is common throughout the state, where it is seen feeding on herbs during the warmer months. It is our largest squirrel and is a strong digger. It is our most famous hibernator, spending the coldest months sleeping in its den. Groundhog Day, a holiday of sorts, is named in its honor. Woodchucks have declined over the past thirty years, as Coyotes have increased in the state. They are, or apparently have been, relatively easy prey for the Prairie Wolf.

Our final two squirrels are the Thirteen-lined Ground Squirrel and Franklin's Ground Squirrel. Both are prairie animals and are found only in the former prairie regions of the state. They dig dens in grassy areas and are active by day in the warmer months, hibernating in winter. The thirteen-liners are most familiar because of their habit of denning in road banks from which we see them scurrying across the highway. Franklin's are about the size of gray tree squirrels, which they resemble except for their slightly shorter tail and a little brown on their backs. They are very secretive. A colony lives on the railroad embankment behind my house with some dens actually in my yard! In spite of their proximity, I only saw three squirrels this past summer.

Our native squirrels are an interesting group that is more available for wildlife watching than our other wild mammals. Take time to enjoy them.

November 1993

AUTHOR'S NOTE.—*Woodchucks have increased in most areas since the Coyote population declined, reportedly because of a heartworm infestation.*

Native Rats and Mice

When I was growing up in southern Illinois, I knew "field mice" as those short-tailed mice that the cat brought to the back door. Only after getting into a mammalogy class at Southern Illinois University did I realize the full diversity of native rats and mice in the Prairie State. I was amazed to learn that we had our own pack rat, mice that jumped like kangaroos and hibernated like bears, and other mice that climbed up into vines and shrubs to build nests above ground.

Illinois has twelve wild, indigenous species of rats and mice in addition to the Norway Rat and House Mouse that have emigrated here from Europe. Six of these natives are found throughout the state, and six are restricted to either northern or southern Illinois. All of these rodents have sparsely haired tails, but rats and mice have long tails, while voles and lemmings have short tails. Mice and their relatives the voles, lemmings, and rats are the most abundant mammals in the state. This is not apparent to the casual observer since they are so small, secretive, and come out mainly at night. Good grassy or forest cover usually harbors fifty or more of these animals per acre.

Even though we seldom see them, the hawks and owls that depend on them for sustenance have the sharp vision and patience to hunt them successfully. Coyotes and foxes also prey on them. They are important links in many food chains, converting grass, fruits, and insects into red meat. Although many are eaten, they are so prolific that their numbers remain relatively high. Most mice and voles have a three-week gestation period with a litter size of three to four and breed just after giving birth. Often the young of one litter are weaned just in time to nurse the newborn of the next. Young mice are ready to breed at five to eight weeks of age and could have young of their own just eight weeks after their birth! While reproduction slows in winter and summer, it can occur year-round.

One species restricted to southern Illinois is the Eastern Wood Rat, called by some a pack rat. It is found on rocky bluffs along the Mississippi River at the southern tip of the state. It is rare in Illinois and is listed as an endangered species under Illinois law. It is at the northern limit of its native range here, and cold temperatures may restrict its abundance. The Wood Rat collects sticks, seeds, fruits, and sometimes shiny objects and piles them into nests and food caches in crevices of rock bluffs. This habit of collecting and packing materials gives the animal its name—pack rat. Another southern Illinois species is the Golden Mouse, which climbs vines and shrubs to build its nest of bark, stems, and leaves well off the ground. Other southern Illinois specialties are the Cotton Mouse and Rice Rat.

Mice and voles found only in northern Illinois include the Western Harvest Mouse and the Meadow Vole. Both live in prairie or grassy habitat, which is more typical of this region of the state. The Harvest Mouse may have recently expanded its range in Illinois along the grassy rights of way of the interstate highway system.

Statewide species include the long-tailed Deer Mouse and White-footed Mouse and the short-tailed Prairie Vole, Pine Vole, and Southern Bog Lemming. The very long-tailed Meadow Jumping Mouse also occurs statewide. Deer Mice and White-footed Mice look much alike with long tails, large ears, large shining eyes, and white undersides. The Deer Mouse likes forests and brushy areas, while the White-footed Mouse prefers grassland habitat. In addition to their shorter (and hairier) tails, the voles and lemmings are larger than Deer Mice and have short ears that barely exceed their fine short fur. Except for the Pine Vole, they prefer grassy habitat and are noted for population declines after fire decreases the density of the grassy habitat they need in order to hide from predators. Their numbers recover rapidly as the grass regrows.

The Meadow Jumping Mouse is one of our most remarkable mice. Its tail is extremely long, apparently to balance it as it hops up to three feet per jump. It lives in wet areas and has been observed to jump into water and dive to escape capture if it fails to outrun a predator. It is our only hibernating mouse, sleeping from October to April. I have seen it most often around seep springs. Studies of its food habits found that it relishes the seeds of Touch-me-not, a common plant in and around seeps.

When afield, we may find what appears to be a dead mouse or vole lying on a rock or log where it has been left by a predator. Such animals are invariably shrews that a hawk or owl has mistaken for a mouse. Shrews resemble mice but are very musky in odor, and many predators will not eat them. Many shrews have short tails like voles, but they can be told from both mice and voles by their sharp, pointed teeth, which differ greatly from the two chisel-like gnawing teeth of the rodents.

The next time you see a hawk perched or hovering over grassy habitat, remember that his odds of finding food there are good. With hundreds of animals per field, lunch is just a matter of time and effort.

December 1996

~~~~~~~~~~~~~~~~~~~~~~~~~~~~~~~~

Reptiles and Such

I am sure most of us are aware of the wildlife rescue and rehabilitation centers around the state of Illinois that care for orphaned and injured birds and mammals, but did you ever wonder who cares for snakes, turtles, and salamanders needing nurturing and a home?

Well, one who does much of it in Illinois is a natural heritage biologist of the Department of Natural Resources, Scott Ballard of Alton. A herpetologist, or amphibian and reptile biologist, by training, Scott spends a lot of his evenings and spare time caring for an assortment of alligators, turtles, snakes, and salamanders (collectively called herptiles) that have been seized in violation of various laws or that simply need a home. While it is legal to pick up a nonendangered native turtle, snake, or other herptile for a personal pet, collecting for the market is a violation of Illinois law.

Except for a two-headed snake, which he nurtured to health after injury by road construction equipment, Scott Ballard does not treat injured animals. At any given time, Scott's house is home to some

Adult male Five-lined Skink in breeding condition, as evidenced by its red-orange head. This specimen is on a cypress tree in Heron Pond Nature Preserve. The duckweed on its back indicates that it can swim as well as climb trees.

forty reptiles and amphibians and a colony of over two hundred rats and mice to feed them. The fact that he is single helps here. The bathtub in his extra bathroom is home to a two-foot alligator at present, while various aquaria, cages, and a cattle-watering tank house the rest. Most are protected species seized as a result of law enforcement investigations of pet dealers or owners without permits, animals formerly owned in violation of the Dangerous Animals Act, and animals seized from persons who collected them in Illinois for sale. Often Ballard is holding them as living evidence pending a trial. Some are former pets in need of a home. These are frequently exotic tropical or desert animals that cannot be released in the state.

Animals seized under the Dangerous Animals Act include the alligator, a Gila Monster, rattlesnakes, and a six-foot Caiman alligator. The Caiman was too large for Scott's facilities, so he arranged a home for it at the St. Louis Zoo. Some species confiscated for violation of the Endangered Species Act include an Indian Python, a Galapagos Tortoise, and many Illinois natives like Alligator Snapping Turtles, River Cooters (turtles), Eastern Ribbon Snakes, and Timber Rattlesnakes. Various snakes and salamanders are the most common native herptiles that are seized after being collected from the wild for sale. Scott has a lot of native salamanders on hand that were being offered for sale. Once they have been used as evidence, they will be released where they were collected. He also houses a forty-year-old desert tortoise that was raised as a pet from a hatchling and then outlived its owner. Another pet he is housing is a Florida gopher tortoise. He also once had custody of a small alligator that a fisherman caught in Randolph County's Lake Baldwin.

Scott says raising food for the carnivorous species is the biggest chore in caring for them. While the herptiles themselves are fairly easy to clean up after and require feeding only every week or so, the rats and mice he raises as food for them require daily feeding and watering. Most species eat the rodents, some requiring live prey. But his aquatic turtles, such as the Cooters, eat "trout chow," and the tortoises eat fresh leaves and fruits.

Scott's deep concern for this part of our natural heritage shines through when you realize that caring for this menagerie is a spare time avocation. After a hard day out burning prairies or censusing birds, it takes dedication to care for these interesting creatures.

March 1994

Salamander Time

Watch out for those salamanders on the road on rainy spring nights. They are an interesting part of the state's natural heritage that many Illinoisans are unaware of and lots of folks have never seen. The heavy rains of early spring bring many of these subterranean creatures crawling to the surface in search of a pond in which to breed and lay eggs. This is the best time of year to observe many of these amphibian cousins of the frogs. Unlike the frogs, whose singing choruses catch our attention, salamanders are silent. The easiest way to see them is to watch for them crossing the road in rural areas on rainy nights. Roadside ditches and borrow pits are often ideal breeding ponds. It is only natural that many will wander onto the road as they search for the ponds where others of their kind are gathering.

Salamanders are an ancient group. Their forebears were the first vertebrates or back-boned animals to move out of the water to live on land. However, their break with water remains incomplete even today. Like all amphibians, they lay eggs without shells that often are laid in water or at least have to be kept moist. Many have a larval or tadpole stage that lives in water, and some adults have totally returned to the water. If you think "when you've seen one salamander you've seen them all," you could not be more wrong. Illinois' twenty species are divided among six families, which have greatly varying life histories and habits.

Members of the mole salamander family are generally considered "typical" of the group. Illinois has eight species from this family, which gets the name mole from their habit of burrowing in soil and under logs. These are the salamanders most likely to be seen on the roads in spring, when they mostly lay their eggs in water. The eggs hatch into aquatic larvae, which transform during summer into adults that leave the water to start their life in the soil. The Tiger Salamander is the most widespread and common member of this group. The

Spotted Salamander, a mole salamander that ranges throughout eastern and southern Illinois. It lays eggs in ponds in early spring where its larvae will develop before transforming into adults.

Marbled Salamander is an exception to the typical breeding behavior of the state's mole salamanders. In the fall, it moves to areas that will be shallow ponds in spring and mates and lays eggs. The eggs are laid under logs or other debris, where the female stays with them, until they are covered by the rising water of fall or winter rains. The eggs hatch in spring.

The lungless salamander family (*Plethodontidae*) also has eight species in the state. All members of this family have no lungs and absorb oxygen through the skin and roof of the mouth. These animals are also called brook salamanders because of the preference of many species for small, often fishless, streams and springs. Most species lay their eggs in or along small streams, where the tadpole-like larvae may live up to two years before losing their gills and transforming into adults. However, Illinois' three species of woodland salamanders of the genus *Plethodon* live under rocks and debris away from water. They lay their eggs in cavities in soil, logs, or rocks, where the female stays with them until they hatch. These salamanders develop completely within the egg. Rather than hatching into larvae that must spend time in water, these eggs hatch into miniature replicas of adults. The appropriately named Slimy Salamander is the most widespread and abundant member of this group. They come out of hiding at night to forage for food. As a boy camping in the woods of southern Illinois, I recall being awakened in the night by a slimy salamander crawling across my face!

The true salamander family is represented in the state of Illinois by a single species, the Eastern Newt. Illinois' newt has a complex life cycle that involves a completely aquatic adult laying its eggs in water followed by hatching in late spring into a larva that then transforms in midsummer into a rough-skinned terrestrial salamander called an eft. After living on land for two to three years, the eft returns to the water, where it develops a tail fin and the ability to breathe through its skin, and where it spends the rest of its life.

The Hellbender is our only member of the giant salamander family. These totally aquatic animals reach three feet in length. They are wrinkled, ugly, and very slimy. In the Prairie State, they live only in the relatively swift currents of the Ohio and Wabash Rivers, so are not apt to be seen by many Illinoisans. But if you canoe the clear, rocky rivers of the Missouri Ozarks, you will probably encounter this creature. The Illinois Hellbender has a sister species, the Chinese

Giant Salamander, that reaches six feet in length. It is the largest salamander in the world. While visiting a clear mountain stream in China I observed a four-foot long specimen of it.

The mud puppy and siren families each have a single species here that is totally aquatic, with "fuzzy" external gills. The Mud Puppy has both front and hind legs, while the siren only has front legs. Their gills make these salamanders resemble larvae or tadpoles; however, their ability to reproduce clearly distinguishes them as adults. The Mud Puppy and Tiger Salamander are the only salamanders found throughout the entire state of Illinois.

In the interest of keeping Illinois' interesting and diverse salamander fauna, we should all keep some simple conservation measures in mind. Since fish readily eat salamander larvae, most salamanders need small fishless ponds to successfully reproduce. Avoid introducing fish where they do not naturally occur, especially small ponds with no potential as a sport fishery. Also leave logs and downed branches in woods rather than cleaning them up. They are important components of salamander habitat.

With due consideration for their needs, we may always have the opportunity to count salamander-watching among the rites of spring in Illinois.

March 1993

AUTHOR'S NOTE.—*Two additional species of mole salamanders, the Jefferson and Silvery, have been discovered in east-central Illinois since this was written.*

Frog Calls

One of the sure signs of spring is the calling of frogs that can be heard on the first warm days after frost has left the ground. The Illinois landscape is wet from snowmelt and spring rains, providing abundant habitat for chorus frogs and spring peepers that mate very early in the spring. These early spring frog calls are often noticed more than those at other seasons because these early breeders congregate in large numbers and often use ditches along highways, where you can hear them as you drive along. Frog calls are notable for their resonance and carrying ability considering the size of the animals. This is achieved by use of their throat pouch as a resonating chamber. Take the time to slip up on calling frogs and observe or record this interesting behavior. It is not easy to do.

Frogs call mainly to find each other for the purpose of mating and laying eggs. Only the males call, and this vocal activity occurs both day and night for many species. Some frogs also have a short call when fleeing danger, as when they are spooked and jump into water. I am not sure that this is understood as a warning call by other frogs, but it may be. Gray Tree Frogs, Green Frogs, and other species call back and forth during the day, where calling seems to be just to reassure other frogs that more of their kind are in the area. Illinois has two species of Gray Tree Frogs that are absolutely identical in appearance but different in their calls. In this case, voice is used to identify the species. While the calls are similar, one is much coarser than the other. Perhaps the rarest and most seldom-heard frog call is the "death call." I have only heard this four times in a lifetime spent afield. Each time, the call was being given by a leopard frog being slowly swallowed, rear-end first, by a snake. Frog expert Ron Altig advises that many frog species make essentially the same call while being swallowed. It appears to be a warning to other frogs.

Illinois' earliest spring-calling frogs are our three species of chorus frogs, and their name says a lot about their behavior. The croaking calls of two abundant species occur in large, loud choruses in both fields and woods. They often call in broad daylight on warm days, and one species or another is found throughout the state. They can be heard up to half a mile away when wind conditions are right. It is hard to believe that creatures averaging just over an inch long can make so much noise. Another widespread early spring caller is the Spring Peeper. Its call is a single "peep," but can be quite noisy in large choruses. Being a tree frog, it usually calls from ponds in or near woods.

Illinois' eighteen species of frogs have a wide variety of calls, and we cannot discuss them all here. In addition to the croak and peep, they are variously described as trills, snores, clicking sounds, and banjo strums. One sounds like the "baa" of a sheep, and another has a wavering bird-like whistle. The state's loudest frog must be the Crawfish Frog. It emits coarse croaks, often in choruses, that I have heard up to a mile away on warm spring nights. Listen for it in open habitats in the south half of the state. The American toad's call is a long-drawn-out trilling that lasts for up to half a minute. It almost has insect qualities, and some people do not recognize it as a frog call. These toads usually call alone or in small numbers and are common throughout the state. They are the easiest frog call to hear in Illinois, being present in most suburban and rural settings. Listen for a trill in your backyard on a warm night this spring.

The widespread Leopard Frog has a call like a wavering snore with one or two barks at the end. It calls in spring, mostly from open sites. The Cricket Frog's call resembles stones clicking together. Listen for it along creeks throughout the state in summer. The wavering whistle of the Bird-voiced Tree Frog can be heard in cypress swamps like Heron Pond, south of Vienna, in summer. The sheep-like baa of the Narrow-mouth Toad is heard around upland ponds in southern and southwestern Illinois in spring. The call of the Green Frog, a three-inch-long species that resembles a small bullfrog, is described as the strum of a single banjo string heard in woods and wetlands in summer. It avoids the prairie areas of the state. The bullfrog's call sounds like he is saying "belly deep." Their call is a common sound around Illinois ponds on summer nights. They are very aggressive defenders of territories, so they never gather in choruses but are scattered around a pond in their individual patches of turf.

Listening for the calls of frogs and toads can add to your enjoyment of time spent in the out-of-doors. Take the time to listen in the coming months. If your interest is piqued, most nature stores or supply catalogs offer recordings of calls to help you identify them.

March 1994

Rattlesnakes

When Hernando Cortés visited the zoo of the Aztec Empire in Tenochtitlan (Mexico City) in 1520, among the animals that impressed him most were the "snakes with castanets on their tails," which we know today as rattlesnakes. Rattlesnakes were totally new to these Europeans, since rattlesnakes are restricted to the Americas, and Europeans had only recently discovered our continent. Some thirty species of rattlesnakes are now known to exist in the range from southern Canada to northern Argentina. Their venomous nature is not unique among snakes, but the existence of a rattle on their tail and the habit of rattling it to warn off threats is unparalleled in the animal kingdom. It fascinated Cortés and the Aztecs and continues to hold this fascination for us today.

Illinois has two native rattlesnakes, the Eastern Massasauga and the Timber Rattlesnake. Both were once widespread in the state, but their populations in Illinois today are so reduced that the Massasauga is officially designated an endangered species, and the Timber Rattlesnake is a threatened species.

The Eastern Massasauga is primarily a wet prairie and marsh species that prospered in the northern two-thirds of Illinois before the draining and plowing of our prairies. It also inhabits woodland. Its decline is certainly due to human destruction of its habitat. Surviving Massasaugas are scattered throughout its former range, with possibly only six or seven populations remaining. Adult Massasaugas average only about two feet long, and are active during the day from April until early October. Where remnant populations remain, they are often seen sunning on hummocks of grass. They feed primarily on mice. They are not aggressive toward people, and give a warning rattle if approached.

Timber Rattlesnakes are larger, measuring up to six feet long. They prefer rocky forest habitat, where they den (overwinter) in rock crevices. Like the Massasauga, they are relatively inactive and venture forth only for short periods when hunting. They spend most of their time basking, waiting for prey to come by, and digesting the last meal. They often can be seen resting in the same spot day after day. In Illinois, Timber Rattlesnakes range from the Shawnee Hills, at the southern tip of the state, northward, along the Mississippi River bluffs, to Wisconsin. They are also known from the Wabash drainage of Illinois to as far north as Coles County and at scattered sites along the Illinois River. Much timber-rattler habitat is too rugged and rocky for farming and remains intact, but these snakes have declined due to indiscriminate killing and collecting. They often congregate at favored overwintering dens in spring and fall, making them vulnerable.

With their listing under the Illinois Endangered Species Act in January 1994, both of Illinois' rattlers are now protected by law from killing, capturing, or possessing. But law enforcement personnel

Timber Rattlesnake, which occurs at scattered locations in rocky bluff habitats in Illinois. These snakes are most common in bluffs of the Mississippi River and across the Shawnee Hills of southern Illinois.

cannot be everywhere, so legal protection alone may not save this wild and fascinating part of the state's natural heritage.

Those of us with an interest in nature, who spend time in the field, are the most likely to encounter these creatures in their wild and remote haunts. We can help them by giving them a wide berth when encountered in the field and by reporting any illegal killing or taking of snakes to a Conservation Police Officer. Any sightings of live rattlers and other known active populations should be reported to the Department of Natural Resources' Natural Heritage Division. The advent of springtime wild turkey hunting over the past few decades has increased the number of people in remote forests when timber rattlers are emerging from hibernation. The cooperation of turkey hunters in protecting these fascinating creatures is also paramount if we are to save them from extirpation.

We have a long history of fear and persecution of rattlesnakes. Much of this was due to the potential danger they posed when, as farmers, we often lived side by side with them. Now we have become an urban society, and the rattlers have been pushed back to the wildest remnants of habitat. It is time that we grant them their space—their right to live on with nature's other creatures in wild Illinois. We enter their domain by choice, let's go with an understanding that they are peaceful and will issue a warning if we get too close.

April 1995

AUTHOR'S NOTE.—*Both of the state's rattlesnakes remain protected by the Illinois Endangered and Threatened Species Act, which has helped reduce the killing of these reptiles.*

~~~~~~~~~~~~~~~~~~~~~~~~~

Turtles

One of the sure signs of spring is a line of turtles sunning on a log. After a cold winter spent buried in the bottom of a stream or pond, these cold-blooded reptiles love to bask in the warming rays of the first sunny days of spring.

Turtles are the oldest living reptile group, having changed little since first appearing in the fossil record over 200 million years ago. Their long survival with little change is a testament to the success of their shell as a protective structure for a relatively slow-moving animal. In addition to their shell, their lack of teeth is also a distinctive feature of turtles. They have a beak, with sharp cutting edges, but no chewing teeth. The River Cooter is an exception to this general rule, having peg-like "teeth" inside of its mouth.

While everyone recognizes turtles as a group, few realize the diversity of turtle species found in Illinois, and even fewer can iden- tify the state's sixteen native kinds. Illinois' turtle fauna includes two softshell species, two snapping turtles, two mud turtles, two box turtles, the Common Musk Turtle, and seven others that fall into the general category of basking turtles. The baskers are flattened, aquatic, hard-shell turtles with names like Spotted Turtle, Blanding's Turtle, Painted Turtle, Slider, River Cooter, Map Turtle, and False Map Turtle. The two box turtles are dry land species, while the others spend most of their time in or near water.

Illinois turtles range in size from the little Spotted Turtle that reaches a shell length of four and a half inches to the huge Alligator

Snapping Turtle weighing up to 160 pounds in this state and reaching 220 pounds in the southern states. Illinois' turtles have some interesting behavior traits. The Alligator Snapping Turtle has a tongue that resembles a worm. It sits with its mouth open and wiggles its tongue to lure fish into range of its jaws. Illinois' two mud turtles emerge from hibernation in the spring and forage in shallow temporary ponds for a few months before laying eggs and then burying themselves in mud or sand for most of the summer. Together with the time they spend in hibernation, they spend most of their lives just sitting buried in the ground. The Common Musk Turtle has a unique defense of musk glands in its skin just below the shell that can emit a strong stinking odor when it is threatened.

The Smooth Softshell Turtle is a flattened species of creeks and rivers that buries itself in sand and gravel on the bottom with only its head exposed. It can lie hidden like this for hours as it waits for fish or other prey to come within catching range. It breathes through its skin at these times so it does not have to surface and expose its ambush.

Human use of Illinois turtles centers on keeping them as pets and using them as food. The land-dwelling box turtles are the most commonly kept pets. The Eastern Box Turtle is an animal of forests throughout the south half of the state, while the Ornate Box Turtle is a prairie animal. It is found in south-central and western Illinois and in sand areas in northern Illinois. The most important turtle for food is the Snapping Turtle. These large aquatic animals are listed as game species and yield meat that makes good soup and is also good fried.

Four turtles are listed as endangered or threatened species under the Illinois Endangered and Threatened Species Act and are protected against taking. Endangered Species are the Spotted Turtle, Illinois (Yellow) Mud Turtle, and River Cooter. The Alligator Snapping Turtle is listed as threatened. Of the nonprotected species, persons with a valid fishing license may take eight turtles per day per species. These turtles may be used for personal consumption or as pets, but may not be sold or traded. Taking from the wild for the commercial pet market was a threat until it became illegal.

Dr. Ed Moll of Eastern Illinois University is one of Illinois' leading turtle experts. He and his students are presently studying the endangered River Cooter along the lower Wabash River. I asked Dr. Moll just where the name "Cooter" comes from. He advises that "all turtles are called Cooters in the southeastern states where the river

Cooter is most abundant." Using money from the Wildlife Preservation Fund, Moll and his students have discovered new populations of the River Cooter and are studying the size and makeup of the populations. The Lee County Natural Area Guardians, an affiliate of the Lee County Soil and Water Conservation District, has used Wildlife Preservation Fund monies to support surveys for turtles in their county. Their search resulted in the discovery of two new populations of the endangered Illinois (Yellow) Mud Turtle.

This spring when you see turtles on a log or crossing the road, keep in mind that they are an ancient group of animals struggling to survive in a changing world. One way Illinois residents can help them is by donating to the Illinois Wildlife Preservation Fund when you file your Illinois state income tax return.

May 1996

AUTHOR'S NOTE.—*As of 2015, the Smooth Softshell, Blanding's, Spotted, Yellow (Illinois) Mud, River Cooter, and Alligator Snapping Turtles are currently listed as endangered in Illinois. The Ornate Box Turtle is listed as threatened. A recovery program is under way to increase the population of Alligator Snapping Turtles in Illinois.*

Freshwater Mussels

Have you seen a Purple Wartyback, Pink Mucket, or Monkeyface lately? How about an Elktoe, Deertoe, or Fawnsfoot? If you have, you have been spending time in or near the waters of Illinois, as these colorful names are attached to the state's freshwater shellfish, the mussels. On a worldwide basis, freshwater mussels are most abundant in eastern North America where some three hundred species are known. Seventy-eight species have been recorded in Illinois.

Mussels are known as bivalves, since adults have two shells hinged on the back that are capable of being closed for protection. A muscular foot pulls mussels slowly through stream- and lake-bottom sediments. Mussels are filter feeders. Holding their shells slightly open while partly buried in the bottom, they draw water through their bodies, filtering out and feeding on microscopic life known as plankton. This same water movement aerates their gills. Mussels have a unique reproductive system. The male releases its sperm into the water where it is taken in by the female as she circulates water through her body. Her fertilized eggs grow into larvae within specially adapted parts of her gills. At the appropriate stage of growth the larvae are expelled to attach to and parasitize fish. Although most mussels move only short distances as adults, they can move many miles as parasites on fish. After spending a few weeks as a cyst on the fish's gills, skin, or fins, the larva grows into a miniature mussel and drops off to begin life on the bottom of a stream or lake. Only a few species are known to skip the parasitic stage.

Their names give some hint of their diversity of appearance. The Washboard is large with a rough surface; the Spectaclecase resembles its name; the Pink Heelsplitter has a sharp "blade" on its back; and the Hickorynut is short and rounded. Some, such as the Floater, are named for other features. Under certain conditions, its large, thin shell can fill with gas and float.

Mussels have declined more at the hands of humans than perhaps any other animal group in Illinois. A status survey by Kevin Cummings of the Illinois Natural History Survey, and by others in other states, reveals that thirteen eastern American mussels have become extinct, including four native to Illinois. The Leafshell, Round Combshell, Tennessee Riffleshell, and Wabash Riffleshell have joined birds like the Passenger Pigeon and Carolina Parakeet as former members of Illinois' fauna that lost the struggle to survive human development of the state. In addition to these four extinct species, eleven others have been completely eliminated from Illinois; twenty-one of the state's surviving species are endangered; and four are threatened. Specific streams can be cited to demonstrate this decline. The Illinois River formerly supported forty-seven mussel species but now only has twenty-three. The Kaskaskia River has declined from thirty-nine species to twenty-four, and the Embarrass from forty-four to twenty-seven.

Most mussel decline is related to habitat destruction and pollution, especially siltation caused by plowing of the land. Silt or mud caused by soil erosion has buried many sand and gravel stream bottoms needed by mussels and indeed may have buried and killed mussels. Unlike clams, which have siphons that can extend up through sand and mud to bring in water for feeding and breathing, most mussels have to have part of their shell above the bottom to live. The mining of sand and gravel by dredges, the dredging of boat channels and harbors, and the impoundment of flowing streams by dams all have taken their toll. Many species require flowing water, so just think of how much mussel habitat was lost when Rend, Carlyle, and Shelbyville Lakes were formed.

Another impact of dams is the elimination of certain fish species needed for mussel reproduction. The Ebony Shell larva parasitizes only the Skipjack Herring. This migratory fish comes up the Mississippi River from the Gulf of Mexico each summer and has been eliminated from the upper Mississippi by navigation dams. Without its host fish, the Ebony Shell has stopped reproducing there and has essentially disappeared. An occasional living Ebony Shell is found in the Mississippi above Pool 25 as testimony to the longevity of mussels, which have been reported to reach fifty years of age.

As bad as the mussels have had it in the past, they are now faced with severe new challenges from exotic animals. The Eurasian Zebra Mussel was accidentally introduced into Lake Saint Clair at Detroit and has spread rapidly to Illinois and the Mississippi River basin. It kills native mussels by adhering to them with threads. The Zebras get inside the native mussel and prevent it from closing or adjusting its shell opening, which prevents it from feeding and breathing. Another threat is the Asiatic Black Carp, which is reported to have escaped from fish farms in Missouri and Arkansas this spring. These fish are capable of crushing and eating young mussels and aquatic snails. If they become established in Illinois they could greatly reduce native mussel populations. Efforts are under way to bring many of our native mussels into hatcheries and protected habitats to guard against a threatened mass extinction by the zebra mussel. The plight of our native mussels is a sad commentary on humanity's stewardship of the natural world.

June 1994

AUTHOR'S NOTE.—*As of 2015, the Black Carp has not become established, and the native mussels seem to be surviving impacts from the Zebra Mussel. The control of sewage by the Clean Water Act has improved water quality and enhanced mussel habitat, especially in the Illinois River. The Slippershell and Little Spectaclecase have improved their status from endangered to threatened. However, the Pink Mucket, Scaleshell, Northern Riffleshell, Elephant-ear, and Ebony Shell have been added to the endangered list, and the Purple Wartyback and Black Sandshell have been added to the threatened list.*

~~~~~~~~~~~~~~~~~~~~~~~~~~~~~~~~~~

Mussels That Fish

It is fishing time for a group of native Illinois mussels that depend on lures to attract fish as hosts for their parasitic young.
I was reminded of this in mid-July as I walked quietly along the
shore of the Embarrass River in eastern Illinois. A rapidly vibrating
white object just two feet from shore in six inches of water caught
my eye.

I knew that our group of mussels called pocketbooks have a lure
that they use to attract fish, but I assumed that this occurred in deep
water far from human eyes. As I eased closer to the object, I realized
that I was seeing a unique natural phenomenon for the first time. The
mussel was a Plain Pocketbook, found throughout Illinois. In order
to display its lure it was literally standing on its head, with its front
end sticking straight down into the river bottom.

The "lure" was two parallel flaps of white tissue extending just
over a half inch from the rear of the mussel. It had a black "eye" spot
at one end and a tail-like flap of tissue at the other. The whole lure
resembled an inch-and-a half-long minnow struggling to swim, as
the mussel vibrated it, with most of the movement in the tail. The
lure was being displayed to attract a fish that could serve as host
to the mussel's parasitic larvae called glochidia. Although visible
in detail only under a microscope, the tiny glochidia of most native mussels resemble miniscule butterflies in having two wing-like
valves connected with a hinge that allows them to clamp together.
To develop into an adult mussel they must clamp on the fins or gills
of a fish and absorb nourishment for two to three weeks. During
this parasite phase, they change into a small mussel that drops to
the stream bottom to begin growth into an adult. In addition to
providing nourishment for development, the parasitized fish gives
the little mussel a ride that distributes the mussel much farther than
it could go as an adult.

The glochidia of the lure-wielding pocketbook mussels are gill
parasites and need to get into the fish's mouth so they can grab
onto a gill as they are exhaled in the fish's breathing process. This
is where the lure comes into play. After a fish is attracted by the

lure, the mussel senses its presence and releases or exhales a cloud of larvae that get into the fish's mouth. Release of glochidia may be triggered by the shadow cast by the fish or perhaps by the fish striking at the lure. Since mussels have no eyes, just how they do this is a mystery.

With this in mind, I eased up close to the displaying pocketbook mussel and passed my hand over it, being careful not to touch it. It immediately stopped moving but resumed displaying about twenty seconds after my shadow was removed. I saw no evidence of glochidia being released. I then hit the displaying lure lightly with my finger and it stopped displaying, but I still saw no glochidia being released. Since the water was a little murky and the glochidia are so small, it is possible that releases were made that I could not see.

Three of Illinois' pocketbook mussels' relatives from the southeastern United States have taken the lure strategy even further and actually fish with a lure on a line. These species place all of their glochidia for a year in a single, elongate packet—shaped and colored like a minnow. This packet, called a superconglutinate by biologists, is attached at the head end to a transparent mucus strand that remains attached to the female mussel. She can let the strand or line out as far as eight feet. Since these mussels live in areas of relatively swift current, the lure swings and dances about at the end of the transparent line appearing like a live minnow. When a fish strikes or takes the lure, it breaks open the packet releasing the glochidia in its mouth. As these glochidia are flushed through the fish's gills, many attach to begin their parasitic stage. Other mussels place their glochidia in white conglutinates that resemble white meal worms, which are expelled on the stream or lake bottom and break apart when host fish try to eat them. The tiny Liliput Mussel, which is common in Illinois, extends two red, worm-like lures that it waves to attract a host fish. The Flat Floater, a common lake-inhabiting species in Illinois, extends a sheet of mucus containing glochidia into the water like a net. When a fish swims through the net, the glochidia clamp down on its fins or skin.

It is amazing that these intricate behaviors and life strategies have only been discovered and described in the last few years. One has to ponder what other wonders Mother Nature has hidden.

August 1996

Spiders

Everyone knows the eight-legged critters that we call spiders. They all have a poisonous bite, and we avoid them when we can. But did you know that spiders use hydraulics to walk, cannot eat solid food, and have no ears but communicate with each other by sound? Read on if you want to learn more about these interesting creatures.

Spiders are ancient animals appearing in the fossil record about 318 million years ago. These were primitive spiders similar to today's

Fishing Spider, one of Illinois' largest spiders, with a leg spread of about three inches. This ambush hunter is waiting for prey on a block of concrete at the edge of Mermet Lake in southern Illinois.

tarantulas. More modern types of spiders, including the web spinners, appeared about 200 million years ago. Spiders differ from insects by more than the number of their legs. Their body is made of just two segments rather than three as in insects. The head- and leg-bearing segments are fused into one body part called the cephalothorax. The eight legs are attached here, and the spider has up to eight eyes on its front end. Smaller appendages near the mouth called pedipalps bring food to the mouth and contain the poison fangs.

Behind the cephalothorax is the abdomen, which contains the lungs, stomach, reproductive organs, and spinnerets, which produce the silk or webbing that spiders are famous for. Depending on the species, as many as four different spinnerets produce up to six different types of silk or web material. All spiders produce at least one type of silk.

The two principal types of spiders are orb web spiders, which spin sticky webs to catch flying prey, and wolf spiders, which ambush or run down prey. The latter species include wolf spiders, trap door spiders, and tarantulas. Wolf spiders are common in Illinois and hunt along the ground or on trees in search of prey. Trap door spiders are present in Illinois but are seldom seen as they only come out at night. Tarantulas do not occur in Illinois but come surprisingly close to us with a good population in the Ozarks of southeast Missouri.

One little known fact about spiders is revealed by the way that the eyes of wolf spiders and trapdoor spiders reflect a light at night. Unlike mammals whose eyes reflect reddish light, a spider's eyes glow green. This is because spiders use copper as the element to carry oxygen in their blood, while mammals use iron. Iron is what makes our blood red and gives us red eyeshine.

Unlike insects that have a hard exterior skeleton that provides an anchor for muscles to extend and retract their legs, spiders have a relatively soft exterior that does not provide for good muscle attachment. Spiders do have muscles to retract their legs, but to extend them they use hydraulics. Their thorax contracts and blood pressure extends the legs, and then their leg muscles can retract them. While walking, blood is not circulated through the lungs, making it necessary to stop in order to breathe. Notice that a wolf spider hunting along the forest floor or crossing a road has to stop occasionally to literally catch its breath. Essentially all spiders are predators, with their principal prey and food being insects and other spiders. Spiders are only able to take in and digest liquid food; they prepare this food by injecting the prey they have killed or captured with liquefying digestive enzymes. After the enzymes have done their work, the spider ingests the liquid food by sucking it from the prey.

Most spiders are silent, but some, especially the wolf spiders, make calls by stridulating or rubbing legs or parts of the body together. Spiders have no ears, but feel the vibrations caused by sound waves. My wife, Martha, has very acute hearing; while sitting in the woods one day, she heard faint sounds coming from the forest floor. She eventually spotted a wolf spider that would stop and make the sound by rubbing its pedipalps together. Later, while fishing in an oxbow lake along the Ohio River in Massac County, I heard loud clicking sounds coming from a cypress tree growing out in the lake. I pulled my boat right next to the tree but could not see what was making the sound. Finally I determined it was coming from beneath a loose piece of bark. When I tapped on the bark, a wolf spider popped out and ran up the tree. It appeared to be using the bark as a resonating chamber as well as an area to hide. The call made by these spiders is so loud that it can be heard from eighty yards away. Loon Lake, opposite Paducah, Kentucky, is the best place I know to hear these "clicking" spiders. In addition to Massac County, I have also heard them at Horseshoe Lake near Cairo, Illinois. When in their habitat, I can just make a clicking sound with my mouth, and often a spider will answer me. I can then click back and forth with the spider. Just imagine, communicating with a spider! I have corresponded with several spider experts, and no one seems to know about this species.

Many insects have wings for flying, but not spiders. The small young of many spiders fly by ascending to the top of a prominence on a day with a good breeze. They point the end of their abdomen to the sky and send out a strand of silk until it is long enough for the wind to catch it and carry them away. On days when weather conditions are right, the air can be filled with the gossamer or silk of flying spiders. Spiders offer many unexpected opportunities for nature watching.

March 2015

Dragonflies

Dragonflies (called snake doctors when I was young) are one of the first groups of flying insects to appear on earth. Their fossils are found within the coal age deposits from 300 million years ago, long before the age of dinosaurs. When Illinois' swamps were forming the coal beds we mine today, earth's atmosphere contained 35 percent oxygen, compared to the 21 percent we have today. This oxygen allowed insects to grow much larger than they do now, with one fossil dragonfly having a wingspan of twenty-nine inches! Typical specimens in Illinois today have a wingspan of about four inches and a maximum length of three and a half inches. Fossils show that the Gray Petaltail dragonfly now alive in Illinois was living among the dinosaurs 150 million years ago. It is a tame species, which doubtless landed on dinosaurs that entered its seep-spring habitat—just as it will land on you if you do the same!

Gray Petaltail dragonfly, a "living fossil" descended from an ancestor that once lived side by side with dinosaurs. These dragonflies lay eggs in forested seeps where their larvae forage in moist soil rather than in water like most dragonflies.

Dragonflies have two pairs of horizontally held wings that operate independently of each other. With wings beating as many as thirty-five times per second, they can hover and can accelerate to about thirty-five miles per hour in a few seconds. They have large compound eyes, with the more advanced species having the eyes meeting on the top of the head. More primitive species like the petaltails and clubtails have the eyes separated.

Both adult dragonflies and their larvae are predators, eating mostly insects, but their aquatic larvae also eat small tadpoles and fishes. Many adults feed on small insects, such as mosquitoes and midges, which they take on the wing, but others take larger prey, such as butterflies and even other dragonflies. Instead of cruising for prey, some, like the clubtails, are ambush hunters that sit near the ground and dart up to take insects flying overhead. The Dragonhunter is a large clubtail that hunts only other dragonflies.

We see dragonflies near water because their larvae live in water for up to three or four years as they grow big enough to emerge from it and transform into adults. The dragonflies we see at water are mostly laying eggs or mating. Typical adults live for seven to eight weeks and during that short life feed on insect prey, mate, and deposit eggs in water, damp soil, or a place where water will collect in springtime. Dragonflies emerge and fly at different seasons. A few are early spring and late fall fliers, with the great majority flying in summer. Common Baskettail and Springtime Darner are spring fliers; most of the skimmers, clubtails, and pennants fly in summer; and meadowhawks fly in the fall.

Illinois has about ninety species of dragonflies that offer a wide variety of sizes, colors, and behaviors. The large groups are skimmers, clubtails, darners, pennants, and meadowhawks. In addition we have some small but interesting groups like petaltails, dashers, emeralds, gliders, and shadowdragons. Let's take a look at some of these. Skimmers are the "typical" dragonflies that we see most often flying and perched near water. They perch with their bodies horizontal and with their mostly clear wings held rigid. Pennants perch with their bodies horizontal but with their wings held up where they flutter in the wind. Their wings often have black and colored spots on them. Darners are large and rarely land where you can see them. When landed they hang vertically. Meadowhawks often land and feed away from water and feed near the ground. They include most of our red-colored species. Each group has its own characteristics.

Some dragonflies are migratory, and others wander widely and are widespread in the world. The migratory species include one that is both. The Wandering Glider is the most widespread dragonfly in the world and occurs on all continents except Europe and Antarctica. They fly at sea both day and night by gliding with their wide wings. They are reported to have flown up to ships at sea a thousand miles or more from the nearest land. They arrive in Illinois from the south or west in late July and deposit eggs in small temporary pools. Their larvae must transform in a month or so, when new adults emerge and migrate to the south. They are golden in color and perch by hanging vertically. The Wandering Glider's relative, the Spotwing Glider, also lives in Illinois and ranges down to the Amazon basin of South America. I once photographed a specimen of it on the Galapagos Islands six hundred miles west of South America.

The shadowdragons have unique behavior in their habit of flying and feeding only for the last half hour of daylight in the evening and the first half hour of daylight at dawn. They skim along the surface of the water feeding on insects that hatch from the water's surface at these times. The males then search for females and fly to shoreline trees for mating. After mating they spend the day or night on the tree. Two of Illinois' three species live in large rivers, while the third is a creek species. They are difficult to study and photograph because of their unique behavior. I have paddled out into the Ohio River after sundown with net and camera trying to catch or photograph one on the wing. Blurred pictures are all I managed to get. Then one day I spotted a Smoky Shadowdragon spending the day on the foundation of my home near the Ohio River and got its photo.

Photographing dragonflies is easy for skimmers and others that perch along the shore of ponds and streams. However, darners, cruisers, and others that seldom land in the open must be caught in an insect net and then placed in a cooler or brought back to the refrigerator until they are too cold to fly. You can then pose them and take their picture. As they warm up they vibrate their wings to warm up flight muscles and soon fly away.

February 2015

FURTHER READING.—Dragonflies of Indiana, *James R. Curry, 2001, Indiana Academy of Science.*

CHAPTER 7

PLANTS OF ILLINOIS

The essays in this chapter describe interesting facts about Illinois plants. Fall color, edible plants, and poisonous plants are covered, along with plant groups, such as prairie grass, vines, and evergreens. Wildflowers such as wild orchids, violets, roses, and trilliums are also discussed.

~~~~~~~~~~~~~

Our Autumn Color Show

Illinois lies within North America's eastern deciduous forest region and shares in its rich heritage of fall foliage coloration. Fall leaf coloration is part of the leaf-shedding process wherein deciduous woody plants drop their leaves that would not survive the freezing temperatures of winter. We mostly think of trees as changing color, but many shrubs and vines also change color and are among our most colorful plants.

As cool temperatures and shorter days herald the coming winter, plants begin moving sap to their roots to avoid freezing damage to their stems. The veins that carry sugars made in the leaves to other parts of the plant are narrowed at this time in preparation for leaf fall. Green and yellow pigments are always present in the leaves, but the green of chlorophyll covers the yellow during the active growing season of summer. As the days shorten, green chlorophyll that dies is not replaced, and the yellows gradually become visible. Sugars produced in the leaves, which normally flow out to nourish the plant, are restricted in movement by the narrowing veins and are held in the leaves. Here they convert to red and orange pigments that join the yellow to color the leaves until freezing kills them.

Hikers on the hundred-foot-high sandstone cliffs that tower above the creek at Lusk Creek Canyon Nature Preserve in Pope County. The yellow leaves of the Tulip Tree in front of the hikers contrast with the red leaves of the Scarlet Oak trees around them.

The yellows appear annually, but the reds, oranges, and purples are dependent on the weather to some extent. Adequate moisture during the growing season assures abundant sugar production, and bright sunny fall days with cool but not freezing nights are needed to convert some of this sugar to colorful pigment. Thus, color intensity in a given area will depend on weather throughout the summer as well as the fall. Severe drought and early freezes are major culprits in dimming Mother Nature's show. Early-to- mid-October is usually best for northern and central Illinois color, with southern Illinois usually hitting its peak the third weekend of the month.

Predominant trees turning yellow in Illinois are ash, hickory, aspen, Tulip Tree, and some Sugar Maples. Leaves of the native Bittersweet vine also turn yellow. Trees with leaves turning orange-red to orange include Sugar Maple and Sassafras. Many Sugar Maples take on the orange-red appearance but with some yellow leaves and some pure red leaves also present. It is probably our most brightly colored, widespread native tree.

Trees with red leaves include Red Maple, Scarlet Oak (and a few other oaks), Black Gum, Sweetgum, and Flowering Dogwood. Sweetgum is native in Illinois only in southern Illinois and the Wabash River valley but is planted as an ornamental tree throughout the state. Sweetgum is one of our most colorful trees with some leaves turning red, while others on the same tree turn purple or yellow or even remain green. Black Gum, on the other hand, always turns bright red. Some of our most interesting and attractive red foliage comes from shrubs and vines. Common and widespread shrubs like Smooth Sumac, Winged Sumac, and Aromatic Sumac all turn bright red. They are especially visible because they like to grow on road banks where their colorful dark red seeds are also attractive. The Virginia Creeper vine is common throughout Illinois and turns dark red in early autumn. This member of the grape family has the habit of clothing old dead trees and fence posts, which make them appear to be painted red. If you see a red-appearing tree trunk or fence post, you can be certain that closer inspection will reveal the five-leaflet leaves of Virginia Creeper.

Take the time this fall to enjoy the color and to remember the natural functions involved with its production. Get out the camera for some of the most spectacular scenery shots of the year and take along a field guide to identify as many colorful species as you can.

October 1996

~~~~~~~~~~~~~~~~

Plant Defenses

Plants are nature's producers. They use sunlight, air, and water to produce sugar, starches, and cellulose; food for the rest of us. Just about everything alive except plants consumes plants or something else that has consumed plants. With so many creatures just waiting to eat them, plants would not last long if they were defenseless. Given the handicap of being rooted and immobile, plants do a remarkable job of defending themselves. A wide variety of plant defenses are found in Illinois.

Thorns and spines are obvious physical defenses on many of our plants. They make it very hard for a grazing or browsing animal seeking an easy meal. Woody plants like trees and shrubs are naturally protected against being eaten by many animals because their tough woody tissue is coarse and hard to digest compared to tender herbs and leaves. Wood also enables many plants to raise their leaves beyond the reach of earthbound grazing animals.

Another physical protection plants use in Illinois is latex. By having large quantities of rubber in their abundant sap, plants like the milkweeds and spurges "gum up" the mouth parts of many of the caterpillars that might otherwise eat them. Several native Illinois plants of the pea family defend themselves by their behavior! The Leafy Prairie Clover has compound leaves with numerous leaflets that it folds up at night. It is a very palatable species, especially relished by rabbits. Just as the rabbits come out in the evening it folds up its leaves and is much less visible. Other peas such as the Partridge Pea also fold their leaves after several bumps or pulls as would happen if an animal was eating them.

Aside from all of the physical and behavioral protections, however, chemical protections are the most widespread. They take the form of poisons, taste-altering compounds, numbing chemicals, stinging compounds, skin irritants, and eye irritants. Dr. David Siegler of the University of Illinois, an expert on the defensive chemicals of plants, considers tannin to be one of the most ancient and widespread chemical protectors. Tannin in the form of tannic acid makes leaves and other plant parts bitter to the taste. "The reasons for its effectiveness,

Leafy Prairie Clover, which protects itself from nocturnal grazing animals like rabbits by folding its leaflets into a thin stalk at dusk.

other than its bitter taste, continue to elude us," he says. Theories that tannin inhibits digestion and utilization of plants by animals have recently been proven false. The fact that squirrels love those bitter, tannin-containing acorns that people cannot tolerate points up one common fact about plant defenses. In virtually every case, there are some animals that develop a tolerance for them. Terpenes in pine trees serve several functions. Volatile terpenes such as turpentine protect against feeding animals while the thick terpene we call rosin also seals wounds against fungal spores and diseases. Terpenes are not confined to pines. Rhododendrons and other plants also have powerful terpenes in their tissues.

The root of Jack-in-the-pulpit is so hot to the taste it is rarely eaten by anything. The "heat" in hot peppers is also a repellent to would-be eaters (except Mexican food fans). Our common little tree called Prickly Ash has a second name—Toothache Tree. This latter name is derived from the natural novocaine in its bark. Any deer or other animal that browses it gets a numb mouth and does not taste much for a while. Early settlers used its bark and roots to treat toothache. Pale Coneflower (Echinacea) contains similar chemicals that numb the pain of toothache. Some chemical repellents do not require eating to be effective. Hairs filled with irritating chemicals protect the Stinging Nettle plant. The hairs inject their poison into animals that brush up against them, causing severe irritation. The repellent effect of Poison Ivy is well known as is the strong odor and eye irritation of wild onion.

The most widespread of Illinois' native plant poisons is probably cyanide. It is effective in prohibiting feeding on plants by a wide range of animals. Dr. John Ebinger of Eastern Illinois University has screened many Illinois plants for this chemical. He thinks that at least three hundred kinds of plants in the state, and probably many more, use this poison to protect their leaves from being eaten. Wild Black Cherry is a common native tree with high levels of cyanide in its leaves. Many of us have noticed black cherry trees with nearly all their leaves eaten off by tent caterpillars. These caterpillars are yet another example of how animals have developed tolerance of the strongest of poisons when there is a meal to be gained.

Many toxic alkaloid chemicals are produced by wild flowering plants, such as Indian Tobacco. When eaten by mammals, including humans, overdoses can cause death. Alkaloids are probably the largest and most diverse group of defensive chemicals, but remain among the least known. One plant defensive chemical many of us ingest daily in our coffee or cola is caffeine. Dr. Siegler says that plants apparently use this chemical as a defense of their territory against other plants. Caffeine leaches into the soil from the plant or its leaves that have fallen to the ground. Once in the soil, it inhibits the growth of other plants that could compete with the defending plant for space, nutrients, and moisture.

The next time you hear about the vast array of chemicals and potential medicines in the plants of the tropical rainforest, just remember that Illinois' plants have a rich chemical heritage of their own.

April 1993

Vines

Vines, or lianas as they are called in the tropics, comprise an interesting part of our native flora. Climbing on other plants and just about any other natural support, they forego the need of providing their own support tissues by grasping others for this purpose.

Vines climb by three main means—twining, tendrils, and aerial roots. Twiners simply wrap themselves around a stem or other round object as the growing tip grows upward. Morning glories, Bittersweet, and Japanese Honeysuckle are prominent twiners. Tendrils are special branches believed to be developed from modified leaves that are adapted to twining around support while the whole vine does not. Grapes and greenbriers are among the many vines that climb by tendrils. Vines that climb by sending out many short rootlets or aerial roots that attach the vine to a tree, rock, or building are creepers. Prominent in this group are Virginia Creeper, Trumpet Creeper, and Poison Ivy.

Vines are most common in the tropics and decline or disappear in colder climates. Their distribution in Illinois follows this trend, with vines being more common in southern Illinois than northern Illinois. The moonseed family exhibits this trend within its three Illinois species, all of which are vines. Cupseed is found only at the southern tip of the state; Carolina Snailseed is found in the southern fourth of the state; and only the Moonseed is found throughout Illinois.

Vines are the only growth form in some Illinois plant families such as the grapes and morning glories. But other plant families, such as the pea family, have trees, shrubs, and herbs as well as vines. Illinois even has one vine (Climbing Hempweed) in the sunflower family. In the eastern states, there is also a fern vine. One of Illinois' most peculiar group of vines is dodder, a parasitic relative of the morning glories. Its orange-colored leafless mats of stems twine and attach themselves by their parasitic connections to a variety of herbaceous host plants. In late summer they are conspicuous on low vegetation.

To my knowledge, no one has ever added up the total number of wild vines in Illinois, but we can do that here for some of the principal vining families. There are ten grapes and their relatives, nine smilaxes or greenbriers, six native morning glories, ten dodders, and five wild clematises. Perhaps the most important vine to Illinoisans is Poison Ivy. Its potential to harm us is significant since 80 percent of all people have an allergic reaction to its touch. It is probably the most common and abundant vine in the state, and everyone venturing outdoors should learn to recognize it. Its three pointed leaflets on stems with short aerial rootlets are diagnostic. Its stems can be creeping and attached to trees or can be free-standing shrub-height stems.

There are two categories when we consider which of the native vines of Illinois is most beautiful—those with beautiful foliage and those with beautiful flowers. I feel there is no competition for Virginia Creeper in the foliage division. Its interesting leaves with five finger-like leaflets are beautiful in themselves. Add to this the creeping stems, which allow them to coat tree trunks and walls with a solid ivy-like covering, and they are indeed a source of natural beauty. If this were not enough, the leaves turn a bright red in the fall. If you see a solid red fence post, snag, or telephone pole this fall, it probably has a coating of Virginia creeper.

There is much more competition for most beautiful flowering vine. If showy flowers, abundance, and widespread distribution are considered, I think the Trumpet Creeper wins hands down. Its abundant orange-red flowers trumpet from fence posts and road banks as well as forests and fields. It flowers throughout the heat of summer and attracts an abundance of hummingbirds as well. The white-flowered blankets of the Virgin's Bower Clematis have to come in a close second for a statewide flowering vine.

But if you are looking for flowering beauty in vines of restricted range in Illinois, the Mountain Clematis of northwestern Illinois and Wild Wisteria of southern Illinois are near the top. Two of the most unusual wildflowers of Illinois are also vines. The Dutchman's Pipe has tubular flowers with a downward bend resembling a pipe, and the Large Purple Passion Flower has two-inch-diameter lilac blossoms with a colored, fringed structure in the center. Both are found primarily in the southern third of Illinois.

Of course, if we ask our wildlife what their favorite native vine is, I predict the fox, Raccoon, Opossum, and a myriad of songbirds would vote for wild grapes. They probably provide more wildlife food than any other vine.

August 1996

Evergreens

Winter is the time of year when a splash of green on the landscape catches the eye. In sharp contrast with the gray of Illinois' deciduous woods and the brown of the state's dormant prairie, the occasional native evergreen plant adds color and gives promise of the green spring to come. While all mosses and liverworts are evergreen, as are occasional violets and grass and herb leaves, our subjects in this essay are Illinois' native evergreen trees, shrubs, and woody vines.

There is considerable difference in native evergreens between northern and southern Illinois. The northern part of the state has more evergreen conifer trees and shrubs, while southern Illinois has fewer pines and some broad-leaved evergreens that are lacking in the north. Even Illinois' most common evergreen tree, the Eastern Red Cedar, comes in northern and southern varieties. The Red Cedar is commonly found along bluffs, on roadsides, and in idle fields throughout the state. However, careful examination discloses different growth forms in our northern and southern plants. In the north half of the state it grows with a strong central trunk with branches more or less at right angles to the trunk. In the southern half of Illinois it is usually multiple-trunked with ascending branches. Northern Red Cedars shed snow well and are not deformed by snowfall, while the southern form often splits apart under a heavy load of snow.

Other native evergreen trees in northern Illinois are White Pine, Red Pine, Jack Pine, and Arbor Vitae. White Pine is widespread across the region in bedrock outcrop areas, while Arbor Vitae is restricted to northeastern Illinois, especially the Fox River valley and the Illinois River bluffs at Starved Rock State Park. Red Pine is found only at one spot on the Fox River bluffs, and native Jack Pine survives only on the dunes along Lake Michigan in Illinois Beach State Park. Both of these pines have also been used for reforestation in northern Illinois. The principal evergreen shrubs of northern Illinois are Canada Yew, Ground Juniper, and Trailing Juniper. The best place to see the latter two are on sand dunes along Lake Michigan at Illinois Beach State Park, while the yew is most easily seen in northwestern Illinois on bluffs at Apple River Canyon State Park and White Pines Forest State Park.

Southern Illinois' only native pine is the Shortleaf Pine. In addition to its two native stands, it has been widely planted for reforestation in the region. The best place to view this tree in its native habitat is the Pine Hills Ecological area of the Shawnee National Forest in northwestern Union County. The common broad-leaved evergreens of southern Illinois are five vines and one parasitic shrub. Four of the vines are greenbriers—thorny vines with toothless, oval-to-elongate leaves, which grow mostly in upland forests and fields. The other is Cross Vine, a creeping vine related to Trumpet Creeper, which is at home in upland and lowland habitats. Cross Vine has opposite deep-green-to-purplish evergreen leaves that are narrow and with "ears" or backward projections at their base. A cut stem reveals a cross in its center, which gives the plant its name. The evergreen parasite is the shrub Mistletoe. It grows on the limbs of maple, elm, and other trees, mostly those growing near lakes and rivers. It is occasionally found on upland Black Gum trees as well. It can be killed by extreme cold, but usually sprouts back the next spring. Mistletoe is collected in southern Illinois for Christmas decorations.

American Holly, is a rare native evergreen tree in southern Illinois, which has begun spreading in recent years. I have found it at Fort Massac State Park, and there are recent reports of it from the Cache River Area and Shawnee National Forest. In the future, this beautiful, native evergreen may become common in forests at the southern tip of the state.

Another plant on the southern evergreen list is Giant Cane. This woody grass forms clones or "cane breaks" mainly in lowland forest and open lowlands. It is evergreen through most winters, but can be killed back to the ground by temperatures of about twenty degrees below zero. The evergreen nature of this highly palatable forage plant made it extremely valuable to the early European settlers of southern Illinois. It provided cattle with grazing through the winter without the need to make and store hay. The area covered by cane brakes is greatly reduced in southern Illinois at present.

Native evergreen plants are relatively few in Illinois, but their presence adds interest and a little color to an otherwise drab winter landscape.

January 16, 1996

AUTHOR'S NOTE.—*American Holly has continued to increase in southern Illinois forests but is still an uncommon tree.*

~~~~~~

Edible Wild Plants

In Illinois, Mother Nature provides many edible wild plants. Wild greens predominate in the spring, with berries in summer, but with autumn providing the biggest harvest of all. As the days shorten and cool weather approaches, tree fruits ripen, nuts begin falling, and tuber-bearing herbs complete formation of their underground morsels.

King of the wild fruits ripening in the fall is the Persimmon. They are found throughout the southern half of the state and extend northward to Peoria in the Illinois River valley. The checkered bark of this small tree is distinctive. After complete ripening, some say after the first frost, persimmons are delicious right off the tree or prepared in sweet breads, preserves, or pies. This is one fruit that everyone should try.

Another widespread fall-ripening tree fruit is the Paw Paw. They are found throughout Illinois except for the row of counties bordering Wisconsin. These small, large-leaved trees grow in rich woods in ravine bottoms and lowlands, where their smooth gray bark is distinctive. They grow in groves—thus the term Paw Paw patch. The fruits or Paw Paws are about the diameter of a banana but only half the length and blunt on both ends. Their flesh is very sweet and sweetly aromatic. They fall to the ground when ripe. Paw Paws are quickly eaten by wildlife on the ground so you have to be fast and first to get naturally ripened fruit. Try shaking some down or even picking green fruits and ripening them at home. It is best to ripen them outdoors, as the sweet odor can smell up the house. Most people eat them fresh, but they can be used in cooking and puddings.

The most prized of our wild nut trees is the Pecan, a native, thin-shelled hickory of riverside bottomlands. It is common along larger rivers like the Wabash, Ohio, Mississippi, and Illinois and even along the lower reaches of smaller rivers like the Kaskaskia. Pecan does not occur naturally in the eastern states and was first discovered by botanists when they reached Illinois. It was given the scientific name *Carya illinoensis*, Latin for hickory of Illinois, in honor of the state. Many other hickories are also choice and edible, particularly the Shag Bark and King Nut, both of which have very shaggy barks. Some of the tight or smooth-barked hickories have bitter nuts, so when collecting them, sample a few before collecting in quantity. Black Walnut and Hazelnut are also good eating. The latter is our only important nut from a shrub rather than a tree. It often grows on road banks, where you have to be early to beat the squirrels and birds. All of these wild nuts are good in candies, frostings, baking, and just for nibbling. Pecan pie is my favorite.

Wild tubers are perhaps the least known and least used of our wild edibles. There are many that can be eaten, but only two of the best, Groundnut and Jerusalem Artichoke, are discussed here. Groundnut is a vine in the pea family. It is our only vine with an elongate compound leaf with five leaflets. The leaf with five (sometimes seven) leaflets, together with its preference for low, moist ground help to locate and identify it. It is common throughout Illinois. Its tubers occur along roots just below the soil surface like beads on a string. Some reach the size of a hen's egg, but most are smaller. Many consider them superior to potatoes, which they resemble in appearance and taste. They can be boiled or roasted and should be eaten hot, as they harden on cooling.

The Jerusalem Artichoke is neither an Artichoke nor associated with the holy city. It got this name by a variety of circumstances in Europe after being sent back by early American explorers and becoming a popular food plant in the Mediterranean region. It is actually a native perennial sunflower that is common in moist soil throughout Illinois. Look for it in low open areas along streams and at the edge of bottomland fields. Its rough, hairy stems commonly reach six to eight feet in height. The leaves are opposite on the lower part of the stem but usually become alternate in the upper part. While narrower than cultivated sunflower leaves, they are broader than other wild perennial sunflowers in the state. Their flowers at the top of the plant are yellow and about two to three inches in diameter with a yellow center. Their sizable tubers are formed at the end of short roots at the end of summer. They are best if dug after the first frosts of fall. Cook them by covering with water and simmering them until tender. They can then be peeled, buttered, and salted to taste. They are even said to be good raw.

If this has piqued your interest, take the time this fall for an outing to collect and sample some of nature's bounty. It is there for the taking.

October 1994

~~~~~~

Chicory

One of the most commonly seen wild plants in Illinois is Chicory, an escaped garden plant from Europe. It is seen so often because it chooses to live in that narrow strip of sterile soil at the edge of the pavement of many highways where it can scarcely be missed by the motorist. Its spikes of large bright blue flowers border many of our paved roads from July until frost, living where few other plants can eke out a living. White-flowered plants are occasionally seen and rarely pink-flowered forms.

Chicory is a close relative of the Dandelion, and, except for color, the flowers are similar in size and structure. But the whole plant has an altogether different appearance, with its flowers scattered along an upright stem that reaches three to four feet in height, whereas Dandelion flower stalks arise from the ground. Chicory leaves are sparse on the stem but a large cluster of leaves occurs at the base of the stem in spring. It is widely cultivated in Europe as a green, as it is closely related to lettuce and endive. Most Chicory cultivation is in Belgium. Although a good wild salad plant and green, few Illinoisans use it. Like Dandelion, it has a little stronger taste than lettuce. If cooked as a green, this strong taste can be eliminated by thorough cooking and pouring off the water. The best leaves are obtained early in the spring, because the undesirable taste gets stronger the older the leaves get. By early summer the basal leaves die and disappear completely.

The plant grows from a stout tap root that penetrates deep into the soil. This root is the source of the Chicory used to flavor coffee or even as a substitute for coffee. The roots are dug, scrubbed, and roasted in an oven until dried. Some manuals say that the oven door should be left open during the roasting process. The roasted root is ground to a consistency similar to ground coffee beans and is simply added to the coffee grounds before perking. One can drink straight Chicory or any combination of Chicory and coffee depending on taste preference.

Chicory is most often used in the south, a practice that began during the Civil War. Imported commodities like coffee were hard to get during the war, so the government promoted the use of Chicory as a substitute. The Civil War developed a following that persists to the present day, and Chicory-flavored coffee is still readily available in many parts of the South.

Plant physiologist Dr. Marian Smith and her students at Southern Illinois University at Edwardsville have undertaken studies of this unique member of Illinois' wild flora to learn why it likes the roadside when few other plants can survive there. They found that it is highly drought tolerant and needs high levels of bright sunlight to thrive. It is also a poor competitor with other plants in moist fertile habitats. These characteristics make it obvious why they succeed in the roadside habitat that features seasonal drought, few competitors, and bright-light conditions. Drought adaptations are found in its leaves, stems, and roots. Leaves are great transpirers or losers of moisture, so chicory has an abundance of basal leaves early in the season when moisture is abundant, but they die as the hot, dry days of summer begin. The few small and scattered stem leaves remaining in summer transpire little moisture as chlorophyll in the stem takes over most photosynthesis. Using stems rather than leaves to produce food from light is a fairly common adaptation for arid climate plants like Skeleton Weed, but is somewhat unexpected in a European plant like Chicory. Even more unexpected was their discovery that its stem has an endodermis, an unusual internal structure for plants of its type that restricts moisture loss from the stem. The thick taproot stores moisture early in the season to support growth and life processes during the hot, dry summer. It also reaches deep for moisture when the upper soil dries out.

Taken together, these drought adaptations make the edge of a slab of pavement in sterile graded soil a fine home for this immigrant. Look for its bright blue flowers as you drive the highway this fall. If you are curious about how chicoried coffee tastes, dig some roots this autumn or winter and roast them. They are best if dug after the first frost but before spring growth begins. I plan to give them a try.

September 1994

~~~~~~~~~~~~~~~~~~

Plants Poison to Touch

Before you venture outdoors this summer, be sure you know which plants are safe to touch. There are only a few that can hurt you, but a surprising number of people still do not recognize them. I am not talking about injurious plants that bear thorns that everyone can see and avoid, but rather plants that cause skin irritation or dermatitis if you touch them. We will not cover plants that are poison to eat in this essay.

There are two kinds of dermatitis plants—those that cause a delayed rash, such as Poison Ivy, and the irritant dermatitis plants that let you know on contact to "back off." Primary in the latter group are the nettles, which impart toxic compounds into the skin that directly damage skin cells or stimulate immune system (allergic) responses, which cause the body to damage its own skin. The leading irritant dermatitis plants in Illinois are the stinging nettles. The alternate-leaved Wood Nettle is a two-to-three-foot-tall perennial herb that is abundant in lowland woods statewide. The less common opposite-leaved Stinging Nettle is taller and is found along streams in the northern two-thirds of the state. Both have stinging hairs on their stems and leaves that inject histamine-like substances on contact that cause burning and itching. The hairs can penetrate clothing, even heavy denim, so avoid them by staying on trails during the summer and fall months. They are not a hazard in early spring as they reach stinging size only in late spring.

There are two kinds of the delayed reaction plants, those that cause photo dermatitis and require light to activate the response and contact dermatitis, which only requires time. The light-triggered plants act by increasing the skin's sensitivity to light, resulting in sunburn-like patches or allergic responses. Contact dermatitis usually acts by leaving antigens on the skin, which are attacked by the body causing an itchy rash. The delay in these is caused by the time it takes the body to prepare the antibodies. The irritating substances are usually in the sap or in oils on the surface of the stems and leaves. This group is the most important for those venturing outdoors to learn, as one can literally roll in these toxic plants without detecting their harmfulness until days later when the response occurs.

Photo dermatitis is caused by chemicals that lack allergic potential or toxicity until activated by ultraviolet light in sunlight. Probably the most common and dangerous photo dermatitis plant in Illinois is Parsnip. It is a member of the carrot family and has leaves dissected into many segments and sports a flat-topped group of small yellow flowers that bloom in spring. It is common throughout the state in fields, prairie, and even lawns where sunlight is high. Its active irritant is in the juice, so just touching the plant will not cause problems. But since it is often a troublesome weed, it imparts its poison to anyone who pulls or breaks it with bare hands and arms. Other photo dermatitis plants in the wild in Illinois are Cow Parsnip (*Heracleum*) and some St. John's worts, mustards (*Brassica*), goosefoots, and buttercups.

Contact dermatitis not requiring light activation is more common, with at least seventeen plants growing in the wild in Illinois having that potential. This list does not include those with allergy-stimulating pollen. Most of these, such as Pennyroyal and Spearmint, are so small and locally distributed that they are not a real threat to most people. On the other hand, Poison Ivy is so common and widespread that it poses a threat to almost everyone out-of-doors, even those in their own backyards! Poison Sumac is a rare northern wetland plant in Illinois, and we have no Poison Oak.

Poison ivy is easy to identify because of its leaves formed of three pointed leaflets. Each leaflet is usually wavy-margined, but lacks sharp teeth. Its greenish flower clusters produce white berries in late summer. The stem or vine has lots of short "rootlets" all along it, which it uses to attach tightly to trees and other objects it climbs. However, not all poison ivy plants climb. They can also grow as low shrubs with no support save their own stems. Such shrubs are commonly knee-high and often waist-high or higher. Poison Ivy is common in all types of woods from dry uplands to wet bottomlands where it reaches its largest size. It also grows in open sunny sites like fences and other bird perches. Its white berries are choice wildlife food, which enables its seeds to be spread widely by birds. I recently found Poison Ivy coming up in my lawn.

About 80 percent of us are vulnerable to Poison Ivy's toxin, which is contained in oils on its stems and leaves. This oil has antigens that stimulate the immune system of vulnerable people to attack and kill the affected tissue. There is a twelve-to-twenty-four- hour delay between exposure and onset of symptoms.

Learning to recognize the few plants that should be avoided is a small task considering the benefit. Learn to recognize them whether you venture afield or not, as they often grow in urban yards and parks as well as wildlands.

August 1994

~~~~~~~~~~~~~~~~~~~~~~~~~~~~~~~~~~~~

Prairie Grasses

The hot "dog days" of August are as timely as it ever gets for a discussion of Illinois' prairie grasses or "warm-season grasses" as they are also known. Illinois' original prairie or native grassland was dominated by grasses that spurt into growth during the hottest and driest days of summer. Big and Little Bluestem, Indian Grass, Switchgrass, and Cordgrass all thrive in the heat, and thus are called our native "warm-season" grasses. When domesticated grasses, such as your Kentucky Bluegrass lawn or that pasture or hayfield of Timothy or Orchard Grass, are wilting from moisture stress, these wild natives are growing their fastest. This characteristic not only makes them ideally suited to growing in our prairies, but gives them special value to agriculture as well.

Where did these grasses come from? We think North American grasslands got their start about six million years ago as the climate cooled and moisture from the Pacific was blocked by the rise of the Rocky Mountain ranges. Paleoecologist Dan Axelrod points out that this is the time that grazing or grass-eating animals increased on the central plains, and there was a great increase in species of grass. These first grasslands were probably dominated by cool-season grasses related to present-day Needle Grass and Porcupine Grass. Cool-season grasses seem to have dominated the North American prairie right up to the start of the ice age about two million years ago. Grasslands as we now know them were largely absent from the central plains during the ice age.

After the ice age ended some ten thousand years ago, a tallgrass prairie established itself on the eastern plains, including Illinois. This historic Illinois prairie was dominated by warm-season grasses that moved out into the prairie from forested eastern and southeastern North America. These grasses became vigorous and able to dominate other grasses, at least in part through a genetic process that plants possess allowing them to have more than the normal two sets of chromosomes. Such plants are called polyploids. Polyploidy gives these grasses the increased size and vigor of hybrids without being sterile like true hybrids. So the hybrid vigor that makes our corn crop one of the largest in the world was at work on our prairies long ago.

Big Bluestem, Illinois' state prairie grass and one of the dominant warm-season grasses of Illinois prairie. It commonly grows to six feet in height and often exceeds this stature by several feet. Legislation to make it Illinois' state prairie grass was promoted by Piasa Southwestern High School in Macoupin County, and it was approved in 1989.

These warm-season grasses are softer, more palatable, and more nutritious to grazers than the cool-season grasses of prairies prior to the last ice age. Their value to landscaping and agriculture has only recently been recognized. As you drive Illinois' highways you will notice more and more native grass plantings by the Department of Transportation. They green up the roadways in August and add color and beauty in the fall as they turn orange and purple. They can provide the same benefits to a homeowner in a backyard planting. Cattlemen are also realizing the value of warm-season grasses as forage during the hot months, when typical pasture grasses go dormant. A native prairie- grass pasture provides highly nutritious forage at a time when it is naturally scarce. Some farmers make such plantings a part of their pasture rotation as their animals graze through the seasons.

While we frequently look to the far corners of the world for agricultural plants, the warm-season grasses remind us that nature has adapted and provided us with plants ideally suited to our area. We are finally beginning to realize just how economical as well as aesthetic this natural heritage can be.

August 1992

Oaks of Illinois

In Illinois' four-and-a-quarter-million acres of forest, the most abundant type of tree is oak. It is also one of the most valuable to nature and man. With twenty kinds of native oaks growing wild in the state, it's little surprise that our most common forest type is oak–hickory, and our state tree is the White Oak. Oak wood is hard and beautifully grained, making great furniture, floors, and firewood. The value of oaks to nature, however, lies in their abundance and the adaptation of different oaks to nearly all of the state's forest environments. Oaks and their acorn fruit provide much of the food and cover for our forest wildlife.

Of the twenty species of oak in Illinois, twelve are in the black oak group and eight in the white oak group. Black oaks can be identified by their dark, smooth-to- furrowed bark, and the sharp tips on their leaf lobes, or the tips of unlobed leaves, as is typical of Shingle Oak

213

and Willow Oak. After pollination takes place, Black Oaks require two growing seasons to develop acorns, which are bitter to the taste because of their high tannin content. Black oak acorns germinate in the spring. White oaks generally have pale gray bark, often in relatively broad slabs or thick and corky ridges. Their leaves have rounded lobes, and they ripen acorns in the fall after just one growing season. Their acorns are often sweeter to the taste and germinate in the fall, just after falling. The Chinquapin Oak is so low in tannin that some people can eat it right off the tree. Illinois' state tree, the White Oak, is also in this group.

Oaks flower early in the spring, just as their leaves are unfolding. For this reason, they are vulnerable to occasional late freezes that can kill the flowers and, with them, a season's acorn crop. However, the delayed second-year development of black oak acorns gives some protection against a total acorn-crop failure in a given year. A late freeze that kills the current year's flowers will not kill the developing black oak acorns from the previous year's flowering. Thus a killing freeze two years in a row is necessary to generate a complete acorn-crop failure in an area.

Oak "flowers" lack petals and are not showy. Like willows and other catkin- producing plants, they release a large quantity of pollen, which is carried on the wind from tree to tree, thus avoiding the need to attract insect pollinators with pretty flowers. Oak pollen contributes to hay fever in the spring, and the widespread distribution of pollen leads to much hybridization among oaks. With so many oaks to begin with, the abundance of hybrids just complicates the job of identifying them.

The diversity of oak species is greatest in southern Illinois, with fewer species to be found as you go northward. An exception to this general trend is the Hill's Oak, which is found only in the northern counties. There are oaks adapted to most natural conditions of the state. Blackjack Oak will grow on the driest ridges and sand dunes. White Oak likes "typical" upland sites, and Northern Red Oak prefers cool, shaded, north-facing slopes. Of the many oaks that like bottomland or wet sites, Pin and Swamp White are the most widespread. Overcup Oak, found mostly in southern Illinois, can withstand the most permanent flooding. Bur Oak shows the greatest variation in habitats across the state. In southern Illinois, it is a bottomland tree, but in northern and central Illinois it grows more often in upland sites. This is especially true of sites that burned frequently during presettlement times. Its thick corky bark protected it from fires that swept through the dry forests and savannas. This gave it a distinct advantage in these upland sites.

Acorns are very important food for wildlife. They are relished by deer and turkey. Ducks also feed extensively on them, especially the small acorns of wetland oaks, such as Pin Oak. Squirrels and birds such as the Common Crow and Blue Jay are the principal feeders that transport the acorns and plant new generations of oaks. Jays provide much longer-distance movement of the seed than do squirrels. My family wondered where all the oak seedlings were coming from in our "prairie" subdivision that had scarcely been colonized by tree squirrels. When we watched a Blue Jay planting an acorn in the backyard, our confusion ended.

Half the volume of standing timber in Illinois forests today is of oak. This forest reflects the seedling establishment conditions that prevailed in the late nineteenth and early twentieth centuries in our state. Frequent disturbance, especially fire, provided ideal conditions for oak-seedling development then. Oak seedlings need lots of sunlight and little competition from other tree species. Under present conditions of fire suppression in wildlands, Sugar Maple and other tree species are reproducing much more rapidly than oaks. If things continue as they are now, many of Illinois' oak forests will be maple forests a century from now. Both commercial foresters and naturalists are concerned over the fate of our oaks. Research into management to assure their maintenance is currently under way.

November 1992

AUTHOR'S NOTE.—*Efforts to manage forests to regenerate oak–hickory forests have led to more management with fire and selective logging.*

The American Chestnut in Illinois

The story of the American Chestnut tree in Illinois is a sad one that may be about to take a turn for the better. American Chestnut was a common, large, native tree of the upland forests of eastern North America when the first Europeans arrived. Older specimens

American Chestnut, once among the dominant plants in eastern North American forests but nearly exterminated by an introduced fungus disease. Illinois' only native population was last seen in 1942 as a stump sprout such as the one pictured here in the Great Smoky Mountains of Tennessee.

reached four to six feet in diameter. Their wood was valued for shingles, rails, and lumber, and their nuts, while smaller than European Chestnuts, were edible and were sold in markets.

Although planted and thriving throughout Illinois as a shade tree in the nineteenth century, its native range reached Illinois only in Pulaski County at the far southern tip of the state. An eighty-acre grove grew on a high hill overlooking the Ohio River southeast of the present town of Olmsted.

At the turn of the twentieth century, Chestnut was the most important hardwood tree in the eastern United States, comprising one quarter of the standing timber. Its decline began in 1904 when a fungal disease, known as Chestnut Blight, was introduced into North America from Asia in a shipment of Chinese Chestnut nursery stock. The introduction occurred at New York, and the disease began spreading from that city at the rate of twenty-four miles per year. It killed essentially all the trees in its path by girdling them but often left the roots alive to send up sprouts that live only a few years before being killed by reinfection. By the 1950s, virtually all American Chestnuts, even those planted beyond the native range as shade and yard trees throughout Illinois, succumbed to the disease.

The first description of Illinois' native chestnut grove was written by the Reverend E. B. Olmstead in 1876 after his having observed it since 1839. "I took a position in their midst today [Feb. 26, 1876] and counted without moving thirty-five beautiful and symmetrical trees averaging in diameter about twenty-two inches. About twenty-five years ago I saw a tree cut down and worked up into rails. It was immensely tall and four or five cuts were taken off for rails ten feet long. I measured that stump today . . . and found it six feet two inches [across] three feet from the ground." Comparing this giant stump to a recent one on which he could count the rings, Olmstead estimated the age of the large one at 250 years when cut. A Mr. Gault of Glen Ellyn, Illinois, visited the stand in 1900 and photographed the chestnut trees, some reaching four and a half feet in diameter by this time. Perhaps Gault's donation of these photos to the University of Illinois prompted University of Illinois botanist William Trelease to visit the site in 1916. Trelease found that all of the large, old trees had been cut for timber, but an abundance of young trees remained.

A 1927 booklet on Illinois trees indicated that the blight had not reached Illinois at that time. But Indiana botanists recorded the disease in their state by 1940. As far as I can tell, the last live native chestnut found in Illinois was seen at Olmsted, October 14, 1941, by botanist G. H. Boewe. He indicated that it was a stump sprout from a blight-killed tree. I searched for chestnut sprouts at the site several times in the 1970s and none were found.

A few chestnut trees still survive in yards and forests throughout Illinois. Most of the larger survivors are in far northwestern Illinois, perhaps because they are most removed from the abundant range of the blight. The best place to see American Chestnuts today on public land in Illinois is in the southern part of Mississippi Palisades State Park. Here, two fine mature specimens grow at the edge of a picnic area.

Since the spread of Chestnut Blight, many people have been working to develop strategies to overcome it. Searches have been made for blight-resistant trees, a virus which reduces the virulence of the blight has been introduced as a biological control for the disease, and a cross-breeding program is under way to develop a mostly American chestnut with blight resistance bred into it from Chinese Chestnut.

Many of these efforts are in affiliation with the American Chestnut Foundation. The Illinois chapter of this foundation is providing the Department of Natural Resources with twelve blight-resistant seedling chestnuts this spring. These seedlings originated from a resistant tree found in Ohio and were propagated by the American Chestnut Cooperators' Foundation of Newport, Virginia.

The site of the original Illinois chestnut grove was recently purchased by the US Army Corps of Engineers in conjunction with their construction of a new navigation dam on the Ohio River. An adjacent tract of 267 acres, dedicated as the Chestnut Hills Nature Preserve, has been purchased for nature conservation by the Illinois Department of Natural Resources immediately east of the site. In a cooperative effort, the Illinois Department and Corps of Engineers will plant the twelve trees this spring. One will go on Army Corps land near the area they have developed for visitor observation of the construction project, and the remainder will be planted on buffer lands of the Department's adjacent nature preserve.

The American Chestnut Cooperators' Foundation has committed another fifty seedlings to the Illinois recovery effort for planting in the fall of 1995. If all goes well in the decades ahead, Illinoisans will again be able to walk in a grove of American Chestnuts growing within their native Illinois range.

March 1995

AUTHOR'S NOTE.—*None of the seedlings planted in the spring of 1995 survive in 2015, and no additional plants were obtained and planted.*

Illinois' Wild Roses

The rose is a common symbol of love and respect in our society, its beauty and aroma holding special meaning for most of us. But what do we know of our native rose heritage? How many Illinoisans realize that the state is host to six native species of rose that grow wild here, and that another eleven kinds have spread from cultivation into natural habitats. Our native roses grow in a variety of environments from swamps and marshes to woods and prairies. Three are found throughout the state, two others are found generally in the northern half of Illinois, and one is an extremely rare inhabitant of the northwest corner of the state.

Unlike multipetaled hybrid roses, wild roses have but five pink-to-rose-colored petals. Their red fruits, called hips, are collected by many as a rich source of vitamin C and are relished by birds. One or more species of our native roses is in flower from mid-May to early September, so their beauty can be enjoyed throughout the summer. Let this essay be a guide to identifying some of them.

Pasture Rose is our most widespread and common species. It is known in every county in the state and grows in woods, prairies, pastures, and roadsides. It likes open sun to moderate shade. It has the longest flowering period of Illinois' roses, blooming from late May to early September in various parts of its Illinois range. Its height of only about twelve to eighteen inches and its slender, straight prickles and five leaflets per leaf make it easy to identify. The Swamp Rose is also statewide in distribution, but becomes scarce along Illinois' western border. It is one of the state's larger roses reaching five to six feet in height. It grows in a variety of wet habitats. In southern Illinois it grows in cypress swamps and in and around lakes and ponds. In swamps it is frequently found growing on floating logs and emergent stumps with no connection to soil at all. Elsewhere in the state it grows on pond and wetland margins, in bogs and fens, and even in wet prairies. Its size and habitat combined with the predominance of seven leaflets on its leaves and stout recurved thorns make it easy to identify. It flowers from June to August depending on location.

Our third statewide species is our only native climbing rose. Called Prairie Rose, its climbing-to-trailing stems reach six to twelve feet in length. Its numerous attractive blossoms are up to two and a half inches across and vary from pink to nearly white, side by side, on the same stem. I consider it our most beautiful native rose. Its long stems, stout recurved thorns, and distinctively colored flowers aid in identifying it. But its leaves are the most distinguishing feature of the Prairie Rose. They usually have just three leaflets per leaf and distinctly impressed veins on their upper surface.

The densely thorned Sunshine Rose reaches about two feet in height in hill prairies, dry prairies, and roadsides in the northern half of Illinois. It blooms mostly from late May to July and is most easily confused with Pasture Rose, from which it is separated by its nine-to-eleven leaflets per leaf.

Meadow Rose grows in a diversity of habitats including moist prairies, roadsides, dunes, fens, and woods in northern Illinois. Its flowering season from mid-May to late June make it Illinois' first rose to bloom in spring. It is a colonial species up to five feet high. Except for some straight prickles toward the base of the stems, it is essentially thornless. This lack of thorns is usually adequate to identify it.

Our final native rose is the Needle Rose, a northern plant that ranges from Siberia to the boreal forests of North America. It grows in Illinois in a unique cold talus slope and on a north-facing hillside next to a stream, both in Jo Daviess County. It is a beautiful rose with its densely bristled stems reaching over three feet in height. But few can hope to see it here because of its extreme rarity. Its very prickly stems, habit of usually having only one flower atop a flowering stem, and pear-shaped fruit help to identify it.

Of the introduced roses, Multiflora Rose is by far the most common. It is a large alien species whose long branches somewhat resemble our prairie climbing rose. It is easily separated from that native by its leaves, with seven or nine leaflets, and its numerous small whitish flowers. It is a pest to farmers and land managers and is now illegal to plant in the state.

Shakespeare said "a rose by any other name would smell as sweet," and perhaps with the information provided here you can both smell and name them.

May 1995

AUTHOR'S NOTE.—*The Prickly Rose has disappeared in recent years from its only known locations in Illinois due to heavy browsing by deer. Deer are especially fond of eating roses.*

Wild Orchids of Illinois

Orchids are not just for the greenhouse; in Illinois, the state had forty-six kinds of wild orchids at the time of European settlement, and thirty-nine remain today. While it may seem a little cold in Illinois in February to be thinking about plants, the recent publication of outstanding state orchid books in Indiana and Minnesota make it timely. And as you will see, winter is the best time to hunt for one of the state's wild orchids.

With more than fifteen thousand species, orchids are thought to be the most abundant plant family in the world. Most orchids live in moist sites in the tropics, especially tropical rainforests. However, some orchids grow in temperate climates, such as Illinois', while a few even grow in boreal forests and north of the Arctic Circle. Illinois' orchids grow in a variety of habitats, including forests, prairies, bogs, and seep springs. Some Illinois orchids grow with cactus in very dry soil on top of bluffs.

Yellow Lady's Slipper, a large native orchid that occurs statewide. It grows in forests where it blooms in spring often on north- and east-facing slopes.

Even with thirty-nine kinds of orchids growing wild in Illinois, it is not surprising that many Illinois residents have never seen one here. Most are rare, eighteen are endangered or threatened, and only a few have large conspicuous flowers. Even so, the naturalist who knows what to look for and where to look is fairly easily rewarded. Several natural groupings of our orchids exist. Lady's slippers, coral-roots, fringed orchids, and ladies' tresses are the best represented here. All have flowers designed to entice insects to pollinate them.

Our five lady's slippers have a boat or slipper-shaped lower petal (lip) open to the top that is up to two inches long. Different species have the slippers in yellow, pink, and white. These flowers are the largest and showiest of our native orchids. The "slipper" functions as an insect trap. Bees fly into the slipper's opening but crawl to the back of the slipper to get out and pollinate the flower in the process. The Yellow Lady's Slipper is our commonest, and can be found in forests throughout the state. Look for it half to three-fourths of the way up north and east-facing slopes in late April and early May.

There are eight kinds of fringed orchids surviving in Illinois. They have relatively numerous flowers with fringed or toothed lower petals with long "spurs" or tubes of petal tissue filled with nectar. The Purple Fringeless Orchid and White-Fringed Orchid are representative of the group. The first is locally common in wet woods in the southern third of the state where it flowers in early July. The White-Fringed Orchid is rare in prairies in the northern half of the state where it blooms in June and July.

Our four coral-roots are unique in that they have no leaves or green pigment. Like mushrooms, they live off the organic humus in the soil and produce no food through photosynthesis. They lack roots but have knobby rhizomes that resemble coral and give the group its name. All of our species have brown to slightly purplish stems varying from three to eighteen inches tall, depending on the species. They have white lower petals or lips with bright purple spots. The fall coral-root is our commonest and smallest species. It flowers in late September and October in woods throughout the state. Plants are only three to eight inches tall.

Our nine ladies' tresses orchids get their name from the similarity of their densely arranged spikes of white flowers to a braid of hair. The small blossoms are arranged in tight-to-open spiral rows.

Ladies' tresses like open sunny sites and bloom mostly in the fall. The Nodding Ladies' Tresses is common throughout the state in old fields, prairies, roadsides, and dry woods, where it blooms from late September until after frost.

One of our common orchids, the Putty Root, has a unique adaptation to the limited photosynthesis potential caused by deep shade in deciduous forest in summer. It has leaves that function in winter sunlight when the trees have no leaves. When temperature and snow cover allow, the leaves photosynthesize food, which is stored in thick tubers. The Putty Root Orchid is found in dense woods statewide. Its five-to-six-inch long, pleated leaf is half as broad. It is pale green with conspicuous white veins running its entire length. The pointed leaf lies on the brown leaves of winter making it easy to spot. You do not have to wait till next spring to go orchid hunting! As soon as snow cover allows, look for Putty Root leaves in woods where you have seen lots of wildflowers, such as trilliums and Jack-in-the-pulpit, in past years. If you find the leaves, mark the spot and come back in mid-May to find the small yellowish flowers on leafless stalks. You will not find the leaves in May, as they wilt and disappear in the warmth of spring.

One of our orchids is listed as an endangered species nationally. The Small Whorled Pogonia is extremely rare west of the Appalachian Mountains, and Illinois only has a single small population of it.

The two handsome, hardcover, color-illustrated orchid books just published are *Orchids of Indiana* by Illinois native Michael Homoya and *Orchids of Minnesota* by Welby Smith. The 275-page Indiana book has 95 color photos and covers all of Illinois' orchids except the extremely rare Small Whorled Pogonia. The 160-page Minnesota book has 54 color photos and more northern species. I recommend the Indiana book as the best for persons interested in Illinois' orchids.

February 1994

AUTHOR'S NOTE.—*In 2015, the Small Whorled Pogonia Orchid is considered extirpated from Illinois. It was last seen in 1992. The two orchid books are still available from online booksellers.*

FURTHER READING.—*"Illinois' Small Whorled Pogonia Orchids," by John Schwegman.* Erigenia *Number 14, November 1995.*

~~~~~~~~~~~~~~~~~~~~~~~~~~~~~~~~~~

Violets in Illinois

In 1907 Illinois schoolchildren voted on three candidates for state flower of Illinois. The native violet easily beat the wild rose and goldenrod in the balloting and became our official state flower in February of 1908. The children chose a flower that they were familiar with, as violets doubtless grew in most schoolyards and lawns, as they do today. Although small, they make up for their diminutive size by their abundance. Spring is the peak of violet-blooming season and is a good time to examine their great diversity and beauty, which can easily be observed on a walk in the woods and fields.

Violets are widespread and successful plants with about five hundred kinds distributed throughout North America, Eurasia, and the Andes Mountains of South America. Only one species, the Pansy, has been domesticated and cultivated. Illinois has twenty-two kinds of native violets and four introduced alien species. Some are common and seen almost everywhere. For example, the Woolly Blue Violet is so common that it is likely in your lawn. Other kinds have very specific habitat requirements but are common within these restricted areas, and five are so rare that they are on the Endangered and Threatened Species list.

All but one of Illinois' violets are perennials. Only the Johnny-jump-up is an annual that has to come from seed each year. Look for its pale bluish-white flowers in fields in the southern two-thirds of the state. The perennial species come in two types: stemless plants with leaves and flower stalks all arising directly from the ground; and species having leaves and flowers scattered along a stem. The stemmed species are all woodland plants that are seldom seen elsewhere, while those likely to be seen in yards and fields are all stemless.

Most of our violets are blue to violet in color, but some species are white, and others are yellow. One of the commonest violets in woodlands in spring is the Smooth Yellow Violet. It is a stemmed species and is found throughout the state. The Cream Violet is our commonest white species and is another stemmed woodland plant.

It is generally restricted to floodplain areas along streams. Look for it where you see Virginia bluebells. It grows statewide, but is scarce in northwestern Illinois.

The Wooly Blue and Common Blue Violets are the most common species in the state. These stemless species grow in a variety of habitats, although the former is more common in woods. Look closely at some of these blue stemless violets and you will see flower stalks from their bases that have unopened flowers that lack petals. These self-pollinating flowers, called cleistogamous flowers by botanists, produce most of the seed for the violet. The showy flowers are mostly sterile, leaving these inconspicuous flowers to do most of the work of reproduction. Check them late in the spring for seed.

The most beautiful of our violets is the Bird's-foot Violet, sometimes called the wild pansy. Its flowers are fully twice the size of any other native violet and come in two color forms. One form has the three lower petals pale blue and the two upper petals deep, velvety purple. This is the wild pansy form. The other type has all five petals pale blue. Its flowers are all fertile and produce seed, and it lacks the cleistogamous flowers that most other stemless violets have. The leaves of this stemless violet are divided into thin segments that resemble a bird's footprint, thus giving it its name. The Bird's-foot grows throughout the state and is most frequently found on dry mossy ridges in woods. It also grows in sand prairies in central and northern Illinois where the totally blue flower form prevails.

Our only population of the endangered Blue Violet lives along the Mississippi River in an area flooded by a levee break last summer. Department of Natural Resources biologists will soon be visiting the site to see if it survived.

As you head to the woods and fields of Illinois this spring, remember to keep an eye out for the state flower, the native violet. They are an interesting and colorful group that is doing a good job of representing the great state of Illinois.

April 1994

AUTHOR'S NOTE.—*The only known Blue Violet population in Illinois did not survive the 1993 Mississippi River flood.*

~~~~~~~~~~~~~~~~~~~~~~~

Milkweed Pollination

The arrival of summer means it is milkweed-flowering time. For those who take the time to observe, these common plants are among the most interesting members of Illinois flora. Their unique adaptation for using insects to pollinate their flowers attracts many insects and leads to the capture and death of some. It is a pollination system unlike any other in the state. Milkweeds are living proof that close examination of nature can broaden your appreciation of the intricacies of the natural world. Illinois has nineteen kinds of milkweeds, and they grow in all sorts of habitats, from swamps and marshes to forest, prairie, and extremely dry, sandy soils. Four of these are endangered or threatened species, but many of them are among our most common plants.

Milkweeds get their name from the sticky, milk-colored sap that all except the Butterfly Weed possesses. The latter has clear sticky sap. Most milkweeds have leaves that occur in pairs that are opposite each other on the stem, but some have whorls of leaves, and many of the green-flowered species have alternate leaves. The most notable characteristic of milkweeds is their flowers. They occur in rounded groups, with each flower on a long stalk, and with each stalk emanating from a common point. Botanists call this flower arrangement an umbel. Flower colors range from the brilliant orange of Butterfly Weed to white, pink, purple, and green. Each individual flower has five divisions emanating from the base of a rounded, solid, cylindrical, central area, which has five nectar-bearing petal-like structures called hoods growing from its lower sides. Careful examination will reveal five slits in the sides of the central cylinder alternating with the hoods. These slits act as traps for insect feet in the complicated pollination process of the flower.

Now look down on a flower from the top. You should see five dark-colored dots around the margin of the flattened end of the cylinder—one at the top of each slit. Some (or all) may be missing from a given flower if lots of insects have visited it. Take a toothpick or other sharply pointed object and insert it into a slit that has a black dot at its top. Then move the toothpick up to the dot and continue on up.

Variegated Milkweed being visited by a beetle that in seeking nectar has had its left rear foot caught in a slit trap of a flower. A yellow pollinium is attached to that foot.

If you watch carefully you can see two yellow, wing-like masses of pollen that are attached to the sticky dot emerge from their pouches on either side of the slit. Rather than individual pollen grains, like most other plants, milkweeds have fused, slick masses of pollen grains all stuck together called pollinia.

Pollination in milkweeds proceeds as follows. Insects land on the flower and their feet naturally grasp the cylinder between the hoods as they search the hoods for nectar. In grasping the cylinder, their feet sometimes are forced into a slit. Insect legs are slender but with a wider foot at the end. This foot resists easy extraction from the stiff edges of the slit, and, as the insect pulls, the foot slides up to the top, where it comes in contact with the sticky dot and usually comes out of the slit with the wing-shaped pollen masses sticking to it. The insect then moves to another flower, where it gets its foot caught again, and this time the pollinia gets scraped off inside the slit when it pulls its foot out. The slit houses the stigma or pollen-receiving surface, thus

fertilizing the second flower. It is amazing that a system as complicated as this works so well. Many of the green-flowered milkweeds
hold their flowers upside down as in the endangered Mead's Milkweed. They do not depend on flower color to attract insects but rely
on odor. Their inverted flowers make the insect grasp the cylinder
harder to keep from falling off. This apparently increases the chance
of its foot slipping into the slit and picking up or depositing pollen.

Of the many insects that are attracted to milkweed flowers, some
are too small or weak to remove their foot if it gets caught in a slit.
Flies and ants are among the species that become mortally trapped
on the flowers. I have even seen larger bees meet the same fate when
getting their feet stuck in two different flowers simultaneously. They
get caught in a stretched-out position that prevents them from getting
the leverage needed to free either foot from the slit.

So arm yourself with a toothpick and magnifying lens and head out
to the backyard or roadside for a little milkweed watching. Look for
trapped and dead insects on the flowers and insects collecting nectar
with pollen hanging from their feet. Try your hand at extracting
pollen with your toothpick. Nature is truly fascinating.

July 1993

Trilliums

Trilliums are among the most familiar and easily recognized wildflowers in the woods of Illinois. They emerge as a single stalk in
early spring and unfold a whorl of three leaves near their top, with a
single three-petaled flower above the leaves. Trilliums are restricted
to the northern hemisphere, where eight kinds are found in eastern
Asia, seven more are found near North America's western coast, and
thirty-five species inhabit eastern North America. Their flowers are
large relative to the size of the whole plant and range from white to
deep purple in color. One of our white-flowered species turns pink
as it ages. They are among the largest and most beautiful wildflowers
in the Illinois woods.

Trilliums come in two basic types—those with flower stalks and
those without. The stalkless species have the flowers sitting right on
the whorl of leaves. Their flowers are usually purple or with some

purple, and their leaves are blotched with light and dark green color. Purple Wake Robin, Sessile Wake Robin and Green Trillium are the state's species in this group. The stalked trilliums have the flower on a stem, which holds it beyond the whorl of leaves. The flower can be held above or bent below the uniformly green leaves. Their flowers are usually white, but Purple Trillium has both purple and white-flowered forms. Illinois species in this group are Snow Trillium, Purple Trillium, Nodding Trillium, Large-flowered Trillium, and White Trillium.

One or more trillium species occurs in every county of the state, so they are wildflowers that all Illinois residents and visitors can find and enjoy with little effort. Their familiarity and early appearance in spring has led to the name Wake Robin for the stalkless species. While many Illinois trilliums are common in parts of the state, the Nodding and Purple Trilliums are endangered species, and the Green Trillium is listed as threatened. Our endangered and threatened trilliums are species that just barely range into Illinois but are more common elsewhere.

White Trillium, the only trillium with stalked flowers that occurs throughout Illinois. Look for it in rich woodlands that support abundant wildflowers.

Trilliums are peculiar among our wild plants in having a lot of species but with each species having a relatively restricted range. For example, our most common species, the Purple Wake Robin, is widespread and common only in Illinois and Indiana. It exists in the fringes of surrounding states and is only widely scattered to the south. Nowhere does it range into or east of the Appalachian Mountains.

The Green Trillium is our most restricted stalkless species, ranging in a band within a hundred miles of either side of the Mississippi River, from the vicinity of Quincy, Illinois, south to Cape Girardeau, Missouri. It is found nowhere else in the world. The Sessile Wake Robin is abundant in Indiana and Missouri, but is absent from most of Illinois. In Illinois, it ranges along the eastern and southwestern fringes of the state from Chicago and St. Louis southward. It is inexplicably absent from most of the interior of Illinois.

Of Illinois' five stalked trilliums, the Snow Trillium is Illinois' smallest species, reaching a maximum of six inches high, but it is usually much shorter. Where it occurs in the northern half of the state, it is usually the first flower to bloom in the spring, often while snow is still on the ground. Large-flowered Trillium has the showiest flowers of our species but is common only in northeastern Illinois. Its flowers are white, turning pink with age. White Trillium is another beautiful white-flowered species that is more widespread, being found sporadically in very rich forest habitats throughout the state. Its white flowers are usually on stalks that diverge on an angle from the stem. Nodding and Purple Trilliums are our other two stalked species. The former has white flowers on stalks that nod beneath the leaves and is restricted to the northeast corner of the state. The Purple Trillium has mostly purple flowers and is found only in extreme northeastern and northwestern Illinois.

Trillium conservation presents special challenges due to the plant's unique vulnerability to browsing by deer. Deer find them very tasty and eat the entire cluster of leaves, flowers, and fruits in a single bite. Trilliums do not sprout new stems or grow new leaves in a given year once they are eaten. Therefore, the loss of the leaves prevents the plant from making and storing food in the root for the next year's growth. This results in smaller plants each year until their eventual death in areas subject to heavy deer browsing.

Trilliums are both good indicators of deer overpopulation and a good reason to insist on deer population control. Fewer and fewer of these beautiful wildflowers heralding spring in your favorite woods means that deer control is needed.

April 1996

AUTHOR'S NOTE.—*Green Trillium moved from the threatened species list to the endangered species list in 2015.*

~~~~~~~~~~~~~~~~~~~~~~~~~~

Sunflowers of Illinois

Sunflowers are among nature's most beautiful and useful wild plants. Their large yellow blossoms are some of the most conspicuous flowers along roadsides, in prairies, and in woodlands in late summer and fall. They take their name from those few species whose flowers face the sun as it moves across the sky. This group includes the Domesticated Sunflower as well as the wild Downy Sunflower of our prairies. Not counting hybrids, nineteen kinds of sunflowers have been found growing wild in Illinois, and all but five of these are native to the state. The introduced species have all spread here from the western states, usually along railroads.

The "flowers" of sunflowers are really a composite of many flowers growing together to mimic a single blossom. Marginal flowers in the composite or cluster have a single yellow petal appearing as a petal of the apparent larger "flower." The cluster of small flowers forming the central disc of the "flower" can be yellow or brown. Most of our sunflowers have two opposite leaves at each node of the stem, but in some the leaves become alternately arranged in the upper stem, and in some they are all alternate. All have simple or unlobed leaves. Two of our sunflowers are annuals that grow from seed each year, while the others are perennials.

Our largest and perhaps prettiest sunflower is the Sawtooth. It is a plant of moist prairies and roadsides that reaches a height of up to twelve feet. Its long, narrow leaves are all alternate on the stem, and the upper third of the stem has numerous yellow-centered showy flowers. The whole plant has a tall, narrow appearance. It is found throughout the state and is commonly seen on roadsides. Another conspicuous sunflower of roadsides is the Common Sunflower. It is an annual species that reaches up to ten feet tall and has a widely spreading inflorescence and large leaves. Its many flowers have brown centers. It is introduced in Illinois from its native range in the central plains. This is the plant that was domesticated by Native Americans to become the Domesticated Sunflower.

The second sunflower used widely by the Indians for food is the Jerusalem Artichoke. This tuber-producing species of moist, sunny habitats is native to all parts of Illinois. It reaches eight feet in height. Its broad, rigid leaves are opposite on the lower part of the stem and then alternate near the top and help to identify it. This perennial sends out runners, which produce large edible tubers at their end. The tubers are best for eating if dug in the fall. If you cannot find any, try the specialty section of your local supermarket. Cultivated Jerusalem Artichokes are usually available. As its name implies, it has been cultivated in the Middle East and elsewhere around the world. But it is native to Illinois.

Perhaps Illinois' most common sunflower is the Woodland Sunflower. This two-to-three-foot-tall plant grows in nearly every upland forest in the state. Its sandpapery lance-shaped leaves are strictly opposite on its stems and lack leaf stalks. The Downy Sunflower is a colonial plant of prairies and open sunny roadsides. Its broad opposite leaves lack stalks and are covered with dense short hairs that give them a characteristic gray appearance. Its flowers are fairly large for its size and tend to face the sun. Colonies of this sunflower usually have lots of small sterile plants that arise from its underground stems.

Of Illinois' native sunflowers, the Tall Sunflower is an endangered species and the Narrow-leaved Sunflower is threatened. The Tall Sunflower is a plant of wet, open fens and prairies in northeastern Illinois. It is largely alternate-leaved like the Sawtooth Sunflower, which it resembles, except for its slightly shorter stature and the hairs on its stems. It reaches a height of nine feet. The Narrow-leaved Sunflower is a very distinctive and easily identified plant. It reaches three to four feet in height and has peculiar leaves four to six inches long and only a quarter of an inch wide. It is limited to open woods, roadsides, and seeps at the far southern tip of the state.

As you drive Illinois' roads and walk through its fields and woods in the fall, keep an eye out for sunflowers. They are an important part of the state's natural heritage and have been useful to humans, both primitive and modern. You might even take time to dig up and taste a few Jerusalem Artichokes.

September 1996

~~~~~~~~~~~~~~~~~~~~~~~~~~~~~

Asters of Illinois

Autumn is a season with a multitude of striking wildflowers. From gentians and sunflowers to goldenrods, blazing stars, and Ageratum, the list is long and colorful. But for my money, the wild asters take first place in Mother Nature's autumn flower show. Asters take their name from the Greek word aster, which means "star." They certainly stand out like stars on a clear night. All of Illinois' thirty-six native asters bloom in the fall and cover a range of colors from white to pink, purple, and blue. The brightly colored ones usually have a bright yellow center that provides attractive contrast.

Asters have composite flowers consisting of a whole bunch of small flowers growing together to mimic a single blossom. Each flower around the rim of the group has a single petal which functions as a petal of the composite flower. For this reason, asters, like sunflowers and other composites, have many more than the three to five petals typical of "normal" flowers. The Sky Blue Aster may have as few as ten "petals" per flower, while New England Aster has as many as fifty.

Illinois' native asters are all perennials, except the Expressway Aster, and have alternate leaves, which are often heart-shaped, and sometimes have leaf bases that clasp or extend around the stem. Several species spread from creeping rhizomes and form large, often dense, colonies. Most are from knee-high to waist-high, but a few of the wet habitat species reach higher. Our asters grow in a wide variety of habitats. Some are moist-soil specialists, growing in seep springs, bogs, and lowland habitats, such as floodplains. Others like medium-moisture sites, while perhaps most favor dry uplands. Some require the full sunlight of prairie, while others like the shade of forest. They lend themselves well to ornamental plantings around the home, with different species adapted to all sorts of locations. Field guides use a variety of common names for asters, so the following discussion uses the names most commonly used in Illinois. The most notable asters of upland prairies, such as hill prairies, are Sky Blue Aster and Heath Aster. The first has pale blue flowers and arrowhead-shaped lower leaves, while the Heath Aster has narrow, elongate leaves and dense clusters of small, white flowers. Both of these are found throughout the state, with the latter sometimes being found in moist-soil prairies as well. Upland prairies in the western counties and across northern Illinois also contain Silky Aster. This beautiful blue-flowered species has leaves covered with a dense coating of silvery, silky hairs, which make it easy to identify.

Perhaps the most notable and widespread of the mesic or medium-moisture prairie asters is the New England Aster. This waist-high species grows in clumps or colonies on open, sunny roadsides, as well as in prairies, and is sometimes found in the horticulture trade. Its large purple-to-bluish flowers are abundant across the spreading top of the plant. Its leaves have no petioles or stalks and have ear-like projections that extend back around the stem. Among the most common rich woodland asters statewide are Arrow-leaved and Short's Asters. Both have arrowhead-shaped leaves, but the former has them sharply toothed while Short's leaves are smooth-margined. Flowers of the Arrow-leaved Aster are pale bluish to almost white, while Short's are deep blue.

Two common and showy asters in the dry and rocky woods of the southern half of Illinois are Spreading and Top-shaped Asters. Both have large, blue-to-purple flowers. Spreading Aster has clasping leaves not unlike the New England Aster, but its forest habitat and knee-high stature easily separate it from that species. The other gets its name from the thin, top-shaped base supporting the flower. Its leaves are long and taper gradually to each end.

One of the most widespread of our small-flowered white asters is Ontario Aster. It is a colonial species that inhabits floodplain and lowland forests statewide. Due to its colonial nature it often constitutes much of the groundcover vegetation in lowland forests. Many of our small-flowered white asters become weedy and are among the common weeds along roadsides and sidewalks in cities and rural areas of Illinois. Hairy Aster is the most common and widespread of these. Its dime-sized white flowers have pale pinkish-to-yellowish centers and its long leaves as well as its stems are hairy.

As you venture afield in the fall to view nature's beauty, take a closer look at our wild asters. They are truly among autumn's showiest wildflowers.

October 1995

AUTHOR'S NOTE.—*Plant scientists have recently reclassified Illinois' traditional asters into six different genera. None of the native plants traditionally classified as* Aster *now have that scientific name. This essay refers to the asters as they appear in Mohlenbrock's 2002 edition of his* Vascular Flora of Illinois.

JOHN E. SCHWEGMAN is retired from a career in nature conservation at the Illinois Department of Natural Resources, where he worked on inventory, preservation, and management of natural areas throughout Illinois. Decades of fieldwork in all regions of the state give him intimate insights into the natural heritage of Illinois and the adjacent Midwest. The author has not only discovered a natural community and many native species that are new to Illinois but has also described a native plant species from the state that is new to science.